# DISCIPLING THE CITY

# DISCIPLING THE CITY

## A Comprehensive Approach to Urban Mission

Roger S. Greenway, *Editor*

**BAKER BOOK HOUSE**
Grand Rapids, Michigan 49516

© 1992 by Roger Greenway

Published by Baker Book House Company
P. O. Box 6287, Grand Rapids, Michigan 49516-6287

Printed in the United States of America

**Library of Congress Cataloging-in-Publication Data**

Greenway, Roger S.
   Discipling the city: a comprehensive approach to urban mission / edited by Roger S. Greenway. — 2nd ed.
     p.   cm.
   Includes bibliographical reference and index.
   ISBN 0-8010-3849-9
   1. City churches.  2. City missions.  I. Greenway, Roger S.
   BV637.D5 1992
   253'.09173'2—dc20

                                              92-468

# CONTENTS

86733

6

# PREFACE

A billion people have moved from farm to city since the first edition of *Discipling the City* appeared in 1979. For the Christian church, few challenges are more urgent or complex than evangelizing urban populations and multiplying disciples in these teeming population centers.

In the Third World, urbanization turns traditional market towns into growing, small cities. Long-established cities add tens of thousands of people every month and hundreds of thousands each year. In Western countries, a different phenomenon occurs as enormous urban corridors appear, made up of numerous cities and communities of various sizes between them. Such changes demand new definitions of city, urban area, and metropolitan area, and fresh thinking about the uniqueness of urban Christianity. They also add to the complexity of the church's task of transforming cities in the name of Christ.

*Discipling the City* is a reader compiled by urban ministry specialists. We hope to stimulate people committed to Christian ministry in cities throughout the world to think better and work better for Christ.

We understand *discipling* as a comprehensive term embracing all that Jesus meant when he commanded, "Go and make disciples of all nations, baptizing them . . . and teaching them to obey everything that I have commanded you" (Matt. 28:19 NIV). Our concerns are therefore broad. We probe the meaning of Christian evangelism, worship, fellowship, counseling, church development, ministry to the poor, political action, and theological education in light of urban realities and demographic changes occur-

7

ring worldwide. We write as prophets as well as evangelists, for we believe the gospel embraces the totality of life. No part of the city should remain untouched by Christ and his lordship.

We write as evangelical theologians committed to the authority of God's written Word over everything the church does and teaches. In a rapidly urbanizing world, such ongoing reflections are essential if the church is to pursue its mission in ways that please God and advance his kingdom.

This new, expanded edition includes some new chapters and omits some of the original chapters. Subjects range from the very practical to the historical, technical, and theological. To enhance the book's service as a textbook, discussion questions follow each chapter.

The writers are women and men, European-American, African-American, and Hispanic-American. We come from Reformed, Presbyterian, and Baptist traditions and have lived and worked for the church in North America, Europe, Africa, Asia, and Latin America. Our perspectives and emphases differ in some areas, but this adds to the richness of the book and can broaden readers' understanding of the church's common task in the city.

Roger S. Greenway

# CONTRIBUTORS

**Corean Bakke** is a concert pianist, researcher, and writer. She holds graduate degrees from Roosevelt University, North Baptist Seminary, and Chicago Theological Seminary. She travels and performs internationally. Her home base is inner-city Chicago and among her current projects are two new international hymnals and a book about Lausanne II.

**Raymond J. Bakke** directs International Urban Associates, a network of Christian leaders who mobilize the church for more effective urban ministry. He is professor of ministry at Northern Baptist Theological Seminary in Chicago and senior associate for large cities with the Lausanne Committee for World Evangelization. He conducts urban ministry seminars throughout the world.

**Harvie M. Conn** is professor of missions at Westminster Theological Seminary in Philadelphia and director of the school's urban training program. From 1960 to 1972, he served as a missionary in Korea. He is editor of the journal *Urban Mission* and the author or editor of eleven books on Christian mission. He is known internationally for his lecturing and writing.

**Craig W. Ellison** is professor of urban studies and counseling at the Alliance Theological Seminary in Nyack, New York. He is the author of numerous books and articles, both professional and popular, in the fields of counseling and of urban ministry. He is the host of "Perspectives on Personal Living," a weekly nationwide radio broadcast on issues of daily life.

**Edna C. Greenway** is professor of Spanish language and literature at Calvin College in Grand Rapids, Michigan. She has taught church education at Westminster Seminary in Philadelphia, Calvin Seminary in Grand Rapids, and in various schools overseas. With her husband, Roger, she served as a missionary to Sri Lanka, 1958–62, and to Mexico City, 1963–70.

**Roger S. Greenway** is professor of world missiology at Calvin Theological Seminary in Grand Rapids, Michigan. After twelve years as a missionary in Sri Lanka and Mexico, he served for six years as the Latin America Secretary for Christian Reformed World Missions. After pastoring a city church for four years, he taught missions at Westminster Seminary in Philadelphia. Following that he was appointed executive director of world ministries for his denomination, a position he occupied for four years. He has published a dozen books on missions and annually teaches overseas.

**Viv Grigg**, a New Zealander, and his Brazilian wife, Ieda, by their speaking, writing, and personal example (Manila and Calcutta) have inspired a growing number of church-planting teams to live and minister in the slums of emerging megacities. Viv coordinates the Cities Track for the AD 2000 movement and is the international director of the Urban Leadership Foundation based in Los Angeles, California.

**Judith Lingenfelter** directs the doctor of cross-cultural education program at Biola University's School of Intercultural Studies in La Mirada, California. For several years she worked as an inner-city school teacher. More recently she has served with a number of mission agencies in training people for ministry in cities around the world.

**Robert C. Linthicum** is director of the Office of Urban Advance, World Vision International. He has been an urban pastor in Chicago, Rockford, Milwaukee, and Detroit, and he currently chairs the Urban Coordinating Council of the Presbyterian Church (USA) for Southern California. Author of several books on the church in the city and on renewal, Linthicum is involved through World Vision in developing new and creative urban ministries throughout the world.

**Timothy M. Monsma** is the director of Cities for Christ Worldwide and adjunct professor of missions at Westminster Theological Seminary in Escondido, California. He served as a missionary for twelve years in Nigeria. His speciality is urban research, and he writes, lectures, and teaches on urban-related subjects in North America and overseas. He is deeply involved in the Urban Track of the AD 2000 Movement.

**Manuel Ortiz** is associate professor of missions at Westminster Theological Seminary in Philadelphia. He specializes in urban missions and works with students in developing wholistic church planting models in the city. Earlier in Chicago and currently in Philadelphia he has established alternative models of education for young people and for ministerial training.

**Willie Richardson** is pastor of Christian Stronghold Baptist Church, in Philadelphia, an inner-city congregation that he founded in 1966 with 6 people and which currently has an active membership of more than 2000. He is a graduate of the Philadelphia College of the Bible. A specialist in leadership development, particularly in the context of the inner city, Richardson serves as president of Christian Research and Development, an organization that conducts research and holds seminars on subjects related to Christian life and ministry in the city. He is co-author of *The Black Family, Past, Present and Future.*

**Sidney H. Rooy** served in Argentina from 1965–91 as missionary and professor of mission and church history at the Evangelical Higher Institute of Theological Education (ISEDET). In addition, he has taught in numerous seminaries and churches in Latin America and the United States. As a member of the executive committee of the Latin American Theological Fraternity, he is active in various evangelical congresses and publication programs. In 1992 he took up teaching in San Jose, Costa Rica, and Managua, Nicaragua.

**Ruth A. Tucker** is a visiting professor at Trinity Evangelical Divinity School in Deerfield, Illinois, and has taught part-time at Calvin College, Fuller Theological Seminary, and Moffat College of the Bible in Kenya. She holds a Ph.D. in history from Northern Illinois University, and is the author of ten books, including *From Jerusalem to Irian Jaya* and *Guardians of the Great Commission.*

**Charles D. Uken** served for eighteen years as an evangelistic missionary and church planter with the Presbyterian Church of Brazil. In Brazil he worked closely with national pastors and lay workers who were spearheading new church development among the working classes in rapidly growing cities. He holds a D.Min. degree from Westminster Theological

Seminary in Philadelphia. He currently pastors Newman Chapel, a mission outreach of the Christian Reformed Church in Ferry, Michigan.

**Craig Van Gelder** is professor of domestic missiology at Calvin Theological Seminary in Grand Rapids, Michigan. He holds a Ph.D. in administration in urban affairs from the University of Texas at Arlington and a Ph.D. in missions from Southwestern Baptist Theological Seminary, Fort Worth, Texas. He is the founder of Church Services, Inc., a consultancy organization based in Jackson, Mississippi. He ministers widely as a consultant for church extension and revitalization.

# 1

# GENESIS AS URBAN PROLOGUE

## Harvie M. Conn

Looking at Genesis to learn about cities may seem strange to some readers. Those used to thinking of cities as modern industrial centers with tremendous size and population are bound to be disappointed.

The towns and cities of Genesis are closer to those of the most ancient East that arose as cultic and market centers for farmers and herdsmen. Long after the fall of such cities elsewhere, they remained. Amalgams of religion-ritual-government-business, they did not benefit from a large merchant fleet, as did the seafaring Greek cities. Palestine's geography, with its spine of mountains from north to south, provided little room for large population centers.[1]

Other factors also hinder this kind of study. Anti-urban negativism has, in my judgment, stalled research. One wing of biblical scholarship has spent much time in a continuing search for an anti-urban, nomadic bias in the so-called sources of Genesis.[2] Jacques Ellul's 1970 study *The Meaning of the City* set the pace for this negativism. Ellul looked at the city as a symbol of the technology he fears. That controlling perspective, reinforced by his Barthian dialectic, left him little room to see the city as anything but a citadel of sin. Its redemption was left to a radically futuristic eschatology.

Another hindrance to study has been the spotty and sometimes eccentric character of biblical study. Some try to handle the overall thrust of the Bible with a concentration on the history of several cities—Sodom and Gomorrah, Nineveh, Babylon, and Jerusalem. Antioch becomes a model from which to draw strategic principles for contemporary urban church planting and growth.

Using such urban centers for framing biblical constructions has its obvious advantages; they are, after all, the objects of a study like this. But it also has its dangers. The temptation is strong to make restricted biblical passages on the city say more than they do. Hermeneutical carelessness can miss larger biblical themes into which urban concerns are gathered. An urban typology can emerge that is artificially imposed on passages chosen for emphasis. Modern readers' interests can divorce the text from the intentions of its divinely inspired author.

Despite all these potential handicaps, this chapter attempts to trace something of the sweep of urban interests in Genesis. The book's history is seen as the foundation of the Old Testament narrative as a whole. For that reason, we will also provide hints of the wider impact of its narrative on passages throughout the Bible.

Our discussion centers on biblical theology, "the history of special revelation."[3] As general guidelines, we carry on our discussions around the themes of creation, sin and the fall, redemption, and consummation. Will we fall into yet another form of eccentricity? Let the reader decide.

## Creation: God's Original Design for the City

More than one preacher in the city has summarized the Scriptures from Genesis to Revelation with the words, "The Bible begins in a garden and ends in a city." As a one-sentence description of the biblical history, the assertion works well.

The Eden of Genesis 2, the garden of God (Ezek. 28:13; 31:8–9), is a pastoral paradise. Here God places the first man and woman, tenant-farmers at home in the dwelling place of the Lord. They are regents called to rule over a world whose imagery appears uniformly agricultural (Gen. 1:26–28). In naming the animal creation, the man demonstrates his rule, and the Genesis record underlines that he will not do his task alone (Gen. 2:19–20).

The object of the man's and the woman's testing is the fruit from a tree (Gen. 2:9, 17), and the promise of reward for resisting temptation is the fruit from another tree (Gen. 2:9; 3:22, 24). The land is their calling, their blessing (Gen. 1:29–30), and, after their sin, becomes part of their curse (Gen. 3:17–19). From the earth Adam comes by creative act (Gen. 2:7); to it he returns by divine curse (Gen. 3:19).

### God's Urban Intention

Yet there is more to this historical narrative than merely a record, accurate as it is, of the pastoral origins of humanity. The cultural mandate given to Adam and Eve in the garden to fill, rule, and subdue the earth (Gen. 1:28) was nothing more than a mandate to build the city. Human culture to follow them was to take city form.

The couple in the garden was to multiply, so providing the citizens of the city. Their cultivation of earth's resources as they extended their control over their territorial environment through the fabrication of sheltering structures would produce the physical architecture of the city. And the authority structure of the human family engaged in the cultural process would constitute the centralized government by which the life and functioning of the city, would be organized, under God. The cultural mandate given at creation was thus a mandate to build the city, and it would be through the blessing of God on man's faithfulness in the covenanted task that the construction of the city would be completed.[4]

Urban culture, built in perfect obedience to God, would typify our hope in Jehovah.

### God's Urban Apologetic

There is still another urban dimension to these opening chapters of Genesis. The author supplies it by using the original history of the creation to engage in missionary encounter with the urban theopolitics of his day.

When Genesis was written, the cities of the ancient Near East were already in place. How long they had been there is difficult to say, as difficult as trying to define the nature of a city then and now.[5] What is important for our study is their theological or religious significance.

Large or small, not sharply divided from the rural world, the city was a community drawn together by a common religious commitment. It was that territory, generally on an elevated position and surrounded by a protective wall, dedicated to the service of a local deity.

The Canaanite religion, a central concern in the Pentateuch as a whole, illustrates this. The Baal god was a local territorial deity. Each city bore the name of its particular "lord" or "master"—Baal-Gad (Josh. 11:17), Baal-Meon (Num. 32:38), Baal-Peor (Num. 25:3), Baal-Zephon (Exod. 14:2).

The city as a whole was the estate of the city-god. Its "king" or ruler had a threefold duty: "the interpretation of the will of the gods; the representation of his people before the gods; and the administration of the realm."[6] Believed to have been chosen by the gods, the king was responsible to them for the behavior of his subjects. The city was seen as a microcosm, an integration of nature, society, and the divine. Urbanism became a divine activity of the gods.[7]

In this union, cities appeared as the wives of various gods. Many cities carried the feminine form of the god-husband's name, for example, Baalah (Josh. 15:9) and Ashtaroth (Josh. 9:10). The metaphor of the city-as-a-woman became a shared vocabulary. Old Testament terms reflect this. Prominent cities were "mothers" and towns within their sphere of influence were "daughters" (Num. 21:25; 32:42; Josh. 15:45).[8]

Intimately linked to the religion of the city was agriculture. This is reflected even in Old Testament vocabulary. Frequently the Hebrew term *eretz* (land, earth) appears as virtually a synonym for the city (Gen. 11:28; 34:2 [cf. 33:18]; 1 Kings 8:37; 22:36).

In the world of the Ancient Near East, urban worship was concerned with good crops and the productivity of the land. The Canaanite religion in its various rites illustrates the preoccupation of urban worship with the fertility of nature.

Still another literary motif in the ancient Near East helpful in understanding the city is its mythological creation accounts. Perhaps the best known is the *Enuma Elish*, conventionally known as the "Babylonian Creation Myth." That English title, however, may be misleading. Its central theme is not creation (either cosmic or human) but the justification of the supremacy of Marduk and his city Babylon. *Enuma Elish* was a conscious creation for an urban religiopolitical end, a mythological commemoration of city building. Babylon, its argument goes, was built by the gods in primeval times.[9]

Could the Genesis account of creation be intended as a historical counteractive to these literary traditions of mythic creation commonly known in the ancient urban world? Has Moses demythologized these literary traditions in his apologetic against urban mythology? If so, then the parallels between the literary traditions and the biblical account represent urban points of contact that are ultimately urban points of confrontation.

Against this urban background, the pastoral sounds of Genesis 1–3 take on pronounced city hues and undertones. Nature is not deified, and God is not urbanized. The God who enters into covenant with his creation is not a local urban deity like the Baalim. He is the cosmic sovereign who has made the creation his house-city. He is not embodied in or limited in authority to a single city or place. The heavens and the earth are his dwelling place by virtue of his creative act (Ps. 24:1–2). Cities like Jericho fall before him "who is God in heaven above and on earth beneath" (Josh. 2:10–11). Nineveh must bow in worship before Jonah's Lord, "the God of heaven, who made the sea and the land" (Jon. 1:9).

Even the Edenic garden takes on new urban significance in this light. It too had its ancient parallels that would not have been unfamiliar to the first readers. Ancient Near Eastern mythology related the king-god to a role as caretaker in the sacred gardens. G. Widegren argues that it was probably customary for the Mesopotamian temple to have a garden or grove of some sort associated with it. The king was its builder, the owner and caretaker, a symbol of his connection with the divine. In the myths, these gardens are described as the habitation of the gods.[10]

In apologetic response to these myths of a corrupted covenant, Genesis sees creation itself and its microcosm in the garden as the dwelling place of the Lord. Creation is the cosmic house of God, the seal of God's victory over chaos. On the seventh day he sits as king in the archetypal house of his rest (Isa. 66:1). He gives fertility to the earth and its creatures (Gen. 1:22, 24). No earthly king is his representation; all human beings, male and female, are representatives of his image-glory (Gen. 1:27). Our life, our security, lies not in the city but in our covenant attachment to him.

This urban flavor to the *shalom* of paradise was not forgotten in the rest of the Scriptures. Isaiah 40–55, for example, uses the language of the *Enuma Elish* in its counterclaims to the ideology of Babylon the city. Jehovah is the true victor in creation (43:15–16). He emerges triumphant in combat with Rahab as dragon, sea, and great deep (51:9–10). And intertwined with this creation language are the urban metaphors pitting Babylon against Jerusalem. A rebuilt Jerusalem (44:26, 28; 45:13; 52:9), in contrast with a doomed Babylon (47:1, 5; 52:2), becomes the equivalent of God's primeval Eden (51:3), an Eden no longer localized but gathering the nations of the world to itself (2:2–4; 45:14, 22–24; 49:23; 54:3).

Isaiah 65:17–25 gathers all these themes together in its eschatological vision of the coming *shalom*, painted now in terms of the restoration of the urban paradise of the Messiah. The vision is prefaced by a recollection of the language of Genesis 1:1. The new heavens and the new earth are to be an urban re-creation.

Preeminently these eschatological connections between creation and city are drawn in the Book of Revelation. The Edenic features of the presence of God in the garden, of rivers and the tree of life, are intensified in Revelation 21–22 and its vision of the Holy City, and all of this is prefaced again by the Genesis language that introduces the heavenly vision as an urban vision of "a new heaven and a new earth" (Rev. 21:1–2).

Security was the hallmark of the city in the Old Testament. In fact, the most common word for city in the Old Testament, 'ir, found some 1090 times, gives the general sense of "a fixed settlement which is rendered inaccessible to assailants by a wall and/or other defense works."[11] That security, exemplified in the eschatological *shalom* of an urban paradise with open gates (Isa. 26:2; 60:11; Rev. 21:25), stands as the heart of the Genesis Eden. God's urban house is the creation itself, and we live in it in the security of *shalom*.

## The Fall and Urban Rebellion

That security was shattered by the fall of Adam and Eve, recorded in Genesis 3. In rebellion, the image of God seeks more; creature seeks to become Creator (Gen. 3:22). Up-reaching pride breaks the covenant solidarity between God and the first family and between humanity and the creation.

Against this background of rebellious dislocation we are introduced to the Bible's first named city and its creation by the first murderer, Cain (Gen. 4:17). Sentenced to wander as a fugitive, Cain builds a city to bear his son's name, Enoch.

### Cain, Enoch, and the First City

Must we see this history as an indictment of the city as opposed to the Garden of Eden? Was Cain, as Ellul has argued, trying to make the world over again?[12]

Several clues point in that direction. For one thing, Cain had been cursed by God to wander (Gen. 4:12). His building of the city, a metaphor of a stronghold refuge against one's enemies (Pss. 46, 48), appears on the surface to be resistance to that curse. He seeks to find alone the remedy for a situation he created.

Another hint is that this story of the first city falls in the chronology of the line of Cain (4:17–24), not that of the godly line of Seth (5:3–32). Seth's line begins "to call upon the name of the Lord" (4:26). By intended literary contrast, Cain perpetuates his own name in the self-sustaining security of the city. And concluding the chronology of Cain's seed is the proud violence of Lamech (4:23–24), "hinting at the fact that the city is a place where violence flourishes, not least family violence."[13]

At the same time, there are hints of a more positive view of the city. Genesis is doing more here than simply playing off city versus country. The city that flows from the line of Cain is also the place of human achievement, the center of civilization. Art and technology (the invention of harp and flute, the forging of bronze and iron tools) arise within its walls (4:20–22).

Cities, the Genesis record seems to imply, are provisions of God's common grace; they play a remedial role in human life. Through them God restrains the development of evil, blesses his fallen creatures, and works out his sovereign purpose in both judgment and grace.[14] They evidence God's preserving and preventative grace.

> Man may turn the city into something more dreadful than the howling wilderness, but that is another matter. As the provision of God's common grace, the city is a benefit, serving mankind as at least a partial, interim refuge from the wilderness condition into which the fallen race, exiled from paradise, has been driven. . . . Functions that would have been performed by the city apart from the Fall are now modified by being turned to the new purpose of offsetting, to an extent, the evils arising through man's sinfulness and as a result of the common curse on the race.[15]

In all this, the double-edged character of the city is apparent. It is a sign of both God's gracious concern for his fallen creation and rebellious humanity's quest for security apart from God.

### Nimrod, the City, and the Tower of Babel

We next meet the negative side of the city in the history of the Tower of Babel (Gen. 11:1–9). We are prepared for this by the introduction in Genesis 10:8–12 of its builder, Nimrod, the verb form of whose name may mean "let us revolt." "The world's first great conqueror" (Gen. 10:8 TEV), he leaves a trail of urban civilizations in his wandering—Erech, Accad, Calneh, Nineveh, Rehoboth-Ir, Calah, Resen, and, preeminently, Babel/Babylon.

The Babel story is a dialectic of centripetal and centrifugal movements. Humanity seeks to rise up to God, God descends to curse humanity's pride. Humanity strives to maintain unity, God divides and disperses the race. Humanity seeks for a self-center, God counters with divine scattering.[16]

Linked to the dispersion motif of earlier chapters (4:12; 9:19; 10:18), the history of the city and tower of Babel centers on its builders' proud efforts to avoid scattering (11:4, 8, 9) and to make for humanity a name that would defy heaven (11:4).[17] Like Cain's city, Babel is to become a refuge from the insecurity of an open world and the destiny willed for them by God. "They were supposed to fill the world, and the previous chapter has described the scattering of peoples as part of humanity's filling the world after the flood; but these people resist that destiny. They want to stop in one place, and find a unity grounded in . . . excluding God."[18]

This divine dispersion theme continues throughout the Bible. The testing of Abraham's faith in the covenant promise of land is reflected in his wandering, homeless life. The slavery of Jacob's jealous children, exiled in Egypt, parallels the Babel narrative, for like Nimrod and his compatriots, the oppressed Hebrews build cities (Exod. 1:11) with bitumen (Exod. 1:14; cf. Gen. 11:3). The wilderness wandering as a judgment on the spies' lack of faith (Num. 14:20–24), the dispersal of the ten tribes and the Babylonian exile of the remaining two—all these repeat the themes of scattering begun in the enforced departure of Adam and Eve from the garden. The cities of the world are only temporary stops for a people who must learn that security is in residing in the mountain-city of Jehovah and keeping his covenant (Deut. 6:10–12; Ps. 43:1–3).

The city and the tower/ziggurat also had a special and extended significance well known in Mesopotamia. In places like ancient Uruk (in the Bible, Erech; Gen. 10:10) in Sumeria, ziggurats were artificial world mountains of mud-brick and bitumen; like Uruk, they were associated with temples where the priest held his briefing sessions with the city god.[19] They were cosmic mountains, links between heaven and earth.[20] In fact, the Hebrew designation *Babel* (confusion) could very well be an apologetic word play on the extrabiblical designation for the city, *babili(m)*, "gate of the gods."

The biblical Babel narrative, however, "is no mere adaptation of the Mesopotamian ziggurat tradition, lacking in historical facticity. On the contrary, Genesis 11:1–9 is the record of an actual event."[21] The ziggurat ideology of the ancient Near East originated in the event recorded in Genesis 11. But it suffers from radical distortion by mythologization, a guilty suppression of the creature's violation of the Creator's covenant. Genesis brings us face to face with the reality of human autonomy in its flight from God.

Later biblical literature picks up the image of sinful rebellion in lofty towers and, in polemical language, repeats God's rebuke against human pride uttered at Babel. The cities Israel dispossesses by conquest are "great and fortified up to heaven" (Deut. 1:28), but God casts them down. High towers symbolizing human strength are brought low by divine power (Isa. 2:12–17; 25:2–3; 30:25; 33:18; Jer. 51:53).[22]

In apologetic contrast to these idolatrous images of world mountains portraying the dwelling of the gods, Jehovah is pictured as dwelling on the urban mountain citadel (Pss. 87:1–3; 125:1–2). "Great is the LORD, and greatly to be praised, in the city of our God, in His holy mountain" (Ps. 48:1–2). Jerusalem, the citadel on Mount Zion, becomes the dwelling place of the Lord (Isa. 60:14), "the city of our God" (Pss. 48:3; 74:2; 84:7; Isa. 18:7).[23] The prophets expectantly await the coming day when the Edenic river of life will flow from the Lord's house (Ezek. 47:1–12; Joel 3:18) and the Lord reigns as king over the whole earth (Zech. 14:8).[24]

### Abraham, Sodom, and Gomorrah

In narrating the transition from the history of the city and tower of Babel in Genesis 11 to the life of Abraham beginning in Genesis 12, the author paints an intentional contrast. The city builders of Babel express contempt for God by attempting to settle in a city. Abraham expresses his faith in God by following the Lord out of his city (11:31–12:5). The tower builders rebelliously refuse to wander anymore; Abraham wanders faithfully, "looking forward to the city with foundations, whose builder and architect is God" (Heb. 11:9–10). The planners of Babel seek to make a name for themselves (Gen. 11:4); God promises to make Abraham's name great (12:2).[25]

Looking at Abraham's links to the city may sound strange to some. Countless sermons give his wandering an almost rural coloring. Significant biblical scholarship characterizes him as a semi-nomad.[26] But seeing him more as a traveling merchant prince may come closer to the truth.[27] His life of faith and the testing of his faith repeatedly were linked to the city. Out of Ur, the greatest trading city the world then knew, he came. In an urban world whose walls were under the protection of deities, "he lived like a stranger in a foreign country" (Heb. 11:9). He went from city to city along heavily traveled urban trade routes.[28] In covenant commitment to God, he left Haran, the "Caravan City" (Gen. 12:4). In covenant devotion he built an altar near Luz (12:8; 13:3), which—perhaps in anticipation of its later urban history—Genesis names Bethel (35:6–7).

Abraham's urban concerns and faith shine most brightly in the extended history of Sodom and Gomorrah and his dialogue with the Lord over their fate. God promises to judge the wicked cities (13:13) as he judged the city and tower of Babel. The same "outcry" that spoke from the earth when

Cain spilt Abel's blood (4:10) speaks now of the rampant oppression in the twin cities (18:20–21; 19:13). The city, intended for refuge and safety, threatens to transform even Lot's hospitality (19:1–3) into perversion (19:6–8), restrained only by God's direct intervention (19:10–12).

The erotic and orgiastic depravity of Sodom, characteristic of the Canaanite fertility cult of Baal and Astarte (Lev. 18:22–25; 20:13–23), is striking. But there are hints of other twistedness in the city. The weak Lot had chosen it because it promised wealth and ease (Gen. 13:10–12). Abraham had refused the wealth its king wanted to shower on him for defeating the four marauding kings (14:22–23). Ezekiel later condemned the people of Sodom for "pride, surfeit of food, and prosperous ease; they did not help the poor and needy" (Ezek. 16:49).

The Sodomites' violence and oppression toward the angel-strangers (cf. Heb. 13:2) was no isolated incident. Lot's urgent insistence that they spend the night inside his home (Gen. 19:3) hints that he expected what followed; it was but a sample of a regular pattern. This suggestion "is in keeping with the rationale that Genesis gives for Yahweh's revealing to Abraham his intention for Sodom—that Abraham's vocation is to do with 'what is right and just' (18:19)—the classic double priority to which the prophets keep returning."[29] The prophets later speak to this barbarity and injustice in connection with the cities (Isa. 1:10; 3:9).

But God did not write off the city easily—not before listening carefully to Abraham's impassioned plea on its behalf. God responded that he would spare the city if ten righteous people could be found in it (Gen. 18:23–32). He had promised that "all the peoples of the earth would be blessed through" Abraham (12:3). Here Abraham put God's covenant commitment to the test of prayer.

Later Scripture points preeminently to Sodom and Gomorrah as symbols of God's judgment against wickedness (Deut. 29:23; Jer. 49:18; Amos 4:11; Luke 17:29). But God's promise of grace is not forgotten, either. To an Israel likened to Sodom, God promises restoration and comfort (Ezek. 16:53–55). Lot and his family, rescued from Sodom, are reminders of the remnant of grace (2 Pet. 2:6–9).

## Urban Redemption and the Blessing of Grace

Alongside this dark picture of the city in Genesis is the theme of the city's part in the redemptive purposes of God, an exhibition place for God's grace. This redemptive/eschatological strand repeatedly ties the condition of the city to the mercies of Jehovah. The image that brings them all together is the covenant.

Covenant language, particularly the Hittite vassal treaties, had a long ancestry in the cities of the ancient Near East.[30] Urban legal documents—theopolitical affirmations—were shaped by it. Any single treaty might vary from another—an element might be omitted, or the order might differ—but the basic pattern of a covenant treaty between one major power, the suzerain, and his subordinate vassal was uniform.

Genesis, like the rest of the Pentateuch, is embroidered in this language. Shorn of Near Eastern mythology, it underlies much of the material we have examined already. The creation history and the Garden of Eden narrative are good examples.

In Genesis 1, the preamble of the covenant, we meet God, the emperor of the creation. He appears "not as a king among kings for whom the Canaanite term *melek* was proper, but as 'Suzerain,' a technical term in political science for a monarch who acknowledged no other power the equal of his own. In his sphere all power was derivative from him."[31] The royalty of the sovereign Lord of creation is antithetical to that of the local city-kings. He but speaks, and the world comes into being!

Consistent with the pattern of the suzerainty treaties, a historical prologue tells the basis of the relationship of suzerain and vassal. Can we not see here the significance of the repeated history of Genesis 2, this time focusing on Adam and Eve and their covenant responsibility in the garden? Similar to the treaty forms, it is a most unlegal document in the reading. In the free storytelling form of the covenant style, the suzerain God identifies himself as the owner of the garden in which he has graciously placed the man and woman (Gen. 2:8). The context of the whole is the suzerain's goodness, which demands obedient response from the grateful vassal.

Like the treaties, Genesis then tells the vassal's obligations under the covenant to obey the suzerain (2:16–17; 3:2–3) and pronounces a curse on infidelity (2:17) and a promise of blessing on fidelity: access to the tree of life (2:9), from which, however, sin bars the fallen man and woman (3:24).

Genesis also presents a new note: the promise of salvation not by the covenant breaker's own effort but by the suzerain's act of divine sovereign intrusion (3:15). Despite the curse of sin and the violation of the covenant, humanity's urban cultural calling will be fulfilled: Adam's painful labor will subdue the earth, Eve's travail will fill it. All this is by God's sovereign, saving disposition and the covenant victory of the seed of the woman over the serpent.

### Covenant Grace and Urban Rebellion

In keeping with the gracious promises of God in the covenant, Genesis then records the effect of divine grace on each of the urban scenes of rebellion we have drawn. Even in the curse on Cain, God promises blessing. He sets his mark on Cain to spare his life (4:15–16), and Cain's building the city (4:17) reminds us not only of human efforts to escape the divine curse of wandering but also of the divine provision of urban security for wanderers.

The cultural achievements of the line of Cain reinforce this hint of grace promised to the city. Music, forging metals, and building cities—all are samples of God's common grace and patience toward his fallen, broken creation.

We must look at the scattering of the urban builders at Babel in this same light. It did more than merely demonstrate God's wrath against the builders' impious spirit. It also pointed to God's redemptive, covenant purposes for the city. In faithfulness to his promise after the flood (9:11, 15), he does not allow humanity's sinful activity to reach such a scale as to demand another catastrophe on the same scale. "If the whole of humanity had remained concentrated, the power of sin would likewise have remained united, and doubtless soon again have reached stupendous proportions."[32] The very real mercies of common grace provide the field of operation for redemptive grace.[33] By breaking up the city, God saves the cities.

This same theme of God's gracious intervention also explains why the author of Genesis placed the so-called Table of Nations (Gen. 10) not after the Babel narrative, where it belongs chronologically, but before it. "If the material of ch[apter] 10 had followed the Babel story, the whole Table of Nations would have to be read under the sign of judgment; where it stands it functions as the fulfillment of the divine command of 9:1, 'Be fruitful and multiply, and fill the earth', which looks back in its turn to 1:28."[34] The arrangement of the material reminds us that the dispersal of the nations at Babel tokens both the divine judgment and the divine blessing (9:1) of grace.

### Covenant Grace, the City, and the Patriarchs

In this same spirit, the covenant blessing on Abraham includes the peoples and their cities (12:3; 18:18; 22:18). Repeatedly his life touches the cities and, true to God's covenant promise, his name is made great and he is a blessing (12:2–3).

In support of the alliance of the five urban rulers, he recovers the wealth of the cities of Sodom and Gomorrah (14:1–16). Jerusalem finds its first biblical mention when Melchizedek, its priest/king, receives a tithe from Abraham (14:18–20). At Abraham's intercession and for the sake of only ten righteous, the Lord would have spared the cities of the plain (18:22–32). The city of Gerar, through Abimelech its king, pays tribute to Abraham: "My land is before you; live wherever you like" (20:15). The sons of Heth acknowledge him as "a mighty prince among us" (23:6).

The same pattern continues in the lives of the patriarchs who follow Abraham. From the city of Nahor (24:10) come a wife for Isaac and a prediction of urban blessing and rule for her descendants: "may your offspring possess the gates of their enemies" (24:60). Isaac's own encounter and treaty making with Abimelech in the Philistine city of Gerar (26:18–33) parallel his father's history (21:22–34).

The cities and God's covenant promise of blessing meet again in Jacob's life. Where God appears to Jacob during his flight from Esau, the city of Bethel, "the house of God" (28:16–19), springs up. During his return to meet Esau, he encounters the Lord again, and another city, Peniel, "Face of God," grows up to commemorate the event (32:22–30; cf. Judg. 8:8). As they often did in the lives of Abraham (Gen. 13:3–4) and Isaac (26:1–2, 23–25), altars frequently become urban memorials of God's presence, to which the patriarch returns (35:1–7).

Events reminiscent of Abraham's urban experiences occur in Jacob's life as well. As Abraham bought real estate in Hebron (23:17–20), so Jacob buys land from the citizens of Shechem (33:18–19). Just as Abraham's presence was acknowledged as a blessing by the city, so too Jacob's presence is commended (34:20–24). Not intimidated but awed by God's protection of Jacob when he returned to Bethel, the people of the surrounding cities sense "the terror of God . . . so that no one pursue[s]" him (35:5).[35]

The concluding chapters of Genesis (37–50) focus on Joseph. Again the cities of the Gentiles reap blessing from the presence of Abraham's seed. Potiphar's house is blessed "for Joseph's sake" (39:5; cf. 12:3; 28:14). By making use of Egypt's cities as store houses for grain (41:35, 48), Joseph averts a universal famine. His relief program saves not only Egypt but also the children of Jacob.

The Joseph narrative is a bridge to the remainder of the Pentateuch. It explains the presence of Jacob's children in Egypt and prepares us for the history of their slavery and deliverance in the Book of Exodus. At the same time, it is a foil to the history of Genesis 1–11, linking the end of the book with its beginning.

Some verbal and literary parallels have been interpreted in this way.[36] Does Joseph's response to his brothers, "Fear not, for am I in the place of God?" (50:19) recall the phrase from Eden, "you will be like God" (3:5)? Does he allude to the serpent's words "you will not die" (Gen. 3:4) when he acknowledges God's beneficent purpose as "the saving of many lives" (50:20)? Is it by design that the creation formula "and it was good" occurs again in the Joseph cycle (40:16; 49:15), but nowhere else in Genesis?

In similar fashion, "Joseph's expulsion from Canaan parallels the expulsion from Eden, but the movement away from life is reversed in his being sent by God into Egypt 'to preserve life' (45:5–8). The universal famine of the Joseph story is a counterpart to the primeval universal deluge; the strife between Joseph and his brothers, which is resolved in reconciliation, brings to a happy conclusion the fraternal rivalry that begins with Cain and Abel and runs throughout the patriarchal stories."[37]

Most strikingly for our purposes, can we see here allusions, even parallels, to the urban history of Genesis 1–11 and its conclusion in the history of the city and tower of Babel? The Babel narrative tells how God in judgment thwarted humanity's sinful pride to save the earth's cities and his people. That judgment, we have argued, also contained the promise of grace. Joseph's story tells how God thwarted the brothers' jealousy to save the earth's cities and his people. Again, judgment carries the purposes of grace.[38]

As we move beyond Genesis, these themes of covenant redemption and grace revolving around cities enlarge. Cities the Israelites occupy on entering the promised land are gifts from God (Deut. 6:10–11; Ps. 107:36). No human achievements win them (Deut. 8:17); the same divine hand that delivers from Egypt gives them freely (Deut. 7:17–19).

The Mosaic legislation designates cities of refuge as symbols of divine, not self, protection for those guilty of involuntary manslaughter (Num. 35:9–34). So Joshua consecrates six locations immediately after the exodus (Josh. 20:1–9). They are the firstfruits of the redemption of the divine kinsman (Job 19:25; Isa. 41:14; 44:21–22).

Preeminently, however, the themes of redemption and the Edenic return to peace in God's dwelling place focus, in the Old Testament, on Jerusalem. She becomes a sign, a witness to God's work of gracious adoption. Her pagan origins are never forgotten. Like an unwanted child, aborted and abandoned, she lay exposed, struggling in her own blood till the Lord came and called, "Live!" (Ezek. 16:3–6). When she was naked, God, her lover, covered her (16:7–8).

Jerusalem was to stand as a testimony to the world's cities of the unity and peace possible under God's covenant (Ps. 122:6–9). "The Lord builds up Jerusalem; He gathers the outcasts of Israel" (Ps. 147:2). David's capturing Jerusalem from the Jebusites finally united all the tribes of Israel, not merely Judah, under his reign. Fearing that the Israelites' attraction to Jerusalem as the center of worship would lead to reunification of the divided kingdom, Jeroboam erected shrines at Bethel and Dan as substitutes (1 Kings 12:26–30).

Throughout the prophetic literature, Jerusalem also takes on eschatological significance as a sign of adoption. The blessing of the patriarchs to the Gentile cities finds its full meaning as the city of Melchizedek one day becomes the mother of all nations (Ps. 87). Hiram, king of Tyre, helps build her (2 Sam. 5:11); Cyrus, king of Persia and God's messiah (Isa. 45:1), rebuilds a house for God in her (Ezra 1:2–3). Nations will flow to her, remolding tools of war into those of covenant peace (Isa. 2:2–4).

One day Jerusalem will fulfill her role as "the joy of the whole earth" (Ps. 48:2; cf. 68:31; 86:9; 137:1–2, 5–6). At the coronation ceremony of her divine king, Gentiles also will participate in her messianic feast (Ps. 72:10–11, 15, 17, 19). Jerusalem's pilgrims will include the cities of the world (Isa. 60:3). She will be set by God "in the center of the nations, with countries round about her" (Ezek. 5:5).

But even this exaltation for Jerusalem will not be humanly won. Grace must fashion its urban victories in Jerusalem, just as in any other city. The prophets condemn her covenant breaking, her desire to be like the other cities, her injustice to the poor (Isa. 10:1–2). Assyria, "the land of Nimrod," will one day be shepherded with a sword, not a staff (Mic. 5:6). And, like her, the cities of Israel will be demolished (Mic. 5:11, 14). Babylon, "overthrown by God like Sodom and Gomorrah" (Isa. 13:19), will experience a new urban immigration—of jackals, owls, and wild goats (13:21–22; Jer. 50:39–40). Jerusalem's streets will welcome the same populace (Isa. 34:12–15). Like the heap of ruins that was once Damascus (17:1–3), she too will stand desolate, forsaken like the desert (27:10). The joy of the whole earth will be "the delight of donkeys, a pasture for flocks" (32:14). Using the imagery of the Genesis flood, Isaiah pictures her as a ruined city in a watery waste (24:1–12).

But God will not forget his covenant of grace with either Jerusalem or the Gentile cities. Once again covenant blessing will touch them all; they will be included in the circle of grace. Mercy will rebuild what justice broke down. From the purification of judgment will emerge a new day for the

city, and a new citizenship. The day is coming, the Old Testament concludes, when the registry of Zion will include the cities of Philistia, Tyre,
and Cush (Ps. 87:4–5; Isa. 56:3–8). Egypt and Assyria will worship the Lord
with Israel (Isa. 19:19–24). "In that day five cities in Egypt will speak the language of Canaan and swear allegiance to the LORD Almighty" (Isa. 19:18).
Even Babylon, the great archetypal urban foe of Jerusalem (Jer. 50–51), will
have all the birth certificates of her citizens stamped with the Lord's affirmation, "This one was born in Zion" (Ps. 87:6).

## The Consummation and Calling of Urban Grace

These prophetic visions of the future of the city are not without their
hints in the Genesis record. Not so specifically eschatological, there are
still reminders that what the cities experienced of grace, directly or indi-
rectly, is still incomplete without a future fullness and consummation. The
blessings of grace are still incomplete; promises await further fulfillments.

The lives of the patriarchs exemplify this incompleteness. The fulfillment of the promise to Abraham to bless all the peoples of the earth
through him remains mixed throughout the record. Through his intervention the five urban kings are blessed, but at the expense of the judgment of war and devastation on the kings of the four other cities (Gen.
14:8–16). Despite Abraham's intercession for Sodom and Gomorrah, God
destroys those cities. His deceptions about Sarah twice bring divine judgment on his hosts: disease in Pharaoh's household (12:17–20), and infer-
tility in Abimelech's (20:17–18).

Conflicts occur repeatedly in the history. Abraham and Lot's possessions require their separation (13:1–9). The city of Beersheba takes its
name from the site of a treaty demanded by Abimelech, who fears that
Abraham will not show kindness to him (21:22–31). Isaac's wells provoke
conflict with the same Abimelech (26:12–20). Jacob's encounter with God
and his raising altars at Bethel and Peniel are occasioned by his conflicts
with Esau and his fears of their outcome. At Bethel, the Abrahamic
promise of blessing "all peoples on earth" through Jacob must be renewed
(28:14). In retribution for the rape of their sister Dinah, Jacob's sons kill all
the males in Shechem and carry off the city's wealth, women, and children (Gen. 34).

The end of Genesis underlines, in the deaths of Jacob and Joseph, this
perception of promise still unfulfilled. Jacob, bearer of the promise, is
buried not in Egypt, where he died, but in the land of promise not yet

possessed (50:12–14). Joseph, confident of the same promise (50:24–25), arranges for his burial in that same land (Exod. 13:19; Heb. 11:22).[39]

Where will we find the final fulfillment of this consummation promise? What links the images of city and house, king and creation, grace and covenant in Genesis? To whom will we look in that day when Zion lifts up its voice as the bearer of good news and says "to the cities of Judah, Behold your God!" (Isa. 40:9–10)?

The good news of the New Testament is that in Jesus the redemptive expectations of the city are fulfilled. In closing we will try to demonstrate this, using themes, motifs, and images from the Gospels especially.

### *Jesus the Diaspora Pilgrim*

The patriarchal wandering theme of Genesis arises again in the ministry of Jesus. The only period when he was settled—growing up in Nazareth—is passed over in silence. Luke's introduction to Jesus' life takes him from Nazareth to Bethlehem in his mother's womb. Matthew records his early flight into and exile in Egypt, the place of Genesis's conclusion (Matt. 2:14–15). His public ministry takes him from city to city, but he settles in none. He is not deterred by their urban pleas to settle down (Luke 4:42–43).

Could there be a reflection here of Jesus not only as the last Adam (1 Cor. 15:45) but also as the last Cain? "Cain was placed under a curse and told he would be a wanderer, but he refused to accept this and built a city instead. Jesus, who came to undo every curse on humankind, took Cain's place and accepted a life of wandering, trusting as Cain failed to do in the promise of his Father's protection and provision. In doing this he declares his freedom from the city and breaks the hold of the city and its false security that has beguiled the human race."[40]

In his work as Savior of the city, Jesus moves as a pilgrim wanderer, calling the cities to follow him. "Foxes have holes, and birds of the air have nests, but the Son of Man has nowhere to lay his head" (Luke 9:58). Not in complaint but in recognition of the divine curse on the sins of the city, Jesus bears the curse of wandering that Cain and the Babel tower builders had sought to escape. What theologians will later call Christ's active obedience is capsulized in his acceptance of perpetual flight to remove the curse from humanity. In his resistance to the tempting allure of the glory of the world's cities (Luke 4:5–8), he learns obedience and builds the heavenly city where we may, through his atoning work, find that only legitimate place to end our running.

### Jesus the Bearer of Grace and Judgment

As he wanders, like the patriarchs, his presence signals both grace and judgment for the cities and their people. Simeon in the temple/house of the Lord in Jerusalem gazes at the baby Jesus and, in thanksgiving to God, announces, "My eyes have seen your salvation" (Luke 2:30). Jesus raises the widow's only son from the dead in the city of Nain (Luke 7:11–17). A prostitute "from the city" (Luke 7:37) receives his forgiveness of sins. To the cities he sends his disciples, empowered to heal the sick and announce the approach of the kingdom in the approach of Jesus (Luke 10:1, 9, 17). And, at Calvary, "outside the gate" of the city, he suffers "to make the people holy through his own blood" (Heb. 13:12).[41]

But the response to grace is not always repentance and obedience. In the region of the Gadarenes, he drives out demons. But "the whole city" responds by pleading "with him to leave the region" (Matt. 8:34). "The cities in which most of his miracles had been performed" reject him (Matt. 11:20). He warns his disciples about cities where the gospel's good news will not be received (Luke 10:14–15). Chorazin, Bethsaida, and Capernaum will fare worse in the judgment day than Sodom and Gomorrah (Luke 10:10–12; cf. Matt. 10:15; 11:24). They have tasted, in the miracles and words of Christ, the redemptive power of the kingdom of God. They have seen the signs pointing to the coming of God in Christ. But they have rejected God in rejecting Christ.

### Jesus the Kingdom/City/House Builder

Genesis, in introducing Jehovah's relationship to the city, wove together a number of images. Motifs like house, city, mountain, and garden flow together repeatedly in the descriptions of creation and humanity's search for security after the fall.

Later parts of the Old Testament, we have argued, repeat them in a variety of ways. Isaiah describes Israel first as a house shelter in a garden, then suddenly switches the metaphor in the same passage to a city under siege (1:8). A prophecy of the coming of the Messiah speaks of going to the Lord as going to the city of God, and that, in turn, becomes going to the mountain of the Lord, to the house of the God of Jacob (Isa. 2:2–3). Entering into the security of the Lord becomes entering into his urban fortress (Ps. 46:4, 7; 91:2, 9). His coming reign will be urban (Isa. 24:23; Zech. 14:16–17; Mic. 4:7). David's desire to commemorate the reign of God by building a house for the Lord in the city is rejected; instead, the Lord will build a house for David and establish his house and kingdom forever (2 Sam. 7:11–16).

In the New Testament these interwoven motifs emerge again, now in announcing the arrival of that eternal Davidic kingdom of God in Jesus' arrival. The redeeming reign of promise, the royal power of God, is visible in the word and works of Jesus.

To describe that coming of the kingdom of God, our Lord uses many of these Old Testament metaphorical synonyms. Particularly striking is his understanding of the kingdom as the house of God.[42] Thus we "enter (into)" the kingdom as into a city or a house (Matt. 5:20; Mark 9:47; 10:23). Those entrusted with the gifts of the kingdom are house stewards (Matt. 25:21, 23). Teachers instructed about the kingdom of heaven are like house owners in the care of great wealth (Matt. 13:52).

The joy of the kingdom of God as the epiphany of God himself, as king in power and glory, is pictured as a royal banquet feast or supper in a home (Matt. 8:11; 22:1–14; Luke 14:15). We "enter (into)" the feast (Matt. 25:21, 23), and the unworthy are thrown out into the dark (Matt. 8:12; 22:13) or not let in at all (Matt. 25:11; Luke 13:25, 27).

Similarly, the urban metaphor appears in Jesus' teaching, though less overtly. City and house are interchangeable in describing the kingdom defeat of Satan and Jesus' self-defense of his ministry: "No city or house divided against itself will stand; and if Satan casts out Satan, he is divided against himself; how then will his kingdom stand?" (Matt. 12:25–26). From "the streets and alleys of the city" the kingdom feast will call its banqueters (Luke 14:21). A widow "in the city" illustrates the kingdom power of persistent prayer (Luke 18:1–3).

There may be a reason, however, for this minimizing of general materials on the city and kingdom in the Gospels. Their focus turns particularly to one city in its orientation of the ministry of Jesus. That city is Jerusalem.

### Jesus and Jerusalem

Jerusalem stands as a prophetic sign of the coming reign of God, an urban theocracy. In Jesus, the theocratic reality of the kingdom reign of grace appears. Jerusalem's place as the promise of God then recedes in the face of the promise's fulfillment in Christ. The God-with-us role typified by Jerusalem in the Old Testament becomes incarnate in Jesus-Immanuel.

In keeping with these connections, the Gospels emphasize the place of Jerusalem as the goal and fulfillment of the ministry of Jesus. In fulfillment of his messianic work of redemption, he "sets his face to go to Jerusalem" (Luke 9:51). Here his suffering, death, and resurrection inaugurate the kingdom of God (Luke 9:22; 13:33; 17:25; 18:32; 23:42–43). The "city of the great King" (Matt. 5:35) stands before him in terms of the messianic fulfillment of the kingdom plan of salvation. His death and resurrection here are the goal of his urban wandering, the surety of the promise that a new Jerusalem is coming.[43]

Thus even in the gospel message of fulfillment, as in Genesis, Jesus himself reminds us that the redemption of the cities is still incomplete, still awaiting its final consummation. Though Jerusalem's earthly temple one day will be waste (Matt. 25:2), he will come again in glory as the temple incarnate (John 2:19–22) for the final renovation of the heavens and the earth. Then he will bring with him the full inheritance of the people of God, "the kingdom prepared for you since the creation of the world" (Matt. 25:34).

For his disciples, living stones in the new temple (1 Cor. 6:19; 2 Cor. 6:16), citizens of the new Jerusalem (Gal. 4:26), there awaits the final city-temple (Rev. 21:22), the new creation (Rev. 21:1–2), the restored Garden of Eden (Rev. 22:1–3). There the divine badge of protection for wandering Cain (Gen. 4:15) becomes his name on their foreheads (Rev. 22:4). No longer driven from his presence, we see his face.

### Jesus' People and Their Consummation Calling

The Genesis history offers no picture of a passive community of faith waiting in abstraction from the city. The patriarchs were active participants in the economic and political life of the cities. Urban royalty from Pharaoh to Abimelech were touched by their influence. Cities grew up from their altars of devotion. An urban world of famine was saved by their wisdom.

They lived in cities of violence and injustice, flowing from the arbitrary wills of urban kings, representations of the arbitrary gods they worshiped. Cain's path of willfulness and Lamech's excess (Gen. 4:24) were duplicated again and again in cities like Sodom and Shechem. And, against this pattern, the people of God were called to display their faith in covenant through "doing what is right and just" (Gen. 18:19). Establishing justice and peace for the cities of the earth was to be their mission (Ezek. 18:5–9; 2 Pet. 2:4–10). Their prayer was for righteousness (Gen. 4:26; 18:22–33).

As we, like the Genesis saints, await the final consummation, the same calling makes its demands of us. Covetousness and ruthless greed belong to the old age (Col. 3:5). Moderation is the quality of life that says to everyone, "The Lord is near" (Phil. 4:5). The tyranny of self-assertion that marked the cities of Cain and Babel is to be swallowed up in the awareness that the new day of the kingdom has come in Christ. We live in the cities now, conscious of our covenant accountability for the whole creation under the lordship of Christ (1 Tim. 3:3; 2 Cor. 7:2). The life centered in Christ must manifest the wholeness, the *shalom*, of the restoration work begun by Christ in his new creation. An urban faith without works is as dead in San Francisco and Singapore as it was in Sodom (James 2:17).

## Discussion Questions

1. Identify some of the factors that have hindered scholars from recognizing the urban dimensions of Scripture.
2. What is the connection between the cultural mandate given to Adam and Eve and the development of urban life?
3. How is common grace evidenced in the city?
4. Discuss God's covenant of grace and redemption in relation to urban life.
5. Explain what Conn means by *urban grace*.
6. How should disciples of Christ express *shalom* in Christ in modern cities?

# 2

# CONFRONTING URBAN CONTEXTS WITH THE GOSPEL

*Roger S. Greenway*

## The Context of Poverty

Boys of nine and ten stagger from supermarket check-out counters to glistening cars in the parking lot, carrying heavy shopping bags for a few cents' tip from the owners. Among the children of the poor, carryout boys are privileged: they get to wear an identifying cap or shirt, and the shoppers are generous.

Out on the street, boys of ten and eleven clamor to wash the windshields of cars stopped at traffic lights. Traffic-light boys have the worst time. They may work eleven or twelve hours a day and face a beating at night when they bring home less than their parents expect. Other boys shine shoes or sell newspapers or lottery tickets.

Everywhere armies of children work instead of going to school. They roam the city in search of something to live on. No one knows how many children run loose on the streets. There are tens of thousands, even hundreds of thousands in the largest cities, and their desperate condition is a glaring indicator that things are wrong in Third World cities.

Uninitiated visitors to a great metropolis can be rudely awakened to some of the brutal realities of urban life. In Mexico City's fashionable Plaza

Garaibale, a tourist dining in an open-air restaurant suddenly saw the juicy steak disappear from his plate as a child ran by. The tourist gave chase and the child disappeared into a public lavatory. Foolishly, the man followed. No sooner had he entered the lavatory than he was attacked by a gang of children, beaten, and robbed of his valuables including his shoes. Along with the bruises the visitor received an important lesson about the city: hungry children live here, they will steal to get the food they need, and they will defend one another ferociously.

The overpopulation of Third World cities can be seen in government statistics and in facts and figures about rural-to-urban migration and the shortages of housing and sanitation. But the personal dimensions of urban overpopulation are expressed in other ways, like the appeals parents place in daily newspapers asking for information about missing children. The notices read like this:

> Your help is sought in locating Maria Isabel Martinez. Age: 13 years; complexion: dark; hair: black; forehead: small; eyes: brown; nose: straight; mouth: small, lips: thin; face: broad; height: average; figure: thin. Special circumstances: *does not know the city.*

Prostitution rings thrive on children like this. Daily, young girls arrive by bus or train from outlying towns and villages, hoping to locate a friend or relative and find work. Their parents send them to the city to earn money to send home, and many rural families are supported mainly by the earnings of children working in the city. But for every one who finds work and a way to survive, another gets lost in the city. Not only are jobs scarce, but also the wages of unskilled workers are hardly enough to live on. For thousands, crime and prostitution are the only alternatives.

Government agencies periodically attempt to curb the growth of street begging, violence, and the exploitation of children. But every time the authorities round up a few hundred children and attempt to rehabilitate them, their efforts are frustrated. In a few days, most are back on the street.

These urban armies of desperate children are symptoms of a whole network of problems that are social and economic, religious and political, familial and personal in nature. Rounding up children and keeping them out of sight for a while does nothing to solve the cancerous problems that forced them onto the streets in the first place. Without question, far-reaching and highly interrelated solutions have to be found that will reorder urban life at all levels. That is what urban mission is all about.

## Confronting Poverty Begins with Education

Poverty abounds in cities around the world, and North American cities have their share. For middle-class Christians it is difficult to believe that millions of their fellow citizens, many of them brothers and sisters in Christ, live in desperate poverty and struggle daily with problems that middle-class people never face.

For middle-class Christians in general, and for students in Bible colleges and seminaries in particular, confronting urban poverty's ugly realities begins with education. Middle-class churches cannot be expected to address the cities and expand their ministries to the poor unless church leaders show the way. Before that happens, changes will have to be made in the colleges and seminaries where church leaders receive training.

Harv Oostdyk, a man who has worked for thirty years in the ghettos of North America, observes that very few pastors and professors have even basic urban experience among the poor. They are "experientially deprived," says Oostdyk, no matter how scholarly they may be in other areas.[1] Most Protestant pastors and professors spend their time in suburban churches and comfortable classrooms and offices. They do not really know what life is like for millions and millions of city dwellers. This deficiency shows up in their teaching, rubs off on their hearers, and in the end produces churches and institutions incapable of understanding or ministering to the poor in the city.

One way to address this problem is for professors and church leaders to become personally involved with the poor and with ministry to them. If each Christian leader would become personally acquainted with at least one poor person and involved in one urban ministry among the poor, things would begin to change in our churches and schools. Teaching and preaching would be different. Petitions would be added to our prayers that we had not thought of before. No church or school would be the same after its leaders became involved with the poor. And life in the slums would change, too.

When pastors and professors engage in ministry among the poor, students and church members can be expected to do likewise. Members seldom do what they see their leaders avoid doing. But when leaders show the way and model genuine compassion in their own lives and ministries, it ripples through the institutions. Preaching and instruction take on new credibility, and ministries that were never tried before can be introduced.

# The Context of Cultural and Religious Pluralism

Cities in most parts of the world are grand mixtures of many different peoples, cultures, and religions. Such diversity can enrich human life, but it can also produce hostility and conflict. It can strengthen Christian faith or weaken it. It offers splendid opportunities for Christian mission, and it can also raise problems that threaten the foundations of Christian faith and witness.

My grandchildren have a wonderful picture book entitled *People*, written and illustrated by Peter Spier. The book celebrates the marvelous diversity that we see among the millions of people in the world, over half of whom live in cities. People come in all sizes and shapes: tall, short, and in between. Their hair and skin come in different colors. Their eyes have different shapes, and human noses come in every shape imaginable. So do faces, lips, ears, and almost everything else.

Spier points out to the children that besides their physical differences, people represent a wide variety of races, languages, and cultures. In line with their cultures, they dress differently, style their hair differently, and eat a wide variety of foods. They enjoy different music, different forms of entertainment, and different games and sports. What makes some people laugh makes other people cry. Some people eat and drink things that are forbidden to others.

There are rich people and poor, mansions and shacks. Some people work hard, while others are lazy, and many people want to work but cannot find a job.

Spier's book contains colorful pictures that illustrate the wide variety of religions people practice. There is the God of Luck of the Japanese, and Brahma the Creator that many Indians worship. There is the Hindu Snake God, and the Chinese God of Wealth. Asian sun worshipers are pictured, along with the Sea God from Nigeria, the Buddhist God of Wisdom, the Ten Commandments of Judaism, the sacred Kaaba of Islam, and the cross of Christianity.

Speaking more than two hundred different languages and many additional dialects, people live, work, communicate with each other, and worship the gods they believe in. In the end they all die.

How dull the world would be, Spier points out, if everybody looked, thought, ate, dressed, and acted the same! The book ends with a marvelous picture of a colorful, crowded city street showing an infinite variety of people and cultures. Celebrate diversity! says the book. Show respect and tolerance for people who are different from yourself. Life is more exciting because people are not all the same.

In the hands of wise Christian parents, Spier's book can be an excellent tool for introducing children to the reality of cultural and religious pluralism. Parents should point out to their children something the book does not plainly state, that God put variety into the world for the enrichment of human life and the glory of his name. Each and every person is meant by God to be different from all others, and each is to be respected as an image bearer of God.

At the same time, Christian parents must be careful to explain to their children the nature of the religious pluralism that Spier's book depicts. Children must not be given the impression that all the world's religions are on a par, the only difference being that some people prefer one religion while others choose another. Nor must children be led to think that respect and tolerance remove the need to engage in mission work and to communicate the gospel of Jesus Christ to followers of other faiths.

Nor must children be left in the dark concerning the non-Christian religious roots of many cultural practices. Children growing up in the context of a high degree of cultural and religious pluralism must be taught early in life to exercise discernment. They must learn to interpret their multicultural environment from the standpoint of the Christian faith and the normative teachings of the Christian Scriptures.

Pluralism is unquestionably an urban phenomenon. There are more Muslims in some cities of Europe than Protestants. Buddhist and Hindu centers are located in every metropolitan area of the world, including Latin America, where until recently the old "Christendom" still survived. Religious pluralism affects politics, public education, the financial world, and the military. It is no longer sufficient for Christian leaders to know the doctrine and practices of Christianity alone. An informed global citizen and active participant in community life must understand at least the basics about all the major religions.

The tendency in cities is to treat people's religious beliefs as private matters. Nevertheless, the encounter with new religious alternatives can undermine long-held convictions. Naive and ill-informed faith, the kind with which many peasants arrive in the city, will eventually take a severe beating. This makes the demands for an informed and dynamic discipleship urgent. Otherwise, you end up with a potpourri of religious notions with no authoritative basis in Scripture. It is precisely this kind of eclecticism that is emerging as the personal choice of many sophisticated urbanites.

## A New Age Urban Eclectic

An educated woman sitting next to me on a plane from Miami to South America illustrates pluralism's effect on some people. Her home was in Caracas, Venezuela, and she identified her religion as Roman Catholicism. She was a university graduate, a world traveller, and the distribution manager in Latin America for a Paris-based cosmetics company. The gold jewelry she wore was exquisite. The book she was reading was written by a Hindu guru.

When she learned my profession, her first question was: "What do you think of reincarnation?" It was the first time a South American Roman Catholic had asked me that question! When I inquired about the little cord she wore on her wrist between two heavy gold bracelets, she said that her "spiritual consultant" in Sao Paulo had tied the cord there. It had her name woven in the threads, and she was never to take it off lest it bring her bad luck. As long as she wore the cord, she need not worry about a plane crash, and her business would prosper.

Her daughter was studying in England and had been writing to her mother about the evangelical Christians who had befriended her. Her daughter, it seemed, was at the point of becoming an evangelical believer, and she was warning her mother that the end of the world was near. "I believe my daughter is right, that we are in the last days," the woman said to me in Spanish. She went on to share some evangelical convictions about Christ that she had learned from her daughter.

The woman was a grand eclectic, a true pluralist, with undercurrents of a traditional Catholicism she no longer trusted, a smattering of Hinduism, a dash of shamanism, and a sprinkling of evangelical ideas. She held to no objective source of religious authority—neither priests nor Bible—by which to evaluate the various ideas she encountered. She had only her private feelings and the latest thing she was reading. I believe she represented many urbanites of the new age.

One of the greatest challenges to Christian discipleship in the urban context comes from the inescapable encounters city people experience with other religions. In many ways we have returned to the social and religious context that characterized New Testament times. Christians are pressed daily to define what they believe and the source of religious authority on which they draw. Besides this, they are constrained to engage actively in the kind of religious apologetic that interacts with other religionists, spells out the relationship between the Christian way and the many other ways people choose, and invites them boldly and winsomely to follow Jesus.

This being the case, it is urgent that schools and seminaries that train Christian leaders take steps to enhance the intercultural effectiveness of the education they offer. All students preparing for Christian ministry need to acquire a basic understanding of the religions and cultures of the various people groups they are likely to encounter in the city.

Moreover, they should be equipped to explain the gospel in culturally appropriate ways to people who are different from themselves and to defend Christian teachings against non-Christian beliefs and values. The urban church's inability to penetrate certain cultures may be due in part to our failures in the past to train leaders properly for intercultural and interreligious communication and ministry. Built into every seminary curriculum should be ample attention to the diverse religious beliefs and cultural issues found among modern city dwellers.

## The Context of Rural Faith in the City

Today, throughout the Two-Thirds World, multitudes of Christians are caught in the waves of rural-to-urban migration. They are pouring from tribal villages and remote rural areas into towns and cities, and some to megacities, in what is unquestionably the largest migration in human history. It is estimated that a billion people—some 20 percent of the human race now living—migrated from rural to urban in the 1980s, and the trek continues. The alarming fact, religiously speaking, is that many of them arrive poorly prepared for the pressures and temptations of urban life. (See table 2.1 for a summary of the differences between rural and urban life.)

There are also the refugees who have been uprooted from their homelands and taken up residence in a new and unfamiliar land. Very often they come from rural areas and end up in cities. Their problems are compounded: a new land, a new language, an urban environment, new jobs, new types of housing, and new neighbors, most of whom they do not understand.

It is easy for recent immigrants to the city to fall into ways that wreak havoc on their family faith and morality. It is depressing for those who, on arrival in the new environment, suddenly become aware as never before of their own economic disadvantage and the wide gap between rich and poor. Unfortunately, rural religion generally does not prepare Christians well for urban life and its challenges. Rural religious life has many positive features, but the range of experience of rural Christians is understandably limited. Arriving in the urban ambience, they inevitably have difficulty adjusting to the new and harsh realities of urban life.

Table 2.1

## General Comparison of City and Rural/Village Life with Implications for Pastoral Ministry

(Differences between countries and continents are recognized.)

| Subject | Rural/Village Life | City Life |
|---|---|---|
| Population | Racial, cultural, religious, linguistic homogeneity | Diversity of races, cultures, religions, and languages |
| Family ties | Close ties, intimate awareness of one another; church is like an extended family | Relationships are casual; midweek life of church members is private |
| Church composition | Generally homogeneous in terms of occupation, education, and social scale | Professionally diverse and complex |
| Church schedules | Farm routine determines church schedule with seasonal adjustments | Business, industrial life determine church program, with breakfast and luncheon meetings |
| Spiritual life | Majority are second- and third-generation Christians with generally uniform spiritual experience and expression; few choices | More spiritual diversity, more new Christians with varied backgrounds; many choices |
| Mobility | Majority remain close to home and their traditional church | Constant change, movement, and competition |
| Information flow | Grapevine | Printed announcement |
| Finances | Simple budgets and much volunteer labor | Business approach, services remunerated |
| Pastoral style | Home visits, leisurely conversations | Appointments, most contacts at church, briefer visits |
| Outreach | Via long-term family and friendship ties | Public announcement, first-time contacts, various media |
| Expectations | Tolerant of traditional, often second-rate preaching, programs, services, and accommodations | Higher expectations, less tolerant of mediocrity; professional |
| Issues | Isolation from current social and religious conflicts; changes come slowly | Continual bombardment of new issues and conflicts; faith challenged by new ideas from everywhere |
| Programs | Traditional programs, low-profile advertising, modest posters, grapevine | New programs, high-profile ads, visibility |
| Values | Stability, familiarity, sameness, homogeneity | Change, diversity, privacy, mobility |
| Temptations | Quarrels, gossip, adultery, mostly between members of the community | Vices of many kinds, reinforced by freedom, anonymity, financial pressures, family breakdown, loneliness |

(Adapted from several sources.)

In my observation, pastors, especially those who have not gone through a major uprooting experience themselves, often fail to deal effectively with urban newcomers, and city churches generally behave awkwardly toward immigrants. A whole generation may pass before the newcomers feel they can participate actively in the internal life of the typical urban church. Many, especially young people, become lost in the meantime.

Pastors can help the new immigrants find their way into the church as well as the city if they will keep in mind some of the factors that make the transition difficult.

First, rural religion is largely traditional. It is rooted in the family and the community. Personal choice of a kind that carries the possibility of putting the individual in a minority position plays very little part. A person born in a particular village or town inherits the religious beliefs and practices of his or her family and community. Seldom is there the need to make a personal religious choice that sets the individual apart from the crowd. Some other religion may be adhered to by certain members of the community, but most rural and small-town people throughout the world live their entire lives without ever facing major religious choices. But things soon change when they come to the city. If there is a community of their own folk that they can cling to, they may avoid personal decisions for some time. But the pluralism of the city will not leave them alone forever, and sooner or later they must make choices that may go contrary to majority opinion.

Second, rural faith seldom has the qualities of a conscious world-and-life view. Consequently, it lacks the important synthesis between doctrinal beliefs and Christian responsibilities going beyond the church and activities directly related to it. As a result, when rural Christians arrive in the complex and highly diversified urban context, they find it difficult to transpose their beliefs and their rural-based understanding of Christian social responsibility to the realities of the city. Very often their personal faith undergoes great trauma. They may react by grasping at extreme fundamentalism to protect themselves from what they perceive as a threatening environment. Their ability to reflect on the Christian message and apply it to the problems and challenges of urban life, which are essential functions of urban discipleship, may be minimal for a long time.

Third, rural religion tends to present the gospel in terms that leave vast areas of human life untouched and unchallenged. Strange as it may seem, this weakness has been reinforced by countless city pulpits, especially in conservative church circles where rural attitudes continue to dominate urban congregations and popular pulpiteers keep their members socially tranquilized through rural-oriented preaching and teaching. As a consequence, one of the great weaknesses of some large city churches is that, so far as social consciousness is concerned, they are still living in their rural past.

No wonder many young intellectuals in the student world of Two-Thirds World countries, some of them sons and daughters of Protestant church leaders, turn their backs on the Christian faith as irrelevant to urban life! A survey conducted in the past decade in Central America indicated that nearly 80 percent of Protestant youth who enter the universities are lost to the church. Much of this has to be blamed on the inadequate teaching given in the average church.

The prophetic notes of the Bible are not being sounded as they should be, and young men and women go off to the university ignorant of the Scriptures' total message and unprepared for what they meet in classrooms and dormitories. Anything less than the "whole counsel of God" (Acts 20:27), drawing from the riches of both Old and New Testaments, will suffer heavy losses when subjected to the issues and conflicts raging in urban society.

For that reason, I call for serious efforts on the part of churches, denominations, and seminaries to help pastors and other church leaders come to grips with the struggles and changes faced by Christians in the city, particularly newcomers. At the seminary level, the multicultural and multifaith milieu of the urban world should be addressed not merely in one or two missions courses but throughout the theological curriculum.

For persons already in church ministry, workshops and seminars should be offered that will facilitate reflection on and understanding of urban discipleship. People can be helped to understand that many of the hurts and frustrations they experience in the city stem from their rural backgrounds and the traumatic changes involved in coming to live in the city. And they can be helped to think Christianly about the new issues confronting them and to apply Christian principles to the questions and challenges they now face.

Given the rate of rural-to-urban migration in many parts of the world and the potential loss if newcomers to the city are not helped to make the adjustment to urban Christianity, I can hardly imagine a challenge of greater urgency than the urbanization of church life, worship, ministry, theological education, and everyday discipleship.

## The Context of the Unsaved, Unchurched, Uncared-for

There are several billion people on this planet whose faith is not in the one and only Savior, Jesus Christ, and who worship something other than the one true God. Approximately half of these people live in cities. Some adhere to one of the major non-Christian religions like Hinduism or Islam. A growing number adhere to what is popularly called the New Age movement, which presents a radically different vision of God, the world, and the purpose of life. But whatever their religion may be called, it is essentially different from the message of the Bible. They worship something other than the triune God, and consequently they have no claim to the salvation that the gospel proclaims. The Christian response to these people is *evangelism*, by which I mean making disciples of Jesus Christ.

What cities need most are disciples of Christ, not just "converts," people who at some moment in their lives say yes to Jesus but never go beyond that. The Bible does not talk about converts but about disciples. Evangelism in the New Testament always aims at discipleship, and discipleship requires commitment to the King and to the purposes of the King in the world.[2]

When we call people to come to Christ in faith and repentance, we are inviting them to turn their backs on the old gods they formerly served and on the Babylon of which they were a part. By this turning they join the new kingdom of the Lord Jesus Christ and offer their lives, talents, and energy in service to him. That is what discipleship is about. It means asking with Saul, "Lord, what do you want me to do?" Authentic evangelism produces disciples who are followers of Jesus and citizen-workers in his kingdom. A simple way of defining evangelism is to say that it is a set of activities that have as their goal initiating people into the kingdom of Jesus Christ and to its service.[3]

Authentic evangelism also leads to church membership on the part of those who believe, and to church planting and church growth wherever the gospel spreads. This point needs to be reinforced today. From my point of view, "churchless Christianity" is in most cases something spurious, unbiblical, and empty. I am not here defending denominationalism as we have come to know it in the past two hundred years. But I am saying that it is impossible to read the New Testament, particularly its record of the ministries of the apostles, without seeing how important it makes the planting and growth of churches. We can conclude that any mission strategy for cities that does not emphasize the role of churches is seriously flawed.

## Church, Community, Cosmos

But there is still more. The comprehensiveness of the missionary task in the city requires the proclamation of the gospel, the planting and nurture of churches, *and* the application of the principles of Christ's lordship to all areas of community life. It means concern for all that is city, even for the cosmos above and beneath the city, from the quality of the air people breathe to the purity of the water in the rivers and canals. (See fig. 2.1.)

Figure 2.1
A Comprehensive View of Urban Discipleship:
All That Is City; All That Is Christ's

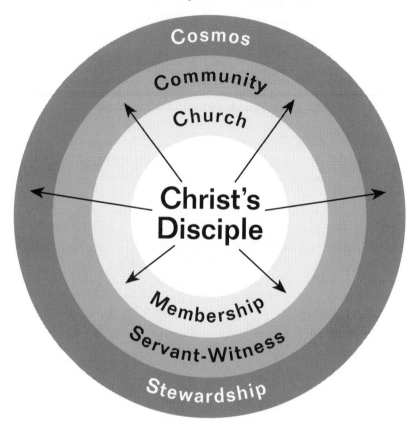

Urban discipleship means getting serious about issues like good schools, responsible government, sanitation and clean streets, fairness in the market-place, and justice in the courts. It means working to eliminate squalor, slums, and every depressing condition that dishonors God by degrading human life. Once urban disciples see the big picture of what it means to be citizens of Jerusalem in cities as they are, they begin to work from a new and enlarged perspective. Obedience to King Jesus takes them to every nook and cranny of city life. They find the challenges innumerable and the cost often high. But they know that while Babylon is great and its dark powers are awesome, Jerusalem is greater, and its advance is worth every sacrifice.

## Renewal for Discipleship and Mission

It is a mistake to think that churches as we know them can undertake what needs to be done in cities without experiencing inward renewal. A great deal has been said on the subject of church renewal, and I will only observe that churches that lack spiritual vitality and concern for truth and moral discipline cannot expect to engage fruitfully in urban discipleship. They may devise all the clever methods they please and spend heaps of money, but they will not make so much as a scratch on Babylon's skin. They themselves must first experience renewal.

To that end, I will briefly sketch a vision of what renewal might mean and where it might start for men and women who want to get serious about urban discipleship. My thoughts on this subject were triggered by a book written nearly thirty years ago by James Smart, *The Teaching Ministry of the Church*.[4] Smart points out that in his ministry, Jesus called people to become his disciples, learners, students of his teaching and his way of life. The learning process that Jesus followed consisted first of confronting the disciples with the reality of the kingdom and calling them to enter it by faith and make it their whole life.[5] The process began during the three years of Jesus' ministry and continued for a lifetime under the tutorship of the Holy Spirit.

Disciple making was key to Jesus' strategy for the salvation of the world. *He made disciples that they might become apostles.*[6] Jesus educated and disciplined them, that through them the movement of God's kingdom might pass on to the world with growing power and scope. Their discipleship was unto apostleship.

In the early church, it was assumed that all those who became Christians had chosen the life of discipleship with the understanding that they would undergo discipline and training. The goal was the expansion of the kingdom of God in a pagan world. Jesus had set the pattern. He never accepted people as his followers who were not willing to commit themselves wholeheartedly to God and God's kingdom. Likewise, in the early church, faith in Jesus meant work as his disciple. To be a Christian involved participation in Christ's redemptive mission. Not all were apostles, nor did all possess special gifts for preaching and teaching. But all who were disciples were expected to be witnesses to their faith before an unbelieving world. This was the source of early Christianity's explosive power.[7]

This is the key to what the church needs today in terms of discipleship and renewal for mission. The world's great cities will not pose such obstacles if in our churches and schools we adopt no lesser goal than what Jesus and his disciples had before them: discipleship for mission. Let us preach and teach with this goal in mind, that God will work in those we instruct to make them disciples wholeheartedly committed to the gospel of Christ's kingdom and possessing a faith that takes them to a thousand cities, witnessing with power through their words and actions.

## Discussion Questions

1. Identify the main characteristics of Third-World urban poverty and suggest ways in which Christians can and should address the issues involved.
2. From what you know about the rich, the "upper 5 percent," how would you define the church's mission to them in their context?
3. Put yourself in the place of a peasant who has recently arrived in a large city. You are poor, bewildered, and dismayed by your new surroundings. You attend a church. What would you be looking for there?
4. Describe some ways in which the following professionals can express their loyalty to King Jesus in specific urban contexts:
   a. a New York stockbroker;
   b. a police sergeant in Mexico City;
   c. a university student in Seoul, South Korea;
   d. a pastor in a poor Los Angeles neighborhood.
5. Explain Jesus' strategy in making disciples. Suggest some ways to apply this strategy to church and seminary education today.

# 3

# THE ROLE OF WOMEN IN DISCIPLING CITIES: A HISTORICAL PERSPECTIVE

*Ruth A. Tucker*

Blood and fire!
The Salvation Army
Two Hallelujah females
will speak and sing for Jesus
in the old chair factory
at Sixth and Oxford Streets
Oct. 5TH at 11 A.M. 3 P.M. 8 P.M.
All are invited to attend.

In 1879, handbills bearing this message summoned the people of Philadelphia to join in what was hoped would be a mighty awakening of souls. The attendance the first night, however, was bitterly disappointing. Only twelve people appeared. But the meetings continued, and within only a few weeks, "every bench in the factory was filled . . . every foot of standing room was taken."[1]

## A Lost History

Nineteenth-century American revivalism is often associated with the frontier and with rugged, raucous, "hellfire and brimstone" male evangelists, but some of the greatest revivals occurred in urban settings and under the preaching of women. Indeed, women played a very significant role in urban mission in America, Britain, and elsewhere in the world. But as in other fields of history, their contributions have been neglected by historians. "As so frequently happens in the writing of history," writes Patricia Hill, "the women have simply disappeared."[2]

Among those who have disappeared in the history books is Catherine Booth, one of the foremost urban evangelists of the nineteenth century. Her husband, William, is usually recognized as the founder of the Salvation Army, but she, no less than he, was involved in inaugurating and sustaining the movement. In addition to her own active ministry in behalf of the urban poor—especially "fallen" women—she paved the way for her female colleagues to enjoy an equal role with men in the Salvation Army. From the beginning, the movement welcomed women into its ranks alongside men, and in 1875 that provision was made official through Clause 14 of the Foundation Deed, which gave women the right to hold "any office" and "to speak and vote" at official Army meetings.[3]

Catherine herself set the example. She began preaching as a replacement for her husband when he was ill, but she later preached regularly to her own congregation on London's West End while he tended his flock on the East End.[4] Her style was evangelistic, and conviction was uncompromising: "Oh! people say, you must be very careful, very judicious. You must not thrust religion down people's throats. . . . Then I say, you will never get it down. What! am I to wait till an unconverted Godless man *wants* to be saved before I try to save him?"[5]

Catherine never ran from controversy. She welcomed it. "Opposition! It is a bad sign for Christianity of this day that it provokes so little opposition. If there were no other evidence of it being wrong I should know it from that."[6] Her controversial views often intruded into the political arena. She was a socialist, according to William Stead, who wrote her biography ten years after her death in 1900. Endorsed by her son Bramwell, the book spoke of her "radical antagonism" and "complete revolt against the existing order" and of her "sympathy" for "all schemes for remodeling society in accordance with humanitarian ideas."[7]

Her ideals for a more humanitarian society were evident in areas like medical relief, housing projects, prison reform, and employment programs initiated by the Army. But her most lasting legacy was the model she offered to other women—including her daughters and daughters-in-law—who followed in her footsteps. Women headed existing missions and opened new branches, and soon "Hallelujah lassies" were stationed all over the world. The work in America was begun by the "Splendid Seven," a team of seven young women led by Commissioner Railton. These women, and the many others who sacrificially served with the Army, prompted William Booth to say, "My best men are women."[8]

By 1904 the Army's work in America was headed by a woman—Evangeline Booth—and its tradition of serving the urban poor continued through her tenure as Commander in the United States and later as General of the worldwide organization. It is indeed a remarkable story. From the founding influence of Catherine and the lengthy rule of Evangeline to the present-day leadership of Eva Burrows, the Salvation Army has demonstrated the competence of women on every level of authority. Long before the Army was born, however, women filled strategic roles in urban mission.

## The Sunday School Movement

The first mass movement to involve women in urban mission came with the onset of the Sunday school movement in the late eighteenth century. Robert Raikes, considered the movement's founder, began his work in the 1780s with four women, and this pattern of women's participation continued in the generations that followed. According to Ian Bradley, "the most active agents in the conversion of the working classes to vital religion seem to have been the females. Most of the teachers in Sunday schools and ragged schools were women." It took time, however, before they were fully accepted in such roles—at least by outside observers. Lord Shaftesbury "was alarmed to find a young woman in her mid-twenties in charge of a class of men in a ragged school in a particularly rough area of London." The superintendent of the school responded that his only fear was "that some day a man might drop in who, not knowing the habits of this place, might lift a finger against her, for if he did so, he would never leave the room alive."[9]

The ranks of the early Sunday school movement in America were also filled with women who volunteered to serve the poor of the cities. Joanna Bethune and her mother, Isabella Graham, organized their first class in 1803, and within a short time others had followed their example, and Sunday schools were organized throughout New York and Philadelphia. In 1816, Bethune organized her Sunday schools on a wider scale. In a letter to a friend, she described how she had been publicizing the cause "in hopes that the gentlemen would come forward in the business, but after waiting a number of weeks, I conversed with several of my own sex, who expressed a wish to unite with me in a Female Sunday-School Union." Word quickly spread among Christian women, and the first organizational meeting drew several hundred women from various Protestant denominations. Classes started the following week, and within a few months there were more than two hundred teachers and more than three thousand pupils.[10]

## The Protestant Missionary Movement

While the Sunday school movement was getting underway in America, the missionary movement was also gaining momentum. In 1812, with great fanfare, America's first missionaries (and their wives—assistant missionaries) were commissioned to go abroad, but at home, mission ventures to the cities were becoming routine. Many women were involved in both foreign and domestic mission—one of the most extraordinary being Mary Webb. Though physically handicapped and confined to a wheelchair, Webb was a dynamic leader. In 1800, at twenty-one, she formed the Boston Female Society for Missionary Purposes and served as its secretary-treasurer for more than five decades, while ever broadening her influence:

> Several societies were spin-offs from the parent group, such as the Female Cent Society in 1803; the Children's Cent Society, first recorded as a society in 1811; the Corban Society, 1811, to raise money to help educate young ministers; the Fragment Society, 1812, to provide clothing and bedding for needy children; the Children's Friend Society, to provide day care for young children of working mothers; and a Penitent Females' Refuge, to help rescue and rehabilitate "those poor unhappy females who have wandered into the paths of vice and folly." She also founded societies to minister to immigrants, blacks, and Jews. No wonder Mary Webb was described as a "society within herself."[11]

It is important to keep in mind that Mary Webb was involved strictly in a support ministry and that the recipients of the support were, by and large, male missionaries. When the city mission work began, two ministers (Mr. Davis and Mr. Rossiter) were employed to do the work, and a five-year review of the work in 1821 showed that six men in addition to Andover seminary students had been employed to carry out the ministry. Webb worked within the prevailing confines of the religious attitudes of her day and did not challenge the accepted sex roles. Yet she contributed significantly to a changing mindset that would slowly open the doors for women in missionary service.[12]

### *Phoebe Palmer and Urban Institutional Work*

Another highly influential woman in urban ministry during the early decades of the nineteenth century was Phoebe Palmer, whose ministry among Methodists earned her the title "Mother of the Holiness Movement." As important as her efforts were in bringing mainline Methodists back to the perfectionist teachings of Wesley, her most enduring ministry was her active involvement in urban ministries. She was one of the most outstanding early leaders of inner-city mission work, and, according to Timothy Smith, her "pioneer work in social welfare projects illustrates the part which urban evangelization played in the origins of the Christian social movement."[13]

She was actively involved in establishing the Hedding Church, a city mission work that represented the early beginnings of the later settlement houses. She also conducted personal evangelism in the streets and prisons and founded the Five Points Mission. This was her "crowning achievement"—a mission project in New York that housed some twenty poor families and provided schooling and religious training as well. According to Smith, the beginnings of Protestant institutional work in the slums can be traced to this mission.[14]

### *Sarah Doremus: Philanthropy and Fund-raising*

Sarah Doremus was another effective organizer of urban mission work in the nineteenth century. She is also remembered for founding the Woman's Union Missionary Society of America in 1861. Prior to this, however, her work was concentrated in New York City, where she was involved in a vast array of Christian endeavors to help the poor and needy. She was the wife of a prosperous New York businessman and the mother of nine children, but her warm heart and compassion extended far beyond the boundaries of her immediate family. She "was the guiding light of practically every benevolent project in New York City," writes Patricia Hill. "Prisons, hospitals, foundling and old-age homes, and industrial schools as well as individual families were the beneficiaries of her personal, meticulous care."[15]

Doremus herself had never known any other life than one of privilege. She was born into wealth and grew up in elegant surroundings, and her marriage further advanced her social prestige. She had every opportunity to circulate among the fashionable elite, but her Christian values came first. "She gave up articles of personal adornment and bestowed the price upon schools and hospitals. . . . On her own feet she walked to hospitals, to city missions, to homes for aged women, to schools for Italo-Americans. . . . She held services in jails and inspired released prisoners to better living."[16]

Doremus's prison ministry began in the 1830s when she started conducting Sunday services in the City Prison in New York. She focused on female prisoners and served as the first director of the Women's Prison Association. She was associated with this ministry for more than thirty years. One aspect of that ministry involved the Home for Discharged Female Convicts, to which Doremus was particularly devoted. Through her prison work, she realized that prevention of crime was the most effective means of helping troubled youth and adults in the inner city, and she began expanding her ministries into other fields. She maintained an even longer tenure with the City Mission and Tract Society, which she managed for thirty-six years. If that was not enough to keep her busy, she served for twenty-eight years as the manager of the City Bible Society.[17]

"The list of enterprises in which she was involved, often as founder and/or first director, is astonishing," writes Carma Van Liere. "It includes the New York House and School of Industry, which provided work for poor women and schooling for their children; the Nursery and Child's Hospital, providing day and hospital care for children of the poor; the Presbyterian Home for Aged Women; the City Mission and Tract Society; the City Bible Society; and the Women's Hospital."[18]

### Urban Rescue Missions

Rescue missions gained popularity as the nineteenth century progressed, and frequently women teamed up with their husbands in these ventures, which focused primarily on indigent men. Among the most noted inner-city missions was Pacific Garden Mission in Chicago, brainchild of Sarah Dunn Clarke, a school teacher from Waterloo, Iowa, who felt called by God to reach out to the masses of needy people in Chicago. In 1869 she organized a mission Sunday school but was hampered in the work after she married Colonel George R. Clarke, a wealthy Chicago realtor. She struggled through "four merry years in the fashionable circle to which Colonel Clarke clung," praying that God would change his heart. That happened while he was on a business trip. "He telegraphed his wife of his change of life purposes and added that he was returning to Chicago at once to join her in founding a mission."[19]

In 1877 they founded the first rescue mission in the midwest—forerunner of the Pacific Garden Mission. Colonel Clarke was known as "the poorest preacher that ever tried to expound God's Word," but he was aided greatly by his wife, and together they became instruments in the transformation of countless lives.[20]

But the formative role of women was certainly not unique to the Pacific Garden Mission:

> Women . . . generously staffed the rescue mission movement, figuring prominently in the origins and continuing operation of Five Points, Water Street, and numerous other missions. Despite the dangerous location of the Peniel Mission's branch in San Francisco, the workers in charge were largely young women, as was also true . . . in Peniel's chain of twenty-six missions. . . . Moreover, like Sarah Wray of the Eighth Avenue Mission, a number of women held positions of leadership within the larger rescue mission movement. Mrs. Whittemore of the Door of Hope, for example, besides exercising leadership in the Alliance, the Salvation Army, and larger evangelism, presided over the International Union of Gospel Missions during the first several years of its existence.[21]

## The Deaconess Movement

An avenue of urban ministry for women during the late nineteenth and early twentieth centuries was the deaconess movement. The diaconate, an important facet of the church during the early centuries of the Christian era, was reintroduced in the early nineteenth century by Theodore Fliedner, a German Lutheran pastor. The movement grew rapidly and spread to America, and by the end of the century there were more than one hundred deaconess homes in the United States representing several Protestant denominations. The young women served in various capacities—most often in urban settings. In the minds of many observers, trained deaconesses were the ideal solution for the desperate needs of the cities. Christian Golder, a medical doctor, wrote in 1903 of the need for women to do evangelism in the ghettos. He cited the findings of George W. Gray, superintendent of Methodist City Missions in Chicago, that in one Chicago district of more than twenty thousand people there were "two hundred and seventy-two saloons, eighty-five wine-houses, seven opium and eight gambling dens, and not less than ninety-two houses of ill-fame," but only three churches. What was Golder's solution?

> More than ever before we are in need today of female power. We need women who will give up the luxuries of life, who will forsake society and friends, and condescend to help this class of men. The only hope and possibility of elevating and saving this class of the population in our great

cities lies in the unselfish and devoted activity of such women. . . . Here is the great and useful field for deaconesses. . . . The time will come when tens of thousands of deaconesses, in city and country, will sacrifice their lives in Christian service.[22]

The need for deaconesses was equally urgent in England, where they were in high demand by the church as a competent, highly-motivated, low-cost, generally compliant work force.

There was no end to the activities of Deaconess House, and the deaconesses were lent out to hard-worked vicars in the slum parishes of Liverpool, where they toiled unremittingly among the Sunday schools, cottage meetings, girls' clubs, bands of hope, and open-air meetings. Each one could be relied upon to do the work of a whole-time curate, without the inconvenience of requiring a stipend.[23]

## The Holiness Movement

Some religious movements were founded primarily to conduct mission work at home and abroad, and in them the work of women was often indispensable. This was particularly true of denominations broadly categorized within the holiness movement. The Christian and Missionary Alliance, founded by A. B. Simpson, is an example. Here women played a leading role in urban outreach. "Ladies teamed up for house to house visitation and special meetings for 'fallen women.' The South Street Mission was one of at least four havens begun through their efforts." One of these women was May Agnew Stephens, who "opened the Eighth Avenue Mission" in New York in 1899.[24]

Another was Sophie Lichtenfels, known as "Sophie, the Scrubwoman." She had wanted to be a foreign missionary but was turned down as too old. She later testified that the Lord called her one night saying, "Sophie, who is your next door neighbor?" That question made her realize that she had a foreign mission field outside her door—Italians, Chinese, and other nationalities. "Sophie was an ardent mission worker, and her life left a marked impression on the work among fallen men and women. Superintendents from almost all the rescue works in New York City and from missions in Philadelphia attended her funeral service as a homage to her support of their work."[25]

### Urban Mission Internship

For many women, and for men as well, urban mission work was a stepping stone to foreign missionary work. Some of the most noted women missionaries of modern times, including Mary Slessor, served initially as volunteers in urban ghettos. When she was in her early twenties and working long hours in the textile mills, Slessor volunteered her spare time to work with the Queen Street Mission that served the blighted neighborhoods of Dundee. Among other things, she taught classes for teenage boys. "The wilder spirits made sport of the meetings and endeavored to wreck them," but she persisted and many of the young men came to faith in Christ. The leader of one of the gangs that gave her the most trouble was transformed by her ministry. Years later, when she was serving in Africa, he sent her a photo of himself and his family that she hung in her thatched hut.[26]

In many ways, this volunteer ministry provided practical ministry that served Slessor well during her years in Africa, as it did other women who are remembered primarily for their ministry abroad. Amy Carmichael worked in the slums of Belfast prior to her decades of ministry in India. Johanna Veenstra of the Christian Reformed Church served in mission work in Paterson, New Jersey, and Grand Rapids, Michigan, in preparation for her pioneer service in Nigeria. Evangeline French, who, with her sister Francesca and Mildred Cable, would become known for extraordinary work with the China Inland Mission, began ministry "in a slum parish" working with "down-and-outs in all their undisguised misery" in Geneva.[27]

### Overseas Urban Mission

One of the most successful and energetic women to work in urban mission overseas was Emma Whittemore of the Christian and Missionary Alliance. She focused her attention primarily on "street girls"—young girls who, in most instances, had been taken advantage of because of poverty or family problems. In many ways she represents the vast army of women who penetrated the cities during the nineteenth and early twentieth centuries with the Bible in one hand and life-sustaining provisions in the other. It was not enough simply to preach the gospel. These young street girls, like so many other homeless victims of the cities, were trapped by their environment and needed a refuge where they could turn their lives around.

Whittemore was a remarkable woman who founded Door of Hope missions in cities throughout the world. She founded her first mission home in New York City in 1890, and by the time of her death in 1931 there were nearly one hundred such homes in major cities in the United States, Canada, Western Europe, Africa, China, Japan, and New Zealand. By some accounts she was believed to be "instrumental in saving more fallen women than any other person."[28]

Whittemore's work overseas was in many instances more desperately needed than her work in North America. In Shanghai, for example, the situation was pitiable. "Very few of the girls in the brothels of the eastern port were there through their own fault of choice," writes Phyllis Thompson. "Most of them had been bought or kidnapped, and brought to submission by intimidation, even torture. One method employed was to string them up by their thumbs until they were ready to give in. . . . They were then dressed up, their little faces painted and paraded on the streets of the red-light district." What hope did they have? "There was only one way of escape for them, and that was through a Christian Mission known as the Door of Hope."[29]

### Ordained Women in Urban Ministry

For many women, urban ministry was a means of having a more meaningful ministry than was otherwise available to them. This was true of Antoinette Brown, the first woman ordained a minister in America. She resigned from her Congregational parish in 1854 after serving less than one year and began ministering as a volunteer in the slum districts and prisons of New York. Through articles in Horace Greeley's *New York Tribune*, she rebuked the "polished, enlightened, civilized, Christianized society" for its "black shadow"—its failure to come to the aid of the poor and oppressed in the cities.[30]

Brown's "liberal" theological perspective was a significant factor in her decision to leave a middle-class parish ministry to serve in a more humanitarian endeavor, but women on the opposite side of the theological spectrum also found deep fulfillment in urban mission work. Florence Crawford, founder of the Apostolic Faith movement, experienced her "baptism" at the Azusa Street revival and became a leading Pentecostal evangelist. She established her headquarters in Portland, Oregon, in 1907 and in the years that followed built an extensive city mission outreach. So successful was her work that an auditorium seating more than three thousand was erected to accommodate her congregation.[31]

Ann J. Allebach, the first woman to be ordained as a Mennonite pastor, also ministered effectively to the urban poor. Her ordination in 1911 was scorned by many in her own denomination, and the only pastoral calls she received were from outside it. She initially rejected such offers and chose rather to serve as a volunteer in humanitarian causes, but in 1916 she accepted a pastoral call to the Sunnyside Reformed Church in New York City. An article in the *New York World* captured the essence of her ministry:

> Should you chance some Sunday morning to visit the Sunnyside Reformed Church, do not be surprised if the service opens thus: "If any of you here present are sick or hungry and need employment or help in your homes, come to me after the service and I will help you." And the Rev. Miss Allebach does help. There are many men and women in New York City who can corroborate this, men and women who know that this woman minister not only preaches but practices the Gospel.[32]

## Changed Lives

That large numbers of Christian women have served sacrificially among the urban poor is not a matter of debate, but the results of their work in terms of the number of faithful disciples of Christ that they produced is an open question. Exciting indications of changed lives sometimes prove to be temporary. Yet there are evidences of great success—especially among women and girls.

Seth Cook Rees, writing in 1907, cites many instances of changed lives in his book *Miracles in the Slums; or, Thrilling Stories of those Rescued from the Cesspools of Iniquity, and Touching Incidents in the Lives of the Unfortunate.* The following are only a few of the "trophies of slum missionaries": Orpha, who "fell prey to a professional procurer . . . [later] became a slum missionary and an ordained deaconess." Little H____, who "had been taken to men's rooms and forced to drink," was later "sanctified and went to Bible School in order to prepare to become a slum missionary." Miss M____ "was put in jail for grand larceny" and later "became a missionary in the New York City slums." Lucy "was ruined by her employer who turned out to be a bartender and was put in a Negro sporting house." After she was rescued, "she began teaching a Sunday School class of nineteen scholars." Dicie, who was "a drunkard, cigarette fiend, and user of morphine, cocaine, and other drugs," later "became a slum missionary." Little Ella, who was "sold as a prostitute for $5.00," later "became a Quaker and started preaching." And Christine, a pregnant teenager who "was forever hopelessly ruined," was "called to be a slum missionary" and "went to Bible School for training."[33]

The scale of women's involvement in urban ministry and the magnitude of their contribution is remarkable, especially in light of the written histories, which have largely overlooked women. But equally remarkable were the benefits to women themselves. They gave selflessly of themselves, but they were not without their rewards. Indeed, it was urban ministry—in organizations like the Salvation Army—where women, according to one widely circulated newspaper, found "perfect equality." Frances Willard, president of the Woman's Christian Temperance Union, agreed. In her opinion, the Salvation Army represented "the nearest approach to primitive Christianity" in modern history, in part because it "placed woman side by side with man as a teacher, worker and administrator."[34]

A comprehensive study of women in urban ministry needs to be done, but this overview indicates that in previous generations women played a very significant role in ministering to the poor in the cities. In most instances this involved lay ministry, and many of the women were wives and mothers doubly burdened with their domestic responsibilities. These women ought to serve as role models for modern women who juggle busy schedules in today's world—women who may not be able to minister full time, as Catherine Booth did a hundred years ago or as Mother Teresa does today, but who may be able to serve in part-time lay ministries reaching out where the needs are greater than ever before.

## Discussion Questions

1. What appear to have been the motivations of women ministering in the slums?
2. How did mission work at home and abroad provide opportunities for women to use their gifts in ways generally closed to them in churches?
3. Analyze and discuss the nature and role of the Salvation Army in city missions, how the Army differs from traditional churches and denominations, and how it continues to reflect the early vision of its founder.
4. What new things might women do in the cities of today's world to address the physical, emotional, and spiritual needs of prostitutes, homeless women, and single-parent families?

# 4

# RESEARCH: MATCHING GOALS AND METHODS TO ADVANCE THE GOSPEL

*Timothy M. Monsma*

Effective research enables a Christian worker to achieve specific goals that promote God's kingdom in the shortest possible period of time. In this book, it means research that contributes to the discipling of cities.

In this chapter I will examine five goals of research and then describe the research methods most appropriate for achieving them. In chapter 14 of this book, Judith Lingenfelter describes the ethnographic method of urban research.

## Locating New Work

Sometimes a researcher is asked to recommend a new city, or a specific area within a city, in which to establish a new witness for Christianity. Even when missionaries feel certain that their work ought to begin in a particular place, research can help determine whether the reasons for the choice are valid. Research at the start can save a mission hundreds of thousands of dollars and spare missionaries a lot of grief. Good research is good stewardship.

The most basic research methods for locating a new work are library research and interviews. Additional methods may be used on occasion.

Library research is not limited to a library but involves reading any material that bears on the subject, including, but not limited to, newspapers, periodicals, pamphlets, and statistics. Although not normally classified as library research, radio and television can also provide useful information for perceptive listeners.

All research must begin with library research. Reinventing the wheel wastes time and money. If researchers conduct surveys, organize data, and write reports, only to discover that someone else researched the same subject a short time earlier, they will have wasted their resources. Even if the earlier study was poorly done, it is better to know what was uncovered.

The best library research on a foreign city begins before you leave home and continues after you arrive. Materials may be available in one place that are not available in the other.

After doing library research, and sometimes even during its later stages, you can begin interviewing specialists for in-depth information. Often this information has never been written or published. Specialists living in cities know them intimately from living and working in them for years. They may be missionaries, pastors, evangelists, government officials, businessmen, or others.

When you arrive in a city for the first time and have few contacts, how do you get to know people and set up appointments to visit them?

First, choose your lodging with care. It will be your first point of contact. Avoid five-star hotels, where you will likely meet only tourists or high-powered businessmen who are foreigners like yourself. Most researchers' budgets don't allow luxurious hotels anyway, but this financial necessity is actually a virtue when conducting research.

Try to stay in a church, a mission guest house, or a non-Western hotel. The supervisor of the guest house may know helpful people to contact. When my wife, Dorothy, and I did research in Jakarta, we stayed in three guest houses to meet three sets of people. This greatly helped us to get to know a large city like Jakarta.

Once we were scheduled to stay at the Baptist guest house in Dar Es Salaam, Tanzania. Because of a medical emergency, the supervisors asked if we would move to the Salvation Army Camp. Staying there exposed us to a much larger circle of people than we had met at the guest house. Every time we went to eat in the dining hall, we met someone new from whom we gleaned information. There were Africans from Tanzania and other east African nations. We learned a great deal just from table conversation and gained contacts for later formal interviews. (Table conversation is classified as an informal interview because no previous appointment was made and no notes are taken at the time. Formal interviews usually involve a previous appointment and note taking or a tape recorder.)

As American citizens, we have found it helpful to go to the American embassy or consulate shortly after we arrive in a new city overseas. We usually try by telephone to get an appointment with someone first. This helps us get through the careful screening at most embassies. Embassy staff give us health tips, describe the political and economic situation, and convey other significant information. Frequently this type of information is not available in writing and comes only through the specialist interview. Researchers from other nations can expect similar help from their embassies.

Interviews with church leaders can reveal the size and location of the churches in a city. They will also help in assessing the amount of evangelism and church growth presently taking place.

If research begins with churches it may also end there, especially in a large city. We have learned to look first not at the number or location of churches, but at the ethnic and social groups in the city. Better to begin with people groups to determine early in your study those which still need the gospel. You may not have time to look at all the churches, but accurate information about people groups will be a basis on which to build as you try to discover which groups still have not heard about Christ and salvation. Unfortunately, many pastors do not think in terms of people groups and so may provide little reliable information about unreached people groups. But we will describe other ways to get this information in the next section.

Socioeconomic groups are usually easier to identify than ethnic groups. But be cautious. The word *poor* is elastic. Always distinguish the working poor from the unemployed or the desperately poor. They may have trouble making ends meet, but at least they have a job and some income. The unemployed are in a desperate predicament in countries without welfare systems. Unless they create their own employment by working as street vendors or scavengers, or by picking up odd jobs, they cannot survive in the city.

You find the poor living in the crowded shanty towns that now abound in virtually every city of the southern hemisphere. In most cities, the poor are an unreached social group. Specific strategies must be designed to reach them.

# Choosing a People Group with Whom to Work

An important question for missionary researchers is, What people groups live in this city? Once the researchers know the groups, they can ask whether they have heard the gospel and whether there is a thriving, witnessing church among them.

Several churches are scattered about in one Indonesian city of about a million people. On the surface, the whole city appears to have been reached with the gospel. But investigation revealed that no churches serve the indigenous community, which includes at least eight ethnic groups. Four of these were on none of the lists of unreached people groups drawn up in the United States. This illustrates the importance of asking, Who are the people groups in this city and how many are unreached with the gospel?

But where can one find information about the ethnic groups in a city? The government may purposely play down ethnicity to reduce intertribal violence. In one city, our questions about the history of the city led Dorothy and me to the "town historian." He had written several small, vernacular books on the history of this city that had not been translated. Fortunately, he spoke English, and we learned a great deal in an interview that lasted over an hour. He even invited us to a meeting where the ethnic groups discussed their differing customs and how they could live together side by side.

Later I was paging through a book on the art of this area. It had a full list of the ethnic groups that had contributed to the city's artifacts. The list agreed with the town historian's list, confirming that we were getting accurate information.

The Nigerian government conceals the ethnic makeup of the Nigerian army. Its reasons are understandable: to minimize tribal identity and promote national unity. But visitors to the museum in Jos, Nigeria, find most artifacts identified by the ethnic group that made them. They can build a long list of Nigerian tribes. The museum also sells books describing the country's ethnic groups. Information that appears threatening to the political establishment seems inconsequential when tied to history or art. Wise researchers dig until they find what they need.

Ethnic groups are not the only groups that need thorough investigation. If we are serious about understanding a city, we must also know its social groups. Often one or more of these are neglected by the Christian community and unreached with the gospel.

For example, virtually all Jamaicans are of African descent, although some are partially of European descent. Inasmuch as Jamaicans all speak the same language—English or some variant of English—and appear to have the same culture, one might conclude that all ethnic groups in Kingston, Jamaica's capital, have heard the gospel. But not all social groups have. The working poor and the very poor are generally still outside the church, and they constitute about 50 percent of Kingston's population. They are a massive unreached social group, and Christians ought to be asking, How can we best approach them with the good news that there is new life in Christ?

Japanese and Koreans are distinct ethnic groups. To find unreached groups in the cities of Japan and Korea, we must look at social groups. In other cities, the primary unreached groups are ethnic, but the secondary unreached groups are social. An example might be the seamen (a social group) of Jakarta.

It is usually not hard for a researcher to identify the social groups in a city. Their houses, jobs, clothes, and transportation all reveal their socioeconomic status. Sociologists, government officials, relief workers, and others are generally willing and able to provide information regarding a city's social groups.

Again, it is better to begin by researching people groups rather than churches. Once the people groups have been identified, whether ethnic or social, we can ask what churches serve them. Gaps will soon become apparent, and intelligent evangelistic choices can be made.

## Choosing the Best Evangelistic Method

No one method is best for evangelizing any city. You must vary your approach according to the needs of each city and each group you want to reach. But how do you know which method is best for each group?

Only intimate knowledge of the group will reveal a method appropriate to it. The largest church in the world, Yoido Full Gospel Church in Seoul, South Korea, makes extensive use of home groups or cell groups for pastoral care. Cell groups do well in Korean culture, and they are being used in many other nations.

But in the United States and Latin America, some churches grew very large before cell groups became popular. Other factors contributed to their growth. Most African cities do not have "superchurches," but in some African cities churches are growing in size and number without cell groups.

Studying a city's cultures may reveal whether cell groups or some other tactic will stimulate growth in a church. Cultural study may reveal the best time for church meetings, preferability of a central house of worship or worship centers scattered throughout the city, people's physical and emotional needs, and a host of other helpful information. The best way to get to know a culture or subculture is to use participant observation and the ethnographic interview described by Judith Lingenfelter in chapter 14.

Certain questions are essential to good observation-interview research:

*How strong is the extended family in this culture?* If it is very strong, the need for cell groups may diminish, and the family may be our primary vehicle for the spread of the gospel. If not, cell groups and other avenues of evangelism will be more important.

*What is the people's economic condition?* Among the poor or extremely poor, evangelism may need to be complemented by programs to help them out of their poverty. If they are wealthy, evaluate how well they will fit into an existing church that is middle-class or poor.

*Are there linguistic barriers to the spread of the gospel among the people?* If the selected group is one ethnic community, it can be assumed that its members all speak the same language. But if they are a social group, they might speak several languages. Even in a single ethnic group there may be an ethnic language and a national language. What then will be the language of worship and instruction?

*Are there religious impediments to accepting the gospel?* The chosen group may consist of adherents to another faith. They may have been misinformed about Christian teachings. How can this misinformation be corrected? They may be hostile to Christianity. How can the hostility be overcome and the truth communicated? Accurate information regarding non-Christian beliefs, attitudes, and practices is needed to present the gospel gently and persuasively.

When these and similar key questions have been asked and answered in participant observation and ethnographic interviews, the researcher will begin to understand the approach to take in presenting the gospel to a specific group of people.

## Evaluating Effectiveness

When people are turning to the Lord, churches are established and growing, and lives are being changed, it is obvious that the heralds of good news must be doing some things right. But there is always the question: Could they do better?

Sometimes things go wrong. Churches are not growing. There are no converts. Standards of living are not improving. Goals go unachieved. Then we ask, What's wrong?

Surveying those with whom you work may clear up some mysteries quickly. It is not difficult for teachers in school to survey their students. Pastors can survey church members. But it is more difficult for an evangelist to survey people who have not yet responded to the gospel. Nonetheless, it is not impossible.

The kind of survey we have in mind consists simply of printed questionnaires handed out to people with the request that they fill out and return them. To encourage candor, respondents should not be asked to sign their names. They should, if at all possible, fill out the questionnaires and hand them back immediately. If they take them home, most will never return them.

Some years ago a missionary in Nigeria wondered why many people who were attending church did not publicly confess their faith in Christ and affiliate with the church. He used a questionnaire to find the answer. But the people he wanted to survey were hard to locate, and some were not fully literate. The missionary solved both problems by enlisting the help of Nigerian assistants, who went out asking questions and recording answers. (They employed the same basic method used by political pollsters in the United States, sans telephones!)

The survey process itself got some people thinking, and some concluded their reasons for not seeking baptism and church membership were insufficient. A surge of people began applying for church membership. Survey responses also helped the missionary to appreciate more fully than before how family relationships kept many people from church affiliation. Especially distressing was the way many husbands kept their wives from fuller Christian expression. As a result of the survey, the missionary and his colleagues gained a clearer picture of where problems lay and began to address them.

Surveys can also test the effectiveness of evangelistic methods. One can form a hypothesis regarding the best methods to use, but nobody knows for sure until methods have been field tested. If surveys indicate that the method you use is not best, you must either choose one (if any) that the survey shows works better, do some fine tuning, or develop a new approach.

Most research is more art than science. It depends to a large extent on the imagination of the researchers and their skills of observation. Done properly, it has immense practical value. To be good stewards of the resources God has given us, we must use research as part of our overall strategy.

## Discussion Questions

1. What practical purposes of missionary research does the author mention?
2. Identify some of the basic questions an urban researcher must ask.
3. Design a simple survey for finding information on a subject about which you are curious. Explain your questionnaire to the class and show how it may produce the desired information.

# 5

# SECULARIZATION AND THE CITY: CHRISTIAN WITNESS IN SECULAR URBAN CULTURES

*Craig Van Gelder*

One of the consistent themes in urban literature during the past several decades is the interrelationship between urbanization and secularization. Secularization is a process of changes in the social order that occur when new technologies or modes of production are implemented. Usually associated with secularization are breakdown of traditional patterns of belief or behavior, disruption of community life, and fragmentation of family relationships.

These processes were given a major impetus in Western culture during the Enlightenment. The intellectual movement that gave its name to the period represented a shift away from the medieval and Christian worldview focused on God and revelation to a worldview focused on the immediate world as the ultimate reality and the individual as the center of authority. This particular philosophy came to be associated with secularism, a philosophy hostile to spiritual beliefs and supernatural explanations of events and history.

The relationship between secularism and secularization appears in the processes set in motion by the Enlightenment orientation toward life. Enlightenment secularism interacted with the rationalism and empiricism of the emerging scientific enterprise to foster changes in the social order in various countries. These changes became labeled secularization.

The combined effects of science-based secularism and secularization are often referred to as modernity, or the modern project. This new reality was rooted in the assumptions of rational order, human progress, and management of the social life. Its product is the science-based culture developed in Western societies in the wake of the Enlightenment.[1]

Secularization wove even deeper into Western culture with the rise of the Industrial Revolution and the accompanying urbanization. Urbanization and secularization emerged together in this context beginning in the 1800s, with the effects of secularization accentuated by the breakdown of traditional patterns of belief or behavior, the disruption of community life, and the fragmentation of family relationships. By the middle of the twentieth century, we witnessed the spread of modernity with its Western-shaped secularization throughout the world as the rest of the world became industrialized and urbanized.

Secularization has changed over the centuries as it has spread around the world. In reality, it has three phases: the secularization associated with the initial labor-intensive industrialization and urbanization (the muscle period) of the mid-to-late 1800s; the secularization associated with the capital-intensive industrialization and metropolitanization (the machine period) of the mid-twentieth century; and the secularization associated with the information-intensive industrialization and globalization (the mind period) of the later twentieth century.

Presently we are in this third phase of secularization. Modernity, or the modern project, appears to be going through a major transition as some of its basic assumptions are challenged. We are witnessing the emergence of a culture that many label post-modern. One of the most interesting features of this new worldview is that it keeps intact the economic mode of production rooted in the science-based technology while it reintroduces (or allows for) elements of the spiritual and supernatural.

This chapter will outline these developments and shifts in the past several centuries and seek to identify the influence of secularization as we now encounter it in a post-modern world. In particular, we will try to understand the different expressions of secularization in the modern world based on different cultures and worldviews.

## The Rise of the Modern Project in Enlightenment-based Culture

The modern Western nations emerged out of a medieval worldview under the influence of both the Renaissance and the Protestant Reformation. The shift was from a world with a fixed social order under a hierar-chical authority that started with God to a world that could be changed and developed based on discovering the natural order of life. The influence of Newtonian physics was evident not only in understanding the natural laws of the physical order but also in trying to understand the natural rights of human life. The core concepts of rational order, historical process, and the management of social life became the emerging worldview.

While the process took time, the new tools of rationalism and empiri-cism in the expanding scientific enterprise gave great hope for achieving a more rational and managed social order. With the technological devel-opments introduced through this same scientific enterprise, there was clear evidence of an improved quality of life and mastery over some of the phys-ical restraints of life. Improved communication systems, faster transporta-tion, and the control or elimination of diseases signaled that the modern project was being realized. Modernity and secularization led to great opti-mism by the late 1800s that the assumptions of the modern project could be realized. But what it called for was the restructuring of the social organi-zation of life. This restructuring took place as economic transformations occurred, driven by technological developments.[2]

Several things, however, were necessary to shape the modern project. First was the development of the modern nation-state, which was con-structed on the premise that the state should be the primary recipient of cit-izen allegiance. The nation-state displaced family, community, and tradition as the primary shaper of human behavior and beliefs. While the state encouraged these dimensions of life, it saw them as subservient to its own authority and aims. In this transition lay a major shift toward what we now call secularization.

Second, the development of a capital-based economy played a crucial role in the emergence of the modern project. Adam Smith laid out the basic the-ory in the late 1700s. He saw clearly the importance of creating a system of mass production and the shift toward a labor-based society if national economies were to break the cycle of their tariff-ridden, mercantile economies. Expanding the production and consumption systems would lead to an expanding economy and increasingly widespread prosperity, especially among people who owned investment capital. Profit, as a return on investment, would seek new opportunities and start more production systems.

Karl Marx and others warned early that there were prices to pay for this system of economic prosperity, most importantly the displacement of persons from the land or their craft trades into a laboring class of wage

earners.[3] The results of this shift, known as secularization, are now clear
to everyone. Urbanization in industrialization broke the bonds and traditions that had shaped communities for centuries and caused workers to
relocate from their small towns or farms to growing urban centers where the
new factory system of production was being implemented.

Third, the development of bureaucracy played a crucial role in shaping
secularization in modern Western nations. The large concentration of
people in the newly emerging factory system and urban centers required a
new form of organization and management. The theory for this new form
came from Max Weber, a German sociologist who, at the turn of the century, wrote about bureaucracy. The basic premise was that the management of systems should be on the basis of rational, legal contracts and the
lodging of authority in positions.

The practice of this new form came in the newly emerging departments
of the modern nations and the growing industrial empires of the entre-
preneurs. Consequently, the influence of personal relationships diminished
and people became associated with the roles they filled in contractual agree-
ments. These practices were but further extensions of secularization in
people's lives.

The coalescence of the developments of the nation-state, capitalism,
and bureaucracy with the emerging modern project set in motion what
might be labeled the first phase of modern urban secularization. It was a secularization shaped by the industrial, urban center based on the labor-intensive factory system. In these centers, secularization became a way of life,
with its breaking down of tradition, disruption of community life, and
fragmentation of family relationships.

It was not uncommon in this context for the assumptions of secularism, with its hostility to the supernatural, to accompany the worldview of
those who had experienced the secularization of the modern, secular city.
This was especially true as churches struggled to adjust their agrarian-devel-
oped lifestyles to the demands of the urban environment, where they often
seemed out of date or irrelevant.

## The Spread of the Modern Project
## and Responses to Its Effects

The modern project was well developed in the countries of Western
Europe and North America by the turn of the century. One dimension
that continued to shape its special Western character was the massive immi-

gration of this period, in which millions moved to North America, first from Northern Europe and later from Southern and Central Europe. This massive immigration of Western people contributed to secularization through the accentuated break-up of traditional ways of life as many of these immigrants took up residence in growing urban centers.

In these centers, centuries of social custom were displaced in a few decades as the emerging generation embraced education, upward mobility, and individualization. This pattern of immigration of Europeans to North America was accompanied by a similar shift in population in most Western countries. Rural residents left farms in increasing numbers in the late 1800s and early 1900s to pursue the dreams of opportunity offered by the city and its capital-based economy. Similar effects to those experienced by the immigrants were felt by these migrants as they settled in the urban centers.

By the turn of the century, these immigration and migration patterns, interacting with industrialization and urbanization in Western countries, gave rise to a literature focused on problems associated with secularization. Sociologist Emile Durkheim wrote a classic study on suicide rates associated with anomie in urban life. His was but the beginning of a whole raft of studies that documented the effects of secularization on modern urban life.

This growing concern was paralleled in the modern mission movement. From around 1850 to 1920, this movement, composed primarily of Western personnel sent to countries of what today is often called the Two-Thirds World, experienced tremendous success in spreading both the gospel of the church and the benefits of modern Western culture. Although many of the missionaries spoke critically of the colonial economic and political system operating in these countries through Western domination, they nevertheless participated in sharing the benefits of the modern project with persons in the countries in which they served by way of the schools, hospitals, and agricultural methods they introduced.

The result of this transfer of Western technology to the Two-Thirds World was the hastening of the collapse of traditional systems of government and social order. The Western practices and institutions soon made their presence felt as most of these countries struggled to begin modernization. Along with the felt presence of these influences came the ever-present secularization. Traditional customs and social mores fell rapidly in many of these countries.

Somewhere between 1910 and the 1930s, two separate but related processes began to emerge in relationship to the massive transfer of Western systems of the modern project to the rest of the world. The first took place in the

Two-Thirds World, where many traditional religions experienced a major resurgence of life as scholars, teachers, and local leaders sought to buffer the effects of the Western influence of the modern project. Some countries, like Japan, sought a middle ground of incorporating modern capitalist economic processes while maintaining traditional forms of social organization. Others, like China, sought to eliminate the evil influences of the modern project and return to an earlier, though obsolete, worldview.

The second took place in the Western world, where there was a growing awareness that the challenge of the modern mission movement was not only winning those of other religious beliefs to Christianity but also finding some way to ameliorate the devastating effects of secularization. The growing awareness that secularization was both a blessing and a curse began to pervade the literature of both the mission movement and the growing ecumenical movement.

The Christian movement in the West faced a major dilemma. How could the church share the gospel as good news in a modern world characterized by industrialization, urbanization, and secularization, especially where the accompanying assumptions of secularism were often tied to the worldview of persons shaped by this new world? During the first half of the twentieth century, the church began to take two divergent directions in trying to answer this question.

On the one hand, the state churches in Europe and mainline denominations in North America sought some way to accommodate the gospel to the basic tenets of the modern project. This accommodation went through a series of theological developments over time, including the social gospel movement, classical liberalism, neo-orthodoxy, and existentialism. One of the key voices that shaped this effort was Dietrich Bonhoeffer, who called for the development of a "religionless" Christianity and a secular gospel in a "world come of age."[4] His call became the watchword for the next generation of theologians who struggled with the problem.

On the other hand, the more conservative churches and denominations sought to maintain the integrity of the gospel in the face of the forces of modernization and secularization. But the price that most of these groups paid was to buy into the separation of facts from values inherent in the Enlightenment worldview. The compromise called for accepting the results of scientific fact as issues of public validity while holding that religious values were a matter of personal or private concern.[5] This bifurcation of the Christian gospel continues to plague the evangelical movement in North America.

# Changes in the Modern Project
# and Its Core Assumptions in the West

During the 1960s, the rising tide of secularization and the spirit of secularism reached their peak in the popular press and Christian literature. In Western Europe and North America, many voices promoted themes like "the secular city"[6]—the church's need to become secular for the sake of the world.[7] They focused on the pervasive nature of the modern project and the secularization of modern life, changes that, they said, required us to rethink and reformulate the Christian worldview in light of modernity. This movement reached its peak with the "death of god" theologians.

Others, like Jacques Ellul, warned of the seductive nature of the modern project with its emphasis on technique and image as the basis of its influence.[8] Still others, like Martin Marty, constructed a historical analysis of the nature of secularization, noting its different characteristics in various Western countries. For example, Marty noted that a process of "utter" secularity threatened to eliminate Christian influence in the European countries; in England a process of "mere" secularity domesticated the church as just another public institution; and in America a process of "controlled" secularity sought a dynamic balance in the separation of church and state.[9]

The coalescence of the core values of the Enlightenment (rational order, historical progress, and the management of society) with the forces of modernity (nation-state politics, capitalist economies, and bureaucratic systems) was creating what many feared would be a controlled society. The shift from labor-intensive industrial cities to capital-intensive metropolitan areas introduced the second phase of secularization in Western countries, a phase characterized by what appeared to be the growth of "Big Brother." The prophesies of *Brave New World* and *1984* appeared to be coming to pass.

In this context, other movements emerged during the 1960s to challenge some basic assumptions of the modern project. The civil rights movement in America, the youth culture throughout the West, and growing concern for the environment called together for an alternative worldview shaped by the core values of human community, justice and equality, relevant relationships, and responsible stewardship of the earth's resources.

All of these movements challenged the impact of the modern project and secularization in the West. The pillars that had undergirded modernism were shown to be inadequate to gain the support of the emerging generation. The call for primary allegiance to the political goals of the nation-state began to unravel, especially in America with the Vietnam war and the antiwar movement. The quest of the capitalist economies to maximize profits through ever-expanding production and consumption of products came to be seen as a disproportionate use of the world's resources by a minority of its population. The bureaucratic rationalism of the modern corporation came to be seen as limiting individual freedom and human value.

The science-based technology that had been reinforced by the assumptions of rational order, historical progress, and management of life came to be seen as part of the problem rather than offering solutions.[10] The mystique of the scientific enterprise was coming to an end, and with it the pervasive presence of the emerging secularism was being moderated. But the shape and character of the values and core assumptions that replaced those associated with the modern project have only become clear in the past decade as we now look back with perspective on this turbulent period as a threshold of change.

The basic shift is best defined by the word *pluralism*. Truth claims become both relative and situational in the face of a growing number of alternatives. The fundamental shift occurred as we began to realize that it was not possible to start with the autonomy of the individual, add to it the methodologies of rationalism and empiricism, and then somehow construct a rational, coherent order based on a common epistemology. In fact, we found that by starting from these points, we wound up with an endless expansion of alternative and competing truth claims, a reality we now label pluralism. We will develop this more fully in the final section of this chapter while discussing the shift to a post-modern worldview.

## The Spread of the Modern Project in the World and Its Influence

As the political landscape of the modern world began to take shape after World War II, scores of new nations came into existence from countries that had previously been under the control or influence of Western colonial powers. Between 1946 and 1969 there was a shift from approximately 95 percent of the countries in the Two-Thirds World being under colonial influence to approximately 95 percent of them being independent nation-states.[11]

Most of these newly emerging nations understood the rules of the economy in the modern project. They knew that, to participate as equal partners in the global community, they needed to industrialize and modernize. For this to take place, they had to turn once again to some of the same Western nations that had been their colonial masters. But the new forms of Western influence this time were loans for capital and concessions to the privately owned and Western-dominated multinational corporations. Some of these mechanisms for "development," especially the various international agencies, were driven by capital available from the World Bank, which had been set up by the International Monetary Fund under the Western-led (and American-dominated) Bretton Woods accord following World War II.[12]

The United Nations labeled the 1960s the Decade of Development, holding high expectations that somehow these emerging nations could achieve self-sustaining economies in a relatively short time through loans and foreign investment. Modernization and the "modern industrial state," what had taken Western countries over 150 years to develop, was now being introduced into underdeveloped nations as a process to be accomplished in 15 to 20 years. The consequences have been dramatic for the people of many of these countries.[13]

Two common patterns appeared in the Two-Thirds World countries that accepted the transfer of the modern project and secularization. First, many nations developed a two-tier economy in which only a small minority gained from the benefits of the infusion of Western capital and technology, while the vast majority continued to live in agricultural dependence or abject poverty.

Second, many nations set in motion processes of economic expansion and urbanization that led to the massive displacement of large sectors of their populations from their traditional patterns of life.

Secularization in the face of modernization has struck most of the nations of the Two-Thirds World with a vengeance during the past thirty years. A few, like Japan and India, were fairly well positioned to incorporate the economics and technology of the modern project without having to displace their traditional belief systems. But most experienced major internal changes from the influences of modernity and secularization on their traditional patterns, local communities, and family systems. The resurgence of fundamental religious beliefs as a global phenomenon in the 1970s and 1980s must be seen in part as a reaction to these changes.

By the 1980s, several additional factors made it difficult for many of these nations to manage both their economies and their social order. First, the oil embargo of the 1970s and the rising price of oil created a major debt crisis for many countries struggling to modernize. The massive debt structure built up by many nations now threatens the stability of the World Bank and major lending corporations in the West. Defaulting on loans, or simply the inability ever to pay off the debt, has become a new reality in the 1990s that the world community has yet to address.[14]

Second, the introduction of Western technologies and industry has, in many countries, fostered what is now labeled hyper-urbanization. In this condition, the massive growth of cities takes place beyond the natural expansion of the economy and the building of the necessary infrastructure. It occurs as a result of people being pushed off the land in the midst of changing agricultural methods, and it is complicated by exploding birth rates. Today's massive growth of urban centers in the Two-Thirds World has to be understood from this perspective. It is a consequence of the introduction of the modern project, but it is not directly tied to its development. Millions of people now find themselves living on the fringes of urban centers in bare subsistence with little hope that the urban economy will ever offer them a better life.

This is secularization with a different face. Direct effects of secularization, like breaking down tradition, disruption of community, and fragmentation of family life, are not the primary issue in hyper-urbanization. These are still an issue for the elite or the emerging middle class, who benefit from the new economic order in these countries. But for the majority, it is the indirect effects of modernity and secularization that impinge on their lives. These effects include the massive dislocation of large numbers of communities and families to the urban centers and the necessity of living in abject poverty.

## The Collapse of the Modern Project: A Post-Modern World

The beginning of the unraveling of the modern project really began in the West during the late 1800s and early 1900s among the avant-garde leaders in the arts and sciences. A gradual awareness spread among the disciplines that by starting with only the rational individual as the center of reality, it was impossible to construct a rational whole for all of life. While empirical truths could be maintained regarding observable "facts," it became clear that no unified field of knowledge could be constructed that included "values."[15]

The inability to construct this rational whole from a common epistemology was first realized in philosophy by leaders like Kant, Hegel, and Kierkegaard. This led eventually to the collapse of foundationalism in this discipline. From philosophy, the awareness spread through the other arts, such as painting, under the influence first of the impressionists, and later of the expressionists and abstract artists. Music went through a similar transition, as did literature and theater, as the avant-garde leaders in each discipline gave up trying to discover the essence or essential principles that were supposed to undergird and guide their work. Their general approach was to offer "shocking" expressions of this truth to the bourgeois (artistic expressions that ironically often became additional marketable commodities in the economy of the modern project).

The shift in this transition was from a worldview that sought to define a rational whole for all of life by defining the essential principles of life, to a worldview that accepted the human condition as relative to any truth claim and contingent on situation or circumstance. All theories of social order and artistic expression came to be seen in the final analysis as only social constructions.[16]

This same shift to a relativistic worldview was also occurring in the physical and social sciences during the twentieth century. In the physical sciences, the development of quantum physics, the clarification of the theory of relativity, and the discovery by Heisenberg of the Principle of Uncertainty challenged the core assumptions of the Newtonian worldview that had undergirded the modern project. The world was no longer just a machine with predictable and measurable natural laws; it was also a place where chance and chaos were parallel realities alongside order and natural laws.

In the social sciences, the new disciplines of Freudian psychology and Weberian sociology set in motion a similar process of relativizing our view of the human condition and the social order. Although the philosophical effects of the Enlightenment and its Newtonian worldview were still strong in these traditions, as expressed in the behaviorism of psychology and the determinism of sociology in the 1960s, another shift was occurring that brought these views into disrepute. The adoption of general systems theory, with its emphasis on the interdependence of all of life, and the development in the social sciences of an open systems approach brought to an end all hope of preserving a rational, predictable social order rooted in the assumptions of logical positivism. Science itself, whether in the physical or the social disciplines, was experiencing a shift to a worldview characterized by the same relativism it had once accused religion of practicing.

These shifts in early-to-mid century in the technical disciplines to a relativist worldview was paralleled in the 1960s and 1970s by similar shifts in the broader culture and the economic and political systems. Production/consumption-based capitalism, undergirded in the twentieth century by the developments of Keynesian economics and Fordist production systems, has begun to unravel as a viable economic system in a globalized economy. No nation is now able to control its own economy and currency in the international banking system that uses the expansion of debt as its basis of maintaining viability.[17]

In similar fashion, nation-state political systems that call for the primary allegiance of the citizen to the state have also begun to unravel with the collapse of specific political ideologies as the basis of shaping the social and economic order. Peoples are now abandoning ideology as a basis for their identity and returning to their ethnic origins as the political organizing principle in the late 1980s and 1990s. The reality of nonideological political pluralism is now pervasive in the world, and, as Peter Drucker noted in his recent work, we do not have the rules as yet to govern these "new realities."[18]

The bureaucratic management of life has undergone a similar transformation to a pluralistic context with the shift in our economy from a capital-intensive manufacturing system to an information-driven service-delivery system. This is what Toffler labels the "power shift" in his most recent work.[19] We rely no longer on muscle and machine power but on the expansion and manipulation of information to manage our lives. This represents the third phase of secularization in the modern West, a phase characterized by the power of information. What is significant about these shifts in terms of bureaucracy is that people are now able, through the technologies of computers and data bases, to individualize their work and shape their own worlds. Rather than massification being the order of the day, as it was for decades during the growth of the modern project, we now live in a world of endless miniaturization, differentiation, and individualization.

The modern project has run aground on both its core assumptions and its reliance on the basic process of modernity. This is what many are now labeling the shift to a post-modern world. The contrasts between the modern and post-modern worlds are shown in table 5.1.

The effects of this post-modern worldview have been accentuated in modern Western culture by the rapid expansion of technology and the changes this brings in the social order. With the rapid changes that now take place, we have seen the collapse of the importance of history. With this collapse have come the endless expansion and multiplication of choices that now challenge our capacity to process information and make decisions. Patterns of relationships continue to expand around rootless associations, rather than around context and place. Change and flux, with their

Table 5.1
## Contrast in Worldviews from Modern to Post-Modern

| Modern Worldview: The "Modern Project" | Post-Modern Worldview: The "Pluralist Reality" |
| --- | --- |
| Machine | System |
| Parts to whole | Interrelated |
| Law and order | Order and chaos |
| Closed | Open |
| Construction | Deconstruction |
| Essential principles | Contextual "truths" |
| Stability | Flux |
| Order | Change |
| Grand narrative | Multiple story lines |
| Truth | Relativity |
| Inner essence | Surfaces and image |
| Historical context | Endless succession of "nows" |
| Purpose of the whole | Participation in the particular |
| Centering | Dispersal |
| Substance | Symbols |

accompanying attention to surfaces and images, are now accepted as normative and endless, in place of substance and principle. The overarching story line has been lost and cannot be reinvented. There is no longer a grand narrative. This is the face of secularization in the contemporary information age.[20]

Some, like Anthony Gidden, want to label this new reality simply a radicalized modernity, with the shifts understood mainly as a difference in the scope and pace of change.[21] But most prefer to give it the label *post-modern*.

Whatever the label, the new reality is now becoming clear. We still have the basic economic processes of the modern project in place, along with the technologies that drive its development, but we have lost the core assumptions of the Enlightenment (rational order, historical progress, and the management of life) that founded its identity, and we have also seen the diminishing of the viability of the central institutions (nation-state, capitalism, bureaucracy) that shaped its development. This means that secularization is still a reality, but it has taken on a new face in the global village, a post-modern face with emphases on change, flux, surfaces, images, and the present moment—all of which operate in the common acceptance of both pluralism and relativism.[22]

However, this post-modern worldview, with its new face of secularity, has reintroduced one element missing from the modern project: spirituality and the supernatural. Secularization is still a reality, but the secularism of previous decades is no longer in vogue. The post-modern worldview is not necessarily hostile to the supernatural. In fact, some dimensions of the emerging worldview are quite compatible with the supernatural, although its content is always defined in pluralistic and relativistic terms. The new reality is that many persons in the emerging generation are both secular and spiritual in their orientation toward life. This offers two challenges to the church, both in the West and around the world.

On the one hand, the church in Western countries will continue to face the deepening challenge of trying to present the gospel as a viable truth claim for all persons and all of life. This claim will need to be made to individuals who are more and more cut off from any conscious memory that such truth claims are either possible or viable. On the other hand, the church in the Two-Thirds World, where it is a minority culture, will face the deepening challenge of presenting Christianity as a viable religion for all in the midst of a growing emphasis on a pluralistic approach to life and truth. Other religions will continue to gain prominence as viable alternatives, and the uniqueness of Christ and Christianity will become more difficult to present and defend.

Secularization has occurred in three phases in the continued growth and expansion of modernity and the modern project: the secularization associated with the initial labor-intensive industrialization and urbanization (the muscle period) of the mid-to-late 1800s; the secularization associated with the capital-intensive industrialization and metropolitanization (the machine period) of the mid-twentieth century; and the secularization associated with the information-intensive industrialization and globalization (the mind period) of the later twentieth century. These three phases of secularization developed parallel with three phases of urbanization.

It is critically important to recognize that there are different types of urban realities, depending on the dominant mode of economic production and technologies being used: urbanization as concentration during the labor-intensive period when the core city held the dominant role; urbanization as decentralization during the capital-intensive period when the extended metropolitan area became the new urban form; urbanization as globalization in the present information-intensive period when the relationship between an urban form and a place has been broken. Urbanization in globalization is a matter of information networks rather than geographic locations.

These different types of secularization and urbanization have spread around the globe. Although some worldviews of other cultures have been able to moderate some of the effects of these processes, all cultures have been fundamentally changed. Secularization and urbanization are inherent in modernity, and modernity is a reality around the globe. What accounts for variations in different countries from these processes are the forms that modernity and secularization take in light of the dominant mode of economic production and the particular worldview of the culture in which the process unfolds.

The church faces a tremendous challenge as we approach the year 2000: how to share a gospel that can bring wholeness in the midst of fragmentation, healing in the midst of brokenness, historical continuity in the midst of the incessant "nowness" of modern life, and ultimate hope in the midst of temporal materialism. This is what the gospel must communicate if it is to be good news at the end of the twentieth century to those who have experienced secularization and urbanization in the globalized world of our day. Are we prepared to disciple the cities of our day?

## Discussion Questions

1. Identify the core values of the Enlightenment and discuss how the Enlightenment has shaped modern Western society.
2. Discuss the relationship between urbanization and industrialization and their impact today on millions of people.
3. Describe the effects of secularization on beliefs and social mores, and how churches (both mainline and conservative) have responded to it.
4. What effects does a relativistic worldview appear to have on Christian convictions, denominational loyalties, and ethical standards?
5. In a post-modern world, what are some of the "fundamentals" that Christ's disciples must cling to, and what is our source of knowledge of these fundamentals? Describe what you see to be the global task of disciple making in the post-modern world.

# 6

# BEING DISCIPLES: INCARNATIONAL CHRISTIANS IN THE CITY

*Manuel Ortiz*

Adopt [then] this frame of mind in your community—which indeed [is proper for those who are] in Christ Jesus. Though He existed in the form of God, Christ took no advantage of His equality with God. Instead, He made Himself nothing by assuming the form of a servant, that is, by becoming incarnate. And having appeared as a mere man, He further humbled Himself by becoming obedient to the point of death—no less than the death of the cross. [Phil. 2:5–8][1]

Our Lord broke through the barriers between history and eternity to be with us. He underwent all the physical and emotional experiences of a Jew in first-century Judaism (Luke 2:51–52). This divine intrusion was necessary to fulfill God's redemptive plan. The Lord became a man, a servant among people who needed salvation. He came to redeem and transform them to a new life of obedience, justice, and worship in the Spirit of Christ.

The manner in which the Lord came among us in his incarnation brought glory and honor to God and achieved his redemptive purpose. Vinay Samuel and Chris Sugden describe specific features of Christ's incarnation:

1. [It] *is specific to a context*. Jesus did not come as a universal man: he came as a Jew to Jews. . . .
2. [It] *is involved in a context*. Jesus did not just speak to Jews; he became a Jew. He identified himself with all aspects of being a Jew.
3. *The cultural context* [is taken] *seriously*. . . . He came into real problems, debates, issues, struggles and conflicts which concerned the Jewish people. . . .
4. *Humanity* [is taken] *seriously*. Jesus did not address the Jews impersonally, as one abstracted from their cultural context. He . . . addressed himself to economic questions, to the political groupings in Israel, and relationships of injustice that prevailed.[2]

I find these observations about Christ's incarnation helpful. Having lived in the cities of the United States all of my life, from El Barrio of Spanish Harlem, New York, to Bartram Village Housing Project in Philadelphia and Humboldt Park, Chicago, I know by experience the awesome task of living out the gospel in the city. How shall we be Christ's hands, feet, and life in our community? How will Christ the Servant become known in contemporary urban America? And what is God's will for our community and neighbors?

These questions provoke us to seek a deeper understanding of our calling and involvement in the communities where God has placed us. We have been purchased by Christ and are no longer our own (1 Cor. 6:19–20). Therefore, we are compelled by his Spirit to be concerned for the present and eternal well-being of our neighbors. We believe that God is disturbed with their condition and desires their reconciliation with himself. He wants peace between neighbors.

The Lord guides us into the streets of the city to bring God's peace, for in shalom there are no lame; all walk. There are no poor; all have sufficient means. The God of Israel is also the God of the poor and needy. Our Lord is committed to shalom, where there is no injustice or oppression.[3] As we enter the barrios and communities of the city, we are conscious of the Lord's presence and power, for we have come in the name of the Lord.

Our prior assumptions about the needs of the community and solutions to the problems must be brought face to face with concrete facts. An illustration comes to mind from my ministry with gangs in Humboldt Park, Chicago, in the late 1970s. Violent crimes were on the increase, and many youths were being killed. The political leaders decided to hold a meeting and invite significant people from the community, like the police, religious leaders, and politicians. The goal was to get at the causes of the problem and attempt to find solutions.

The leaders discussed what they thought were the major issues. As a result, they suggested that paint be provided to clean up the graffiti, schools be opened during the summer for recreation, and equipment be made available for organized sports. After their presentation, a gang representative stood up, walked to the chalk board, and listed in plain and simple words the major problems in the community.

*Education*—students were dropping out, and those who graduated were no more prepared than those who dropped out.

*Health Care*—there was a lack of community health clinics, and the existing ones treated people disrespectfully.

*Employment*—there were high rates of unemployment and unemployables, which led to other economic alternatives (drug traffic, prostitution) harmful to the community.

*Housing*—the houses in the community were extremely bad, and few had any owners living in the community.

Who knew and cared about the community? Obviously, the people who lived there and whose lives were being destroyed by its conditions. This precisely illustrates the problem facing those who want to disciple the city. In order to be disciple makers for the Lord in the city, we need to know our communities well enough and become identified with them deeply enough to be the Lord's continuing incarnation there.

We must heed several warnings as we begin to pursue the theme of serving Christ incarnationally in the city. First, there is a tendency to transfer models of ministry from one location to another without discovering the new contextual situation. Hasty, unthinking transfers seldom work out. Another caution is in the area of felt needs. Peoples' future needs as well as their immediate, felt needs must be determined. Also, our preconceived assumptions about people, needs, and solutions may be inaccurate.

Learning a new community is a process, not a once-and-for-all matter. It goes on internally and externally. The community becomes part of our lives as we walk in it in the Spirit of Christ. As a final warning, we must realize that the Lord of history was and is present in the city. He works in each community in unique ways, and it is for us to discover what he is doing and what he wants us to do.

## Research and Analysis

To be incarnational Christians in the city, we must know the city and, in particular, that part of the city in which the Lord has placed us. This means analysis and research.

James Engel states that research is gathering information for decision making.[4] Dick Taylor indicates that carrying out needs assessments and conducting demographic studies are primarily for the purpose of knowing God's will for your neighborhood. He says that the purpose of research is to discover where people in your neighborhood are being denied shalom.[5] He adds that research leads to shaping your plan for doing God's will. In other words, a strategy is developed that will meet the needs of the people in your community. This is "shaping your research by God's will."[6]

Since research tends to discover the negatives and the shortcomings of a community, it is important to recognize a possible side effect: paternalism, wanting to rescue these "poor people" from their plight. Such an attitude is not likely to provide shalom but may instead bring shame on the gospel of Christ. Therefore, we must recognize the value and significance of the people of the community. God will use them to stimulate our personal growth. We need them just as they may need us.

Needs are an ever-present reality for each person. Not one of us is without needs in one area or another. The astounding error frequently found among people serving in the city is to neglect people's eternal needs. Every living person needs what can only be supplied by Christ and the work of the Holy Spirit in regeneration. To reduce our definition of people's needs to physical and material needs is to undercut the work of Christ in the city.

Certainly the more tangible felt needs are the most recognizable ones. But discipling the city for Christ, in his power and according to his Word, requires that our concerns and involvements in every area include presenting the gospel. The gospel is for the whole person. Needs, therefore, must be defined from both theological and sociological perspectives. When the Scripture declares that all have sinned and come short of the glory of God (Rom. 3:23), it speaks of a need that can be filled only by Christ.

## What Are Needs?

A need is the "measurable discrepancy existing between a present state of affairs and a desired state of affairs as asserted either by an 'owner' of need or an 'authority' on need. In the former instance, need is described as motivational; in the latter instance, prescriptive."[7]

### Clarification 1: Felt Needs and Anticipatory Needs

Most of the time the cry of felt needs is heard so strongly that we are tempted to stop and go no further. However, because felt needs tell us something of a past-to-present reality, they do not present a complete picture. Identifying only the felt needs may be a formula for failure, because it leads us to continue to function on the basis of today's and yesterday's reality. Eventually this will make our ministry irrelevant to major issues and incapable of addressing them.

The felt-needs orientation must be challenged by attention to anticipatory needs, thinking and examining a present-to-future dynamic, which identifies what planning is to be done in order to move toward a specified future. The sharp distinction between these two approaches is extremely critical to those in ministry, because they lead to the development of different programs and relationship patterns within the community.

The following are examples of felt versus anticipatory needs in ministry settings:

1. Churches in transitioning communities might be meeting the felt needs of the current community, but if they are not prepared for the transition that will take place, their programs, congregations, and ability to meet needs will all be in jeopardy. This is one of the biggest reasons why churches have closed down when communities' populations have changed.

2. A Christian health clinic wanted to provide health care for Hispanics in Philadelphia and was looking at a location on the southern end of the Hispanic community. Closer examination revealed that gentrification was relocating the Hispanic community from the south to the north. Therefore, clinic leaders decided to locate much farther north, in the heart of the Hispanic community, where they could minister for at least ten years without a population change.

3. When manufacturing businesses started to leave the north Philadelphia area, churches should have realized that this would cause massive unemployment of formerly stable working-class employees and that this in turn would affect families. If churches had been in touch with anticipatory needs, they would have been prepared to handle the

fear and anxiety of unemployment. They might possibly have offered an alternative to the drugs and alcohol that the poor use as a release from feelings of hopelessness. Churches could have prepared to handle day care for working mothers and counseling to prevent family dysfunctions.

The major question is, How can we foresee anticipatory needs? One way is to use demographics not just for understanding current needs but in terms of trends—trends in population movements, trends in family structure, trends in employment/unemployment. Then, using these trends as predictors, we can foresee what we will be facing one, two, or five years down the road and start planning accordingly. In that way, when the anticipated need arrives, we will have programs already set up and will be able to start addressing those new needs immediately without the devastating time lag we usually see. This is an ongoing process, because trends are constantly changing.

### Clarification 2: Compassion and Programs

There is, in my opinion, a swing today toward the development of programs for community transformation that are moving Christians away from developing personal relationships. The emphasis is placed on proposal writing, fund raising, promotional publicity, and programs that meet specific needs. More and more we are becoming servants from a distance. There may come a time when people will respond to Christians as the Samaritan woman did to Jesus: "'How can you ask me for a drink?' (For Jews do not associate with Samaritans.)" (John 4:9). I am not trying to discredit the new approaches entirely but to call attention to the pitfall of neglecting relationships in bringing God's shalom to a community. The approach too often is like that of a modern corporation—efficient, productive in some ways, but coldly lacking in interpersonal relations and compassion.

Compassion calls for standing with people in their suffering and pain. It is incarnational in the sense of being in intimate touch with hurting humanity. Compassion is a solidarity that is internal and external.

The other difficulty with programmatic ministry lies in the notion that once the felt need has been met, the task is completed. This again puts relationships at a distance and undermines incarnational ministries. Effective urban ministry is built on personal relationships.

### Clarification 3: Causes and Effects

In the social sciences, there is a lot of discussion about causality. We should keep in mind that all research is based on trying to go from cause to effect. In assessing needs, one is often tempted for several reasons to deal with effects instead of causes. One reason is the visible, immediate need presented. We are moved to respond to that tangible situation. Another reason is that causes are often less visible and, since they can be multiple and are often interrelated, difficult to pin down. However, the causes of situations are where we discover the real needs.

We must learn to look deeper than symptoms if we are to see people delivered from dependency. Food pantries and clothing distribution are a popular diaconal ministry in most urban community churches. Without question they are important and worthwhile. However, these questions need to be faced: How do we get at the causes of poverty that make people dependent on outside help? How can we eliminate the causes of the problems while we continue to feed and provide shelter to those in need? It may be that the reason for dependency is the lack of employment or the low wages given in exploitative sweat shops. Another possible reason may be language and work skills. Sometimes it is racism and oppression. In any case, as we minister in the name of Christ, we must face the question of causality.

### Clarification 4: Meeting Felt Needs

Investigating people's needs is an important aspect of preparing and implementing a holistic ministry strategy. Some Christians argue that it is the responsibility not of the church but of public agencies to address the wide range of human needs. But based on my experience, I maintain that public agencies are never as successful as God's people in meeting human needs with love.

Before launching a ministry, we must make sure that we understand accurately the people's need. It is clear, for example, that homeless people need shelter. But we have to determine what kind of shelter homeless people need in terms of what they want and require. Do they prefer, perhaps for reasons that make quite good sense, to live undisturbed over hot air vents on the streets? Should they be granted space in subways and bus terminals? Is a clean bed in a temporary shelter the best thing in view of their desire for mobility? Or is the proper solution a permanent home? How are we to meet their immediate needs in ways that improve their long-term situation?

### *Clarification 5: Interpretation of Needs*

The person who gathers information about a community inevitably begins to interpret the data in the process of gathering it. Opinions are formed about the community that will eventually lead to a plan of ministry for the church in that context. It is important to recognize that data gatherers screen and evaluate information and form conclusions on the basis of their worldview, culture, and experience.

For example, when one person investigates a community where men hang out in bars during the day, large numbers of single mothers are on welfare, children are on the streets during school hours, and the housing conditions are deplorable, she may develop a plan of ministry based on the assumption that when people are evangelized and come to Christ, they will automatically straighten out their lives. They will begin to send their children to school, clean up their apartments, stop drinking, and act responsibly. All it takes to transform the community, therefore, is to get people saved. But another person might look at the same community and discern that behind the poor housing are absentee landlords, the kids' truancy results from an uncaring school system, and outside economic forces are destroying local businesses. Besides turning to the Lord and conforming their lives to his Word, these people need justice, economic opportunity, and education for community transformation to take place. In both cases, the interpretation given to community needs is affected by the investigator's religious, cultural, and social perspective.

## Steps Toward Building Urban Ministries

To develop incarnational ministries in the urban context, several steps should be taken.

*Make a commitment to bonding. Bonding* may be a strange term for many of us, but it is an extremely important concept for Christian living as well as for learning the urban context so that we can minister with integrity. The best analogy to describe this process is that of a child being born and entering a new environment, a new culture, with new experiences, smells, and sights. Similarly, in the city Christian workers enter new communities, even if those communities are in the same city where they lived and served before. They become part of a new situation, bonded to it, just as an infant does at birth.

In the early stages of the bonding process, it is important not to allow other involvements to pull us away from our community. Ministry *teams* may be counterproductive to the bonding process because team members are tempted to spend too much time together, thus failing to build relationships with neighbors. Incarnational ministries begin with our neighbors, people who see the gospel in action through us and our families.

Bonding, as with an infant, begins instantly. The timing, therefore, is important, and we should commit ourselves to staying in the community to enhance the bonding process. We will know that bonding has taken place when we begin to own and feel at home with our city blocks.

An illustration of this is the following account by a young Christian woman who came out of a nonurban community:

> I've lived in this, a largely Hispanic community, for the past eight months. Considering my completely different background, I feel very much at home here. I haven't been conscious of how I've been becoming a part of the community, but as I look back there are several things that have been helping me to feel a part.
>
> I live with a Puerto Rican family in the community whose extended family is very close by. Very quickly I met brothers, sisters, nieces, and nephews. I never really thought of it as first-hand exposure to the culture and neighborhood until now.
>
> Most of my time is spent in the community. I go to church here and work here, and therefore most of my friends are here. It's as if the community is now the base of all my activity. Not that everything is done here, but everything has a connection back to the neighborhood. Usually those connections are people.
>
> I think it has also helped that I knew I was a stranger. I was not only new to the area, but to the culture as well. My background isn't anything like the people I am meeting, but we have been able to enjoy and deal with those differences through humor. My major barrier at this point is the Hispanic language, but they are willing to teach, and I am willing to learn, so one of these days I'll catch on.
>
> The overriding motivation for being involved with this community is that God has called me to the city and given me a peace about being here. That's an exciting base from which to work.[8]

Bonding is extremely important. But too often we ignore the importance of the process because we think all North Americans have the same culture, and we minimize the intense differences between communities. If bonding does not take place at an early stage, our rural or suburban values will remain unchanged and our ministries will suffer the consequences. We will be "in" the urban community but not "of" it.

*Discover your personal biases and stereotypical influences.* This step is often the most difficult due to the introspectiveness and individuality of the matter. But, in my opinion, it is one of the most important. The basic idea is to discover the biases and prejudices we carry around in our minds in respect to the city, to multicultural communities, and to the poor.

Are we ethnocentric? Do we have an oppressive sense of superiority as we perceive other cultures? What are our deep feelings about the poor? The agenda calls for honesty where it hurts the most. Can we be Christians and at the same time racists? What do we think when we see a new car in a poor community, or a welfare recipient who is physically healthy and intelligent, or the welfare mother who solicits men to make ends meet? Many other questions can be asked to discover who we are in relationship to the urban context.

It is important to remember that no cultural, ethnic, or racial group is exempt from this need for self-discovery. Anglos are not the only ones who have prejudices and biases. Ethnocentrism is found in all groups.

*Absorb the life of the community.* In this step the primary concern is active participation in the life of the community. Become involved in community festivities and regular times of play. Learn from each age group. Do something with young people. Become part of the community's fun life. Enjoy special events, eat in community restaurants, and shop in the stores. Notice how people treat each other as well as how they respond to you.

*Gather community information.* Gather information about the community from the people of the community, because they are the primary ones who define it. Ask questions that pertain to the major themes of the community. What are the best and worst aspects of living there? What do the people generally feel about the community? Would they rather live somewhere else? Why or why not?

Feelings are important because they reveal things underlying other perspectives. Always keep in mind that some people will try to please you or provide answers they think you are looking for, especially if you are a stranger or represent a different culture.

Local merchants are a great source of information, and they should be divided into various groups. The first consists of merchants who belong to the dominant culture of the community and live in it. The second is merchants who are of the dominant culture but have moved out of the community. The third is merchants who are of a different culture that formerly was the dominant group in the community. This third type of person, in spite of the cultural transition, decided to stay in the community.

Finally, there are merchants who are of a different culture and live outside the community. Data collected from all these types of merchants will be important to you as you seek to integrate into the life of the community. The community, you will discover, becomes more valuable and exciting as you sit at its feet and learn by interacting.

Another source of information is community agencies. Agencies are divided into two kinds—indigenous and outside professional—depending on who controls them. Indigenous agencies are controlled by community leaders, even though their funds may come from outside sources. Local leaders fit programs to community needs and use people from the community to run them. Because they use indigenous leaders, most of the money earned stays in the community, and because they use paraprofessionals at lower salaries, they operate economically. The professional model, on the other hand, excludes many community workers because it employs people from outside the community who require higher salaries. Information gathered from both kinds of agencies is valuable.

*Gather demographic data.* For urban and metropolitan areas in Western countries, one of the first things to examine is the census tracts and their geographical boundaries. Much demographic information can be gathered from city hall, institutions of higher learning, radio stations, cable companies, and major fast-food companies. Real estate agencies can usually provide information on community transitions and the future of the community. Becoming acquainted with the community is an ongoing process. It prepares us for ministries that honor God as the source of strength and transformation and demonstrate his concern for people.

*Discern God's perspective on the community.* Here God's servant, walking in the Holy Spirit, discerns God's perspective on the community. How do you do this? Think of Paul, who was deeply touched in Athens as he viewed the idolatry of the city (Acts 17:16). Remember how Paul and his missionary friends were kept by the Holy Spirit from preaching the gospel in Asia (Acts 16:6). Philip, you will recall, was instructed by the Lord's messenger to go south, where eventually he met an Ethiopian official who was searching for new life (Acts 8:26–40).

If we are determined to build Christ-honoring ministries in our communities, and if we continually yield our lives to the indwelling, guiding Holy Spirit, we will come to perceive what God wants us to do, and the ministry we develop will be truly of the Lord.

*Put together and interpret the information gathered.* Once you have put together all the information you can find about the community, allow local people to help you evaluate and interpret it. Community people should be part of the evaluating group.

## Words of Encouragement

To be incarnational Christians in the city is, most of all, to be Christ's ambassadors (2 Cor. 5:20), willing to live the gospel as Christ did, willing to speak as Christ did, willing to serve as he did. To be authentic disciples in the city means to empty ourselves and become servants of all. The following are some encouragements to our continued service for Christ in the city.

*Build meaningful relationships.* Programs are important, but they tend to move us away from one-to-one relationships. Personal relationships cannot be replaced by sophisticated strategies. Many Christian workers are becoming "development specialists" who do not participate in the community but only organize resources from a distance. They will not build effective, incarnational ministries.

*Provide hope.* People in our cities have only temporal and momentary glimpses of hope, if any at all. Hope comes through the lives of transformed Christians who are willing to share the saving grace of Christ. Our hope is transformational because it works to bring change in lives and communities. It is hope in word and deed, visible as a city on a hill.

*Pursue reconciliation that leads to a united front.* There is in most North American cities a maze of different racial and ethnic groups. We must pursue reconciliation among them. The need for reconciliation between the white and nonwhite communities has often been highlighted, but we have ignored a major and potentially greater challenge to reconciliation, where the responsibility falls on the shoulders of the Black, Brown, and Asian communities.

Demographic changes are going to have major consequences in matters of resources and how they are distributed among ethnic groups. One group will shortchange the other on the basis of sheer numbers. City Hall will pit the Black community against the Hispanic community. The various groups will fight for funds and eventually find themselves at odds with each other. The city needs a united front that works toward justice and reconciliation, and the Christian church should be at the forefront of this effort.

*Understand systemic evil.* The city needs ministers who can understand the devastating effects of systemic evil on our communities: the planning that comes from City Hall to displace and replace the poor for speculative reasons; the education system that selects winners and losers, those who will never work, those who will at best clean hospital floors and bathrooms for minimum wages. We must understand the power of systemic evil and develop a strategy that will confront and overcome such evil with the authority of Christ.

*Mission in reverse—kingdom values.* This is mission that builds from a base among the poor, with the poor in mind, as the apostle Paul did (1 Cor. 1:26–29). It is not enough to build our ministries among the poor and for the poor. The poor must be incorporated into the family of God and take their place in Christ's kingdom for the mission of King Jesus to advance. The rich need the poor and the poor need the rich, and in the kingdom we recognize our incompleteness without each other (1 Cor. 12:21–26).

*Creative expressions of ministry.* Ray Bakke indicates that he has found three significant elements in successful churches: dynamic worship, compassionate giving, and risk taking—a church's willingness to develop new ministries for the present context. Traditional church models are not effective in changing urban neighborhoods. Our churches and their organizations resist pluralism socially, economically, ethnically, generationally, and through gender stereotyping. How shall we break out of our traditions and, for the sake of Christ and the city, create new forms of ministry?

*Empowerment.* Empowerment for me begins with a kenosis of the minister. The humility and servant heart of the minister are the starting place—a voluntary displacement that makes one willing to become vulnerable for the sake of the gospel, to refrain from grasping for the popularity of becoming an urban worker or developing a unique and famous ministry and to serve unselfishly out of a deep concern for the poor and needy of the community.

As incarnational Christians in the city, we yield to the working of the Holy Spirit in our lives. We are motivated by the Word of God and the Lord of Peace who transforms both life and community. Community is a place where we will live out Christ, with all our shortcomings and imperfections, realizing that at times many of our neighbors' needs are ours as well. We are parents who struggle to care for our children in a manner worthy of the gospel; our bills consume our peace of mind; our marriages need constant enrichment and revival. We recognize our fallen state and yet display hope because Christ will not depart from those he calls his own (Rom. 8:28–39).

## Discussion Questions

1. Explain the motivating power of Christ's incarnation for the kind of community involvement this chapter calls for.
2. Distinguish: felt needs; anticipatory needs; eternal needs. Why does Christian ministry require that all three be addressed?
3. Why are interpersonal relationships so important for building up people and communities? Give examples of some ministries that are strong on relationships and some that are weak.
4. Using ideas discovered in this chapter, suggest five items of serious advice you would offer to Christian workers in the city.

# 7

# COUNSELING AND DISCIPLESHIP FOR THE CITY

*Craig W. Ellison*

Urban life is paradoxical. While it presents city dwellers with many opportunities for economic and cultural improvement, it also presents countless occasions for spiritual diversion and personal disintegration. While there is great spiritual hunger in urban centers, there is also great spiritual warfare. Temptations abound: drugs, drink, and illicit sex are abundantly available. Materialism invites the selling of souls. Poverty pushes people into primitive patterns of survival.

In the face of the intense spiritual warfare, Christian mission to the cities of our world must have a vigorous and integrated strategy of evangelism and discipleship. Strong emphasis must be put on growing believers into strong, healthy, holy human beings. The urban church that reaches to the lost will have the opportunity to minister to the real life needs of wounded people. Urban mission cannot be antiseptic and just deal with the well (as if there were any who are absolutely well!). This is good news according to the Scriptures. Jesus came to heal those in need of a healing touch (Matt. 9:12).

Because of the intensity of spiritual warfare in the city and the prevalence of many who have been physically, emotionally, and relationally wounded, urban mission must strategically involve the coordinated interventions of counseling and discipleship.

*Discipling* is the process by which a person is changed at the deepest level of his being so that both his inner and his outer life reflect the redemptive (saving and sanctifying) impact of Jesus Christ. *Counseling* is the process by which a person confronts the pain and distortions of finitude and sin, and the limits of his psychospiritual resources, so that his thoughts, perceptions, emotions, values, and behaviors are altered and he acquires skills for living healthily.

Discipleship and counseling have several underlying similarities and differences. After highlighting these, we will examine specific commonalities of principle and method and several urban issues in light of biblical counseling and discipleship.

## Fundamental Similarities

Both counseling and discipleship are:

*Transformational.* Both are change-oriented. They both focus on movement from one state of being to another. Discipleship involves remaking a person's basic life commitment, restructuring his underlying value system, revising his motivational core. It is movement from being a child of darkness to being a child of light (Eph. 5:8), from not being a people to being God's people (Heb. 2:10), from the old self to the new self (Col. 3:9–10), from slavery to sonship (Rom. 8:15). Counseling, on the other hand, may seek to transform one's foundational belief, feelings, and behaviors. It attempts to help people move from distortion and distress to accuracy and well-being. It is aimed at changes in faulty ways of viewing life, dysfunctional interaction patterns, emotional immaturity, and self-defeating coping patterns. It provides opportunities for emotional comfort and constructive release in an atmosphere of safety and acceptance. Both involve learning to be different, leaving behind old ways and acquiring new ones.

*Teleological.* Implied in the transformational nature of counseling and discipleship is a commitment to purpose. Both are goal-directed. Both are concerned about becoming. Both are aimed at helping people mature. Discipleship urges followers of Christ to grow up (Eph. 4:11–15; 1 Cor. 3:1–3). Its goal is to change people to reflect increasing Christ-likeness (Eph. 5:1–2, 8–10). Counseling may have several purposes (comfort, clarification, challenge, and change), but its end goal is always greater maturity and ability to function healthily and constructively in the midst of life's upsets and challenges. Even nondirective counseling approaches have such goals as helping people to get in touch with their feelings or to become self-actualized and fully functioning.

*Holistic.* Discipleship is concerned with both salvation and sanctification. Each of these goals involves transformation of the whole person. Unlike twentieth-century Western evangelical views of the person, Hebrew thought in particular, and even Greek thought in the early Christian church, did not see people and faith in fragmented, reductionist terms. It's not just a person's spirit or soul that is saved—it is the whole person. It is not just our spirit that is to love God, but we are to love him wholeheartedly with our whole being (Luke 10:27). Faith is more than belief (James 2:18–19); sanctification is more than knowledge. Indeed, the prayer of 1 Thessalonians 5:23 emphasizes the holistic nature of discipleship: "May God himself, the God of peace, *sanctify you through and through.* May your *whole spirit, soul and body* be kept blameless at the coming of our Lord Jesus."

Counseling is also systemic. It views the human being as an integrated system made up of several systems (e.g., cognitive, emotional, biological, relational, and spiritual). Each subsystem affects the others and is affected by them. Our spiritual life, for example, may be negatively influenced by distorted thinking, overreactive emotions, conflicted relationships, or poor health. Approaches to counseling like multimodal therapy or family systems analysis attempt to intervene in a holistic manner. Counseling aims at correction of dysfunctions within the respective subsystems that automatically alters other subsystem pathology.

*Contextual.* Discipleship paradoxically moves people to reflect the qualities of Christ-likeness while accepting differences in personality. The twelve disciples were very different individuals. Paul and Barnabas were so different that they clashed with each other regarding Mark (Acts 15:36–41). Jesus' methods of discipling varied as well. When Jesus called Peter, James, and John, he referred to their profession of fishing (Luke 5:1–11); they were the only disciples allowed to see Christ's transfiguration (Luke 9:28–36). Jesus' incarnational discipling was unavoidably contextualized as he adopted customs, lifestyle, and communication patterns that were particularized to a specific geocultural setting. The apostle Paul adjusted his approaches to the particular people he touched (1 Cor. 9:22–23).

While much of twentieth-century psychology has been heavily Westernized, there has been growing awareness of the need for contextual sensitivity and adaptation of counseling methods in relation to varied cultural and cross-cultural people groups. It is now being recognized that the ways in which information is processed as well as relational structures and emotional patterns are shaped and governed by one's acculturation. Counseling intervention must therefore be both individualized and contextualized if it is going to reach therapeutically into the souls of hurting people. Such considerations as action versus talk therapy, brief versus long-term therapy, and individual versus family therapy require evaluation of cultural and environmental backgrounds affecting the counselee.

*Relational.* Both counseling and discipleship centrally involve an ongoing relationship. While ultimate responsibility lies with the individual, neither emotional nor spiritual growth occurs in isolation. In both cases a more experienced and (in principle) mature person serves as a guide, confidant, teacher, and source of accountability for a less mature person. The counselor or spiritual mentor helps the counselee or disciple to establish goals, clarify confusion, address obstacles, develop a path and process of growth, face self-deception and irresponsibility, correct errors in thought or behavior, and maintain motivation. The counselor and spiritual mentor help the counselee or disciple see things from different perspectives and imagine the new, the needed, and the "impossible." Both act as stimulants of faith and hope, which are essential ingredients for change. Both encourage steps of risk and courage, which are foundational for spiritual and psychological growth. The accountability inherent in such relationships facilitates integrity, which prohibits the counselee/disciple's self-deceptively hiding from sometimes painful truth.

Although personal piety is an important part of spiritual commitment in Scripture, the framework for discipleship in both Old and New Testaments is clearly interpersonal. In addition to the corporate backdrop of "the people of God" throughout the Old Testament, Samuel had his Eli and Elisha had his Elijah. The New Testament models of Jesus and the Twelve, Paul and Timothy, and the early believers meeting together under the leadership of the apostles emphasize the primacy of the relational framework for building spiritual disciples.

The heart of New Testament discipleship is *following*, or modeling and being directly influenced by a leader. Ultimately, of course, the leader is Jesus Christ. But the thrust of the early church clearly involves following earthly spiritual leaders as well. Following is a relational act.

The example of Jesus' pattern for leadership is essential. He did address large groups of disciples and inquirers, much as a minister might do in congregational meetings. But he did not stop with the corporate entity. He spent most of his time in close personal relationship with a much smaller group. He personally led, guided, corrected, taught, and challenged both the small group and individuals in it.

Interpersonal isolation usually indicates emotional dysfunction. Whether the isolation is due to inadequate social skills, psychotic paranoia, self-absorption in addictions, phobias, or other causes, it is contrary to health. (I am referring, of course, to prolonged patterns of isolation, not to temporary interludes or those with a constructive purpose.) While most people are not interpersonally isolated in the extreme sense just discussed, the stress on individualism in American society has produced a strain of isolation that is spiritually destructive because it removes both accountability and the opportunity to receive support at times of weakness and need.

The blending of secular individualism with evangelical emphasis on piety has resulted in a highly individualized faith. Although there are corporate gatherings for instruction and worship, these are not particularly relational. Spiritual development has been left largely to the individual in a highly privatized, individualistic relationship with God. In recent years this has begun to change with the advent of small groups in a minority of evangelical churches. In an even smaller percentage of churches, one-to-one discipling of less mature by more mature believers is occurring. Interestingly, the Roman Catholic church seems to have caught the vision and value of discipleship through relationship with a spiritual guide better than Protestant evangelicals.

Although the city may work against relationships in some ways, it is not necessarily antithetical to the model of accountability suggested here. Indeed, the value system of most urban dwellers, with the exception of the highly individualized, upwardly mobile, and competitive middle/upper class (and even this is changing), sets a *priority* on relationships. Relational discipleship should be well received among the masses of ethnic and lower-class urban dwellers throughout the world. Counseling that connects with the communal emphasis of many urban ethnic groups[1] and is offered in a less formal setting and framework than traditional psychotherapy will be similarly effective.

*Behavioral.* One major difference between faith and philosophy is in the doing. While philosophy is exclusively cerebral, faith is primarily behavioral. As mentioned in the previous section, faith is simply but profoundly a lifestyle of following Jesus. "Follow me" were the words of Jesus that distinguished people of genuine faith from religious professionals. Discipleship is a matter of action. Although spiritual motivation and desire surge from within, they must be expressed publicly (behaviorally) if a person is to be a true follower of Jesus Christ.

In much the same way, counseling aims at behavioral outcomes. This is not to overlook the importance of cognitive and perceptual restructuring—this is critical. However, psychologists have found that our cognition can be altered by changes in behavior as well.[2] Marital and family counseling usually aim at changes in actions that family members express toward one another. Most counseling that deals with relationships, addictions, and stress management similarly focuses on behavioral change as the criteria for effective therapy.

*Volitional.* Finally, both counseling and discipleship are volitional. They are not effective if forced on someone. Unless they are freely chosen out of a sense of need and desire for growth, they produce temporary conformity at best and reactive regression at worst. Nonvolitional discipleship requires a strong emphasis on rules and surveillance. It is legalistic and spiritually deadening. Nonvolitional counseling rarely makes any kind of positive impact. Without a positive will on the part of the counselee, little positive change is possible. Anyone who has counseled teens who are there under duress from parents or courts knows the futility of nonvolitional counseling.

Both counseling and discipleship are much more likely to be effective when a person chooses help, desires change, and wants growth. Both require perseverance, courage, and discipline, qualities released by the choice to seek change.

## Fundamental Differences

Although counseling and discipleship share some fundamental similarities, they are not identical. They are complementary, not conceptually collapsible. In this section, we will briefly distinguish the two conceptually. Methodologically there are a substantial number of additional differences that space limitations prevent our listing.

*Counseling begins with pain and distress.* Whereas discipleship is a process of nurturing believers from spiritual infancy to spiritual maturity, counseling is a process of healing emotional and relational hurts and distortions. Counselees initially seek help to remove or relieve distress in their lives; their underlying motivation is usually pain reduction. The sources of distress are manifold. Anxiety, guilt, broken relationships, phobias, lack of meaning in life, loss, rejection, loneliness, feelings of worthlessness, addictions, domestic abuse, victimization, and incest are but a sample of common sources of pain.

Disciples, in contrast, seek guidance to enhance their spiritual experience. They are motivated to grow toward an ideal. They want to experience more of God's presence in their lives and to become all that God has intended for them to be (i.e., Christ-like). Instead of movement that is primarily *away* from an unsatisfying state of life, they are focused on moving *toward* greater fulfillment, or *shalom*. Very often this desire is rooted in feelings of deep gratitude for what Christ has done in their lives. (There are times when the motivation comes out of psychospiritual perfectionism or idealism; this is usually identifiable because of general dissatisfaction with one's self. In these cases, counseling is an important ally of discipleship; it helps to introduce tempering perspectives crucial for both emotional and spiritual health.)

*Counseling is consciously psychological, while discipling is consciously theological.* Counseling focuses primarily on emotions, thoughts, relationships, and behaviors that are somehow troublesome. Counselors use a variety of techniques and the power of the counseling relationship to encourage changes in how people feel, perceive, think, talk, and act. They study relationships among these dimensions of a person's soul (*psyche*).

Spiritual mentors focus primarily on helping a disciple to solidify his spiritual commitment, or bonding, to Jesus Christ. Discipling involves helping the disciple to understand and put into consistent practice the truths of the Christian faith. It is concerned with the cultivation of a faith-walk that is dynamic as well as informed. The person, power, and purposes of Christ as they are translated into the life experience of the believer are the main focus. Consistency and growth are the goals.

Christian counselors have an opportunity to disciple, as well as to counsel, to the degree that their view of human nature includes the spiritual, and to the degree that they are open to psychospiritual intervention. While being careful not to preach or manipulate, the counselor can address the intertwined psychological and spiritual needs of the person. In this systemic approach there is recognition that the cognitive, relational, emotional, biological, and spiritual dimensions of human nature affect and are affected by each other. The Christian counselor consciously keeps the spiritual domain in mind and uses spiritually-focused interventions as appropriate, to the degree that the spiritual underlies a particular problem or has the potential to aid healing of a specific hurt.

*Counseling and discipling have different durations.* In general, counseling is of shorter duration than discipling. Traditional psychotherapy tended to involve lengthy and intense interaction—often two or three times a week for several years. More recently, there has been an emphasis on short-term therapy, once a week for eighteen to twenty-four sessions. Most pastoral counseling will be limited to eight to ten sessions. Discipling may be as intense as classic psychoanalysis, especially in more communal situations, and usually lasts at least a year between a given spiritual mentor and a disciple.

## Special Concerns for Urban Settings

Urban counseling and discipleship need to develop a psychotheological framework to take into account three significant issues that are not unique to the urban setting but are substantially intensified in it. These are victimization and suffering, diversity, and transience. In this section we will briefly propose some integrative (psychotheological) perspectives to guide the practice of urban counseling and discipleship.

Western discipleship models have not typically considered victimization, suffering, and persecution as part of spiritual guidance. Rather, our discipleship models tend to assume the absence of such crises. Currently, it is estimated that approximately 250,000 Christians are martyred annually throughout the world; that figure is expected to increase to 500,000 by the end of this decade. Clearly, revisions in our psychotheology of discipleship are needed on that basis alone. In addition, hundreds of thousands of Christians have to cope with acts of violence (e.g., rape, assault, murder) and victimization (e.g., robbery, exploitation, prejudice) as they experience life in urban centers. Every act of violence and victimization rips away one's sense of safety and requires one to work painfully through intense feelings of anger, fear, bitterness, and loss.

Urban discipleship models cannot assume the best of all possible worlds and must prepare people to adjust to a world filled with injustice and inequity. Eastern religions teach fatalism as the way to cope. Christianity offers faith in a caring God who offers the spiritual power to overcome anxiety, unexpected loss, violence, and victimization. Urban discipleship must centrally include preparation for suffering that is often random and senseless.

Violence and victimization need to be seen against the backdrop of a greater spiritual war between good and evil. Satan continues to try to destroy all who bear the image of God, especially the children of God. He uses the self-absorption of sin-dominated people and urges those under his control to attack and assault the people of God. When bad things consequently happen to good people, Satan encourages those who suffer to see God as unjust, unfair, or sadistic. His purpose is always to turn people against God so that he can gain control and make people believe that he is more powerful than the Almighty.

Urban counseling intersects with the necessary concern of urban discipleship for suffering. Because suffering strikes emotionally, the urban counselor must be prepared to help those who have been victimized. Psychospiritual issues of powerlessness, vulnerability, loss, rage, forgiveness, and fear must be addressed by the Christian counselor as ravaged counselees struggle to restore a sense of order and safety to their chaotic and unprotected world.

Beyond helping an urban disciple to deal with the probabilities of suffering, discipleship must address biblical justice. What is the responsibility of the urban believer to confront injustice and oppression? Most current approaches to discipleship assume the status quo and ignore these issues altogether. Is this defensible for urban believers who are regularly touched by or aware of suffering that is due to greed, power plays, and human exploitation? Urban counseling must likewise weigh the possibility of advocacy efforts, rather than being limited to an individualized medical school model that fails to link the suffering of the individual with oppressive conditions perpetrated by a power elite. These issues become especially critical as one disciples poor urban masses. What are the biblical limits of confrontation? How does submission to the constituted authorities (Rom. 13) relate to the cry for biblical and social justice (Isa. 61)?

Urban counseling and discipleship must also address the diversity and differences inherent in major urban contexts. Most current models of discipleship assume sameness. We need to be sure that we are properly contextualizing discipleship methods and goals rather than imposing culturally captivated forms that provide a sense of security for some while coming across as alien to others. Diversity demands flexibility and creativity, not standardization and conformity. For example, is it possible that the more passive, cognitive, word-study model of Bible study needs to be adapted for the more action-oriented lower class of the city? Does discipleship need to be more a matter of observation and practical involvement with one's mentor for the urban masses than dialogue and reporting?

Urban discipleship needs to deal up front with rejection and prejudice, even within the body of Christ, due to the frequent failure of the Christian community to accept differences as reflective of the creative ingenuity and playfulness of Elohim. The struggles over and resolution of prejudice in the early New Testament church recorded in Acts are particularly instructive. As the apostles faced major revisions in their thinking and worship, they consistently chose to let go of their provincialism and accept diversity on equal terms. James 2 makes it clear that attitudes of superiority and prejudice have no place in the body of Christ.

Nevertheless, prejudice is common among evangelicals. There is a rampant anti-urban bias among American evangelicals. The poor are looked down on and avoided, even if they are believers. Many white evangelicals merely tolerate people of color, at best, or overtly reject them, at worst. On the one hand, urban believers must be helped to repent and forsake such prejudicial attitudes; they must be exhorted to reach out and fully accept those who are not carbon copies of themselves, thereby demonstrating the all-accepting love of Christ. On the other hand, those most likely to be the targets of prejudice need to be helped to anticipate and forgive prejudicial treatment so that they will not become bitter or reciprocate rejection.

Urban counseling must deal with diversity by seriously studying and incorporating cultural factors into counseling. Instead of imposing a standardized counseling model that purports to be objective and value free (but is really a reflection of the middle class), urban counseling needs to be contextualized.[3] This may result in shorter-term, action-based, and more informal friendship approaches to certain urban people groups like African-Americans and Hispanics. Methods and models must be adapted and created in view of cultural realities that influence healing. The varied healing approaches of Jesus serve as models for such sensitivity and flexibility.

Finally, the transient and transitional nature of urban life both shapes the practice of discipleship and must be addressed by it. Long-term models of discipleship and leadership development generally will not work in the city because of transience. Three- to four-year curriculum cycles will miss a sizeable portion of potential disciples who move more often. Discipleship must be more intensive than extensive (over time), especially for new believers.

Perhaps the model of the first urban Christians is the key. Acts 2:42–47 indicates that they met together *daily* for spiritual nurturing. Paul devoted less than two years of intensive discipling to most of the churches he planted. Though the process of discipling can (and should) certainly continue beyond that brief period of initial development, infants in the faith will grow strong quickly if given intensive nurturing. One of the implications of this approach is that urban discipling will focus more on the essentials of faith and practice. It will not wander into the wilderness of doctrinal speculation but will emphasize the practical meaning of following Jesus in daily life.

Because of urban transience and transition, counseling will normally need to use short-term therapy models[4] with mutually agreed goals, agenda, and counseling timetable, arrived at in the first couple of sessions by the counselor and counselee.

Counseling and discipling share more in common than evangelicals have typically recognized. While they are different in starting points, focus, and methods, they are both concerned with personal growth and maturity. They are, therefore, complementary activities. This is seen in a number of compatible principles that apply to both. The two are also drawn together around such strongly urban issues as victimization and prejudice. Used together appropriately, they are powerful allies for change, and they dramatically promote whole-person health and holiness.

## Discussion Questions

1. Describe some urban realities that threaten to break down Christian discipleship and frequently make counseling necessary.
2. How does the author define discipling and counseling? What are the similarities and differences between them?
3. Evaluate the proposition that urban discipleship must include preparing Christians for suffering, injustice, violence, and victimization. How does counseling relate to this?
4. Describe the effects of transience and discuss how urban churches must adapt to it in their ministries.

# 8

# AUTHENTIC STRATEGIES FOR URBAN MINISTRY

*Robert C. Linthicum*

Are there authentically urban strategies for urban ministry? Is there praxis that has been developed in the midst of city ministry and matured by years of use?

This is a critical question to ask. The model of the church that presently exists in the cities of the First World is based in that world's rural past. That model is of the parish church—a congregation set in the midst of a small locale and assuming spiritual and pastoral care over that community. That approach to mission evolved out of the church's struggle to be faithful in its ministry in rural and village settings.

Likewise, the model of the church that exists today in cities of the developing world was introduced through eighteenth- and nineteenth-century missionaries who had developed their understanding of church from the rural model they had experienced in North America or Europe. Thus, what has been visited on the church in Asia, Africa, and Latin America is simply a missionary adaptation of the First-World rural church model.

So, are there authentically urban strategies for ministry—models of ministry invented, practiced, evaluated, and matured in the city? Yes. There is an emerging body of urban strategies born in the city. These are the strategies to which we need to pay particular attention as we seek to do truly authentic *urban* ministry. What are these strategies?

## Networking

*Networking* has become a popular term lately. I first heard it used only about ten years ago. But I've been networking since 1955, when I began my first urban ministry among children and teens in a black Chicago housing project. If you have been successful doing urban ministry, the likelihood is that you, too, have been doing a great deal of networking—whether you call it that or not.

What is networking? The term comes from the world of business, and it simply means the creation or maintenance of a "net" of contacts through which one effectively carries out an enterprise. That net can be a human net or a corporate net or even an electronic net (such as in telecommunications). Whatever it is, it is effective only as the contacts in it are used to carry out a given function.

*Networking, in the Christian context, is the intentional and systematic visiting of people in an urban community by pastor and church workers in order to enable that community or church to address more effectively that neighborhood's most substantive problems.* Through networking the church builds bridges throughout the community, bridges by which the gospel and its implications for all of life can be carried to corners that otherwise would be inaccessible.

There are three primary reasons for networking, all of which are interrelated and strategic to each other. One networks to:

learn from the people in that urban community what they perceive are the real issues that dominate their lives and community;

discover the real leaders of the community;

find the people in that community who have a burden either for it or for one of its primary issues.

It is important to note what is *not* the purpose of networking. It is not meant for evangelism. Neither is it making pastoral calls on the community. Most of all, it is not for recruiting for attendance at the church's worship service or any other churchly function. The purpose of networking is to learn about your community from its people.

When I became pastor of Edgewater Presbyterian Church of Chicago in 1969, I discovered through visits in the community that the largely non-resident congregation I served knew little about the Edgewater/Uptown communities. So I challenged the leaders of that congregation to call with me. For three months, fifty-two members of the congregation went out in teams of two and three to call on the pastors, business leaders, politicians, people providing social, educational, and health services, community workers, and scores upon scores of ordinary folk from the community. The result of that calling was a profound sensitizing of our congregation to the needs, issues, and people of that slum community. It provided the data on which the fifty-two built a long-range mission strategy for the church. Applying that strategy set the directions and style of ministry for Edgewater Church for the next fifteen years, so that it became not only a church *in* that community, but also a church *of* and *with* that community in all of its struggles for justice and community betterment.

Networkers seek first to learn what the people consider *their issues*. If a church is to reach out to its community, it is irrelevant what the church perceives as the issues. One must begin where people are, with their issues, and the only sure way to uncover those issues is to ask the people.

Some questions that help identify the people's issues are: "How long have you lived in this community?" If long, then ask, "I imagine you have seen this community change a lot since you first got here!"—and follow up by asking about the changes. If not long, ask, "What caused you to decide to move here?" You might ask, "What do you like or enjoy most about this community? What bothers or most disturbs you about it? What strikes you as the biggest problems here?" As you visit with person after person, you will begin to discover a pattern of response indicating the community's most pressing issues.

The second thing networkers seek to learn is who are the real leaders of the community. Very rarely are the elected or business leaders of a community the real leaders—and that is particularly true of a slum community. They are usually only the titular leaders.

Four types of leaders in every urban community make it function: gatekeepers, caretakers, flak catchers, and brokers. Every community has them. They make it run. Without them, there is no community.

The gatekeepers "keep the gates" of the community. They decide who should be "let in" or "kept out." They are the power brokers. Questions like this will help reveal them: "I understand that so-and-so down the street has just moved in. What do you think of him? How did you get that opinion of him?" (The opinion likely came from the gatekeeper.) "I see you have a hole in your street. If you wanted to be sure that the hole was filled, whom would you go to in this neighborhood to make sure it got filled up?" As you talk to person after person, if the same name keeps coming up, you've found the gatekeeper of that block.

The caretakers provide the T.L.C. of a community. They are the "means," the warm-hearted people of the community, the people in front of whose home the children gather and play. The gatekeeper and caretaker make up together the most powerful leadership force in any neighborhood. One never achieves anything if either of these individuals opposes it. The caretaker can be identified with a question like this: "If you had a crisis at 2:00 a.m. and none of your family was around, to whom would you turn in this community for help?" If the same name keeps surfacing in your interviews, guess whom you have identified!

The flak catcher is the most interesting person in a community. Another name for him is "gossip." Gossips can be as healthy for a community as they can be unhealthy. The flak catcher is on top of what is going on and has the capacity to communicate to everybody in the neighborhood. Do you want to get the word out on any issue? Tell the flak catcher.

The broker is the politician, the power broker who can wield influence outside the community. He is the friend of a friend of a friend of the chief of police or the director of the sanitation bureau. He can make a telephone call or have a strategic conversation with someone, and the issue will get resolved. Your questions to identify this person would deal with the brokerage of power.

The gatekeepers, caretakers, flak catchers, and brokers provide the cement that binds a community together. The church cannot minister effectively in an urban neighborhood and ignore them. No mission outreach will be successful, no evangelistic effort effective, no community ministry supported without these leaders giving at least tacit approval to it. The church may not realize it, but these people make or break every activity it undertakes in that community. Therefore, it is critical that networkers identify not just the issues of the people but also their informal leaders.

The third thing networkers want to know is who in the community cares so much about an issue that he'll get involved in dealing with it. No community issue can be addressed successfully unless the *people* address it. Those who have the fire in the belly will take the risk. How do you discover them? Observe the people you're interviewing. Do they really get animated and speak with conviction about an issue? If so, they're likely candidates. Ask, "What causes you to weep over this community? What just breaks your heart here?" When you discover people who weep with broken hearts, you will have found the motivators and convictional workers of that community.

Why network? What are the benefits of networking to one's church or ministry? They are numerous. Networking can:

inform your preaching and teaching so that it brings biblical insights to issues of greatest importance to the people;

identify the people in the community with whom you need to build a strong, empathetic, and trusting relationship;

provide insights on how to communicate to the people who surround the church building;

shape the programmatic development of your church;

identify possible prospects for later evangelization;

create community awareness about your church and consciousness of your concern.

But the most important function of networking is to enable you and your church to move into the most effective aspect of urban ministry—community organization.

## Community Organization

What is community organization? What does it have to do with the urban church?

*Community organization is the process by which the people of an urban community organize themselves to deal with the primary forces that are exploiting their community and making them powerless victims.* Note the assumptions wrapped up in that definition. The first is that the people who are best able to deal with a problem are those most affected by it. What do I mean by that?

When I was pastoring a church in Detroit, my teenage son was getting himself into a lot of trouble. He was drinking, not getting his schoolwork done, running around with a rough group of friends. Those first three years of his high school life were hell for my wife and me. During that time, I went to see a friend of mine to share my concern. When I began to share that heartache, he said something that seemed terribly cruel. Later I realized his wisdom.

"Bob," he said, "I can listen to what you have to say. I can sympathize with you. I can weep with you. I can even feel great pain for what you are going through. But I cannot solve your problem. Only you can solve your problem for yourself."

What is obviously true in family life is equally true for a community or neighborhood. Those most capable and motivated to solve a severe community problem are the people in that community who have that problem. No one else, not even the church, can know what is best for an urban community.

Now, although that seems self-evident, it is one of the most difficult insights for Christians to practice. Why? Because the church assumes that, because we know the gospel, we have the clearest understanding of the needs of a community. We unconsciously believe that, because we "know what is best" for their souls, we also know what is best for them socially, economically, and politically. Therefore we undertake ministry in that community determining what is best for it, thus robbing the people of taking responsibility for dealing with their own corporate problems. The first assumption behind my definition of community organization is that the people best able to deal with a community problem are the people most affected by it.

The second assumption is that people who are excluded from full participation in the social, economic, and political life of their city or neighborhood can be empowered to participate when they act collectively. As long as people take responsibility only individually, they will not significantly change the course of their neighborhood. If people can be empowered to work cooperatively, as a single unit, they will be able to take responsibility for the life of their community and, consequently, to participate fully in the life of their city.

In light of these two assumptions, a church can respond to its city in one of three different ways.

First, it may see itself as the church *in* the city and community. It will not feel any particular commitment to its neighborhood. It will not particularly identify with the community. It will simply be physically present in it. Its brick and mortar happen to meet the ground there.

Often a church that sees itself as in but not of its community will have had a significant commitment to that community in earlier days. It may have been created as a parish church there. But then the neighborhood began to change. People began to move out, and the community began to deteriorate. So, increasingly the church became a commuter congregation with members traveling into the neighborhood to attend church but living elsewhere. So the congregation lost its stake, its psychological ownership in the community. This is the church *in* the city.

Second, a church may perceive itself as a church *to* the city and community. Some urban churches realize that if they do not interact with their neighborhood, they will die. So they begin to become concerned about the neighborhood and its problems. This, of course, is a more holistic approach than the first, because it recognizes that the church must be present to the people around it and concerned with both evangelism and social action. *It is inadequate to be concerned with people's souls, particularly if the people are poor, unless the church is also going to be concerned about their social and economic needs.*

There is great potential in this kind of approach, but there is also a fatal flaw. *The Achilles heel of this approach is the perception that the church knows what is best for the neighborhood.* These Christians look at the neighborhood and say, "Look at all these teenagers hanging around, causing trouble; what these people need is a youth program for their teenagers to get them off the streets." The church says, "Look at all these children running around the streets; they have no place to play. What the church needs to do is develop a program for those children." Or the church looks at the number of senior citizens sitting on their porches and says, "What our church needs to do is to develop a ministry to senior citizens."

The common element in all of these ministry proposals is that the church is deciding what is best for the community. But has anybody asked the community? The teens may be causing trouble because they have no work; their solution might be to start a job-placement and training program, not a recreational program. The children may play on the streets, not because they have no other place to play, but because their parents want to keep an eye on them. The senior citizens sitting on their porches with apparently nothing to do might *like* sitting on their porches, visiting with each other and passing the time of day!

The people best able to deal with a problem are those most affected by it. They can best determine whether a condition someone from another social class or culture perceives as a problem is actually a problem. Being the church *to* the city is inappropriate because the church does not recognize the capability of the community's people; it makes judgments about their priorities from another culture's perspective and perceives them as objects to be ministered to rather than folk capable of determining their own future. It is, essentially, a colonialist mentality.

Third, a church may be the church *with* the city. There is a profound difference between being a church *in* or *to* an urban neighborhood and being a church *with* that neighborhood. When a church takes this third approach, it incarnates itself in that community. It becomes flesh of that people's flesh, bone of that people's bone. It enters into the life of the community and becomes a partner in addressing its need. This means the church allows the people of the community to instruct it as it identifies with the people. It respects them and joins them in dealing with the issues they have identified as their own. This is the approach in which the most authentic urban ministry actually occurs.

The third response—being the church *with* the people—enables the church to join with the people in addressing the issues of that community, not from a vantage point of privileged insight but from the recognition that the people of the community—the people with the problem—must assume final responsibility for coping with the problem. The church should come alongside them, support and work with them in the endeavor, and share with them the particular gifts and strengths it has to contribute. Community organization is the process that enables the church to actually be the church *with* its neighborhood.

How does community organization work? *It is a process of mobilizing the people in a troubled neighborhood to take action together to identify and defeat the social and spiritual forces destroying that neighborhood.* The church is particularly well positioned to undertake that responsibility and to work alongside the people.

How is community organization done? It is impossible, in the limits of this chapter, to describe the organizing process satisfactorily. Ample material is available for interested readers.[1] Here are a few important elements of community organizing.

### Networking

Networking (which we have already examined) is an initial step of community organizing. The felt needs and issues of the community, its real leaders, and the people who will form the convictional backbone of the organization are all identified through networking. In light of the information gathered on issues, leaders, and people, one can undertake the next stage of organizing—coalition building.

### Coalition Building

Coalition building is simply going to the people in the community who claim a particular issue as theirs and pulling them together into an action group to address the issue. To function effectively, the coalition needs *at least* one gatekeeper, caretaker, broker, or flak catcher. Of course, members of the churches should also be involved in coalitions on issues of concern to them.

Most communities need several different coalitions. One can deal with children, another with sanitation, another with education, and yet another with unemployment. In essence, the coalitions provide a means by which people can deal *together* with the issue or problem that concerns them.

This process, therefore, applies the two organizational principles discussed earlier. By being issue oriented, the coalition gets the people most capable of dealing with the problem—those most concerned about it—to work on it. Bringing these people together enables them to work collectively. That, in turn, empowers them to deal effectively with the issue. This is what coalitions are designed to do: to enable the people concerned with a given problem to deal with it collectively.

Integral to the effectiveness of coalition building is the process of action and reflection. The community organizing team leads the people of a coalition to reflect on and analyze their problem, seeking to understand why it exists, determining together what to do about it, and then doing it. It is important for the coalition to select initial actions on which it can win. But it can take on tougher problems, particularly the systemic causes behind surface symptoms, as it matures and gains strength.

The activities of the coalition will tend to be of two types: projects and mediation. Projects are activities undertaken by the coalition or community to solve a problem directly by themselves. A project might be an income-generating scheme or the creation of a housing program. Mediation is an effort to get the governmental or economic powers of the city to undertake what they are obligated by law to provide but are not providing. Thus, mediation might aim at getting the city to pick up the garbage or install sewers, or getting banks to provide loans in slum communities they consider a financial risk.

A cycle of reflection and action will establish itself. If you get people to think about the issues that concern them, they will analyze them on increasingly profound levels. As they act on their reflection, developing substantive projects or mediations they themselves implement, they will be thrust into deeper and deeper reflection.

## Leadership Development

Also integral to community organizing is leadership development. The organizer stays alert for leaders who emerge from the people. Some emerging leaders will have been identified previously: caretakers, gatekeepers, flak catchers, and brokers. But some may be newly emerging as leaders in coalitions. One of the most important tasks in community organization is to build leadership among the people.

Potential leaders are identified within the coalition. They are equipped through the same process of reflection and action, both within and outside the coalition, as the organizer works directly with the potential leaders and trains them to carry out particular actions. If, for example, they have to appear before a magistrate to present an issue of their community, the organizer might role play the confrontation with them. They will practice how to present their case to the magistrate. That way, incipient leaders are equipped to become strong, sound, enduring leaders of their community. Through the training, development, and empowerment of its leaders, the community will become increasingly empowered.

A strategic part of community organizing is to bring coalitions together into the "community's organization." There may be six, seven, or eight coalitions operating in a given community around issues the people have identified. Increasingly, these coalitions need to draw together to work with each other and share each other's leadership, thus eventually creating one organization for the community.

In a slum in Detroit in which I was involved, several churches were concerned about their impoverished and powerless community. Early on, thirty of us networked the community. We called on virtually every family in the neighborhood—hundreds and hundreds of people. We spent time with each family. In our networking, we gathered information regarding the concerns and issues people cared most about and identified indigenous leadership.

We invited the leaders to join us. They did, and together we identified the issues the community felt were of greatest importance: senior citizens' concerns, children, youth, emergency aid, receiving from government what was legally due but not being provided, unemployment, and housing. So we built coalitions around these concerns and began to work on them. We started with senior citizens. That group of people identified what they wanted to do, set up a senior citizens' program, and began to implement it.

Another coalition developed UPLIFT, a year-round youth and children's program staffed by seventy-five volunteers from the community and churches. This was followed by Crossroads, a ministry developed in conjunction with the Episcopal church, which provided emergency aid, food, and clothing and developed an advocacy effort that represented the poor before city and state government officials.

Finally, the people tackled the truly big issues of the community—housing and jobs. Our housing coalition developed a master plan for the community, pulled together a larger coalition of government agencies, foundations, and fiduciary institutions to provide funding, and purchased and began renovating homes. Built on the sweat-equity principle, community people working on them were able to purchase homes at low cost and with virtually no down payment. A jobs training and placement program was also developed, began training the people in new and marketable skills, and eventually placed three hundred people a year in jobs.

## An Evangelism of Respect

In this approach to urban ministry, what role does evangelism play? How does sharing the faith enter the process of community empowerment?

The church's participation in the community's organization creates a unique opportunity to share the Christian faith with the community's emerging leaders. Consider what happens if the members of a congregation actively participate in the coalitions addressing critical community issues. Christians, members of these congregations, work side by side with the people of the community. And they do this even though they are not necessarily affected by, and so concerned with, the same problems! In this process of shared action and reflection, intense relationships of trust and respect grow.

The very nature of the work of a coalition entails risk, as the political and economic systems of a city are challenged by the powerless and the Christians from the community. The very act of reflecting and acting together around issues intensely important to the people builds trust. It builds strong respect for one another, and in that context sharing one's faith becomes easy.

*It takes two people to do the work of evangelism. It takes the evangelist who is willing to proclaim the gospel. But it also takes the cooperation of the one who hears.* The person who hears the Good News must be willing to hear. If he is not willing to hear, it matters not how much the evangelist proclaims the faith; he proclaims it to deaf ears.

Community organization builds relationships of depth and trust between the people of the church and the people of the community. In such relationships, sharing about Jesus is natural. People who would normally be unreceptive to the gospel willingly hear it from their community partners because they trust them—and the Christians likewise respect them.

Other ministry strategies have been developed in the city, including mission strategizing, evaluation, and social analysis. Space prohibits developing these strategies here. Instead, I have presented the strategies I consider most important to incorporate into one's urban ministry.

It is reputed that during the early years of Christianity, when it was under intense persecution by the state, a Christian leader and a pagan philosopher engaged in a debate. The pagan summarized his case against Christianity with the words, "When most teachers go forth to teach, they cry, 'Come to me, you who are clean and worthy,' and they are followed by the highest caliber of people available. But your silly Master cries, 'Come to me, you who are down and beaten by life,' and so he accumulates around himself the rag, tag, and bobtail of humanity."

The response of the Christian to this pagan's mocking attack stands as a profound statement on the task of the church in the city. "Yes," he admitted, "the Christians are the rag, tag, and bobtail of humanity. But Jesus does not leave them that way. Out of material you would have thrown away as useless, he fashions men [and women], giving them back their self-respect, enabling them to stand on their feet and look God in the eye. They were cowed, cringing, broken things. But the Son has set them free!"[2]

This is the unique work of Christ and his church in the city—to reach out to that city's rag, tag, and bobtail, to join with them in winning back their self-respect so that they can stand on their feet and look even God in the eye! This is the work to which all of us as urban Christians are privileged to be called.

## Discussion Questions

1. How important do you feel it is to develop distinctively *urban* strategies for the city? Can you identify some rural models of ministry that have served well in the city? Besides the networking model, what other authentically urban strategies can you mention?
2. List the types of information the networker seeks to collect. What benefits does he hope to gain for the church's ministry in the city?
3. Identify the four types of leaders found in every urban community and the role each plays.

4. Describe how community organization works and what it tries to achieve. Reflect on your own experiences in connection with community organization.
5. How does community work open doors to evangelize? Suggest some ways you might use community work to gather and train disciples for Christ.

# 9

# PROFILES OF EFFECTIVE URBAN PASTORS

*Raymond J. Bakke*

The 1990 census shows that 51 percent of the United States lives in forty-four metropolitan places. As a nation, we have shifted massively since 1900, when 42 percent of all Americans lived and worked on farms, to 1990, when under 2 percent do.

Equally rapid is the parallel shift from a nation where European Americans were the dominant groups to the realities portrayed in a recent *Time* magazine cover story that indicated that non-Europeans will be the majority in the United States generally by 2050, even as they are already in many large cities.[1]

Both of these macro trends reflect similar movements in the rest of the world. We grow a metro Paris of more than eight million each month on this planet. Most of that growth is moving to large, increasingly pluralistic, cities on all six continents.

Many church and mission leaders, as well as theological seminaries, refuse to acknowledge these realities, even though the evidence is all around. An incredible number of folk still portray urban ministry as a minor issue involving places where only a few rather idiosyncratic pastors and missionaries feel called to serve.

In this chapter, I shall argue that most of the world's unreached peoples are culturally rather than geographically distant from local churches and that local urban churches and their pastors can be at the leading edge of cross-cultural, international mission in our time. I shall also show that the majority of churches and pastors are not ready for this mission. While running the risk of offending some people in the process, I shall point out that ignorance about effective urban ministries is no excuse, because church leaders can find all sorts of contemporary models to learn from, including some maverick mall developers.

## The Changing Context: 1960–1980

In their marvelously lucid book *Downtown, Inc.: How America Rebuilds Cities*, Bernard Frieden and Lynne Sagalyn document the post-World War II decline of inner cities. It was assumed by planners that downtowns were obsolete. The nation demolished huge sections of urban neighborhoods as we rearranged our lives around the automobile. While much of the country celebrated suburbanization, the left-behinds sang "Nobody Knows the Rubble I Have Seen."

> Developers believed that suburbanites had little nostalgia for downtown hit-or-miss retailing, pushy crowds, dirty streets, or dress up shopping rite. Seeing the projections for rising incomes and standards of affluence, they assumed suburbanites wanted something better, though more casual and informal, and they built a shopping environment to match. . . . Merchandise was delivered, garbage compacted and picked up, and the mall cleaned daily—all behind the scenes with the sights, sounds and smells kept away from shoppers. . . . The idea behind the mall was to create a sanctuary for shopping.[2]

In two decades, the American middle class went out of the cities and up market at the same time. They left their old church buildings and recontextualized themselves in the new mall culture.

Mall developers had commercial goals but saw that if you provided "an overlay of entertainment, relaxation, art and sculpture, civic goodwill and space for community meetings, you could increase the crowds . . . and so they built bigger malls."[3]

The marketing technology assumes high levels of control once people drive, park, and enter. In the words of Edward J. DeBartolo, the nation's largest mall developer, as he flew over a prospective mall site in the company plane, "We got 'em! We can write our own ticket down there."[4]

Those of us who teach pastors in theological faculties can attest that it did not take the church and the church-growth movements very long to discover, accept, and join the mall people's migration. If the established urban church metaphor before 1960 was "the general store" with the single pastor as proprietor, the new suburban church is the "mall" in which ministry is boutique and the pastors or elders function as mall directors.[5] For more than a decade this has been the dominant profile of the American pastorate.

Since the mid-1970s, the scene has changed. Suburban land costs have skyrocketed, construction and energy costs have escalated, and the Environmental Protection Agency has been adopting policies to thwart suburban development. "With enough help from city hall, the right developer might be able to cope with the reluctance of the department stores and the problems of downtown."[6] This depended, however, on finding strategic sites and people with two primary skills: vision, and the ability to take risks.

## The Maverick Developers

Because this is a book about evangelizing and discipling cities, it is critically important for church and mission leaders to understand cities. Urban pastoral education aims to equip leaders with skills to read the city for more effective entry into the community and the local church within it. This chapter assumes that we can gain a great deal of insight into the nature and mission of the urban church in the 1990s by unpacking the experiences of what Frieden and Sagalyn call "the maverick developers."[7] So, borrowing heavily and without apology, we can examine their case study of developer Jim Rouse (who is connected with the Church of the Savior in Washington, D.C.), the creator of a new city—Columbia, Maryland— and the primary developer of downtowns in Boston, Baltimore, and numerous other places.

Here are some isolated Rouse principles for urban redevelopment, with my implications for urban pastors.[8] Rouse

is committed to saving the best of the old buildings—so he adds architectural historians to his team. By implication, we assume that urban church leadership is an interdisciplinary team.

learns from international models, for example, Tivoli in Copenhagen. Urban church leadership has an expanding, even global, worldview.

is committed to partnerships. Urban ministry cannot be done in isolation from other agencies in the community.

believes that new structures for decision making, funding, and communicating evolve uniquely in each project. Urban ministry is customized in ways that require adaptive politics and regular accountability to the goals of the project or mission.

experimented with racially integrated neighborhoods in Columbia, even while race conflict was tearing cities apart. Urban ministry should be as inclusive as any other community institutions. Is it not blasphemous to the Holy Spirit to allow churches to be less racially inclusive than the secular schools and grocery stores around them?

adopted an operating style that expected risks, change, complexity, and daily problem solving. City pastoral ministry could hardly contrast with suburban ministry more than at this point. Rouse "cheerfully" expects crisis.

assumed that the major obstacle to overcome was a "negative frame of mind about downtown and its future." Urban pastors need to know that the major barriers to effective urban ministry are seldom in the cities; they are in us and our churches, mission agencies, and international policies.

has great political skills and can mobilize community support. Unquestionably, effective urban pastors need and often use these same skills.

cultivated great patience—urban developments take a long time to construct. Projects described in Pasadena and Pittsburgh took more than a decade. Urban pastors must be in for the long haul.

like other maverick developers, makes deals with the city. In this it has been interesting to watch Moody Bible Institute landbank and work with Chicago's political establishment over the years. They know now, as D. L. Moody himself knew when he was on the Rebuild Chicago Committee after the Chicago fire of 1871, that it is never enough just to preach the gospel and witness to individuals in the city.

tries new ways to fund things, like tax increment financing (TIF). This is a rather complex issue, but the whole discussion reminds us that many urban churches now create their own foundations for ministry and routinely leverage and multiply their mission dollars by development strategies.

uses a blend of theme parks, theaters, open-air plans, and parking options. Urban churches will program for similar mixes. Some city malls are designed so that parts are "scruffy" by intent. "We want graffiti, the winos and the vagrants," said one director of Pike Street Market in Seattle. The local artists decide who is welcome. "The street people are part of the scene. They have a right to be here."[9] Urban churches, by their art, murals, music styles, and other behavioral patterns, communicate who belongs and who does not. Here is a quote with which many urban pastors can identify:

> The (Pike Street) Market's tolerance of vagrants, street people and graffiti makes good business sense. Tourists are attracted . . . precisely because it is untouristy. These practices give the Market a raucous character that is authentic and even refreshing in comparison with the orderly restraint and polite atmosphere of suburban malls.[10]

Over and over again now, we are learning from the experiences of the maverick urban mall developers that "downtown retail centers *can serve low-income customers, without driving away the middle-class.*"[11] designs the pulling power of his malls to depend upon an "intricate blend of light-hearted good taste and restrained but canny design that makes them fun. . . . [T]he atmosphere is refreshingly honest (without) Muzak, fountains, plastic plants or gimcrack fakery to evoke nostalgia. The formula then is a mix of location, design, tenant mix and excitement."[12]

## Other Profiles

The urban pastor as maverick developer is not the only contemporary metaphor we could suggest as a profile. Consider briefly two others: the athletic coach and the symphonic conductor.

Today's athletic coaches come in all sizes, ages, and colors, and in both sexes. Professional coaches are highly skilled and normally serve long apprenticeships. They have strengths and limitations. The physical preparation and handling of players has changed dramatically in recent years as knowledge of the human body has increased. Nearly all coaches work cross-culturally with many and sometimes most of their players. Consider, for example, John Wooden, the Indiana-born basketball player who as a Christian coached mostly Black players at a mostly Jewish state university

(UCLA) and won national championships twelve years in a row. Retired now more than a decade, Wooden is a model of how a white midwesterner can and must adapt his coaching strategy to the different kinds of players on his teams.

There are, however, coaches all around us who cannot or will not adapt. They have one system for all times, places, and personnel. You adapt, leave, or sit on the bench. Some urban pastors are like this. They expect the whole church to adapt to their worship styles, operations, and music forms, and they lose lots of folks in the process. Like some coaches, some pastors have a high need to control.

The symphony conductor is another model from whom pastors can learn. Like the Bible, music scores are often ancient, and the audiences often are traditional. Conductors know who pays the bill, and they program accordingly.

Orchestras have all the diversity of the body of Christ. The ability to bring woodwinds, brass, strings, and percussion into disciplined yet creative harmony separates the great conductors from the pretenders. There is no one way to interpret and conduct. It is an art rather than a science. Orchestras, like old churches, have institutional constraints and traditions, like musicians' unions. The best conductors are international and multilingual. Many represent ethnic minorities.

Symphony conductors, athletic coaches, and maverick developers are urban models in transition in our era. So, we might add, are physicians who operate in an urban medical service delivery system that may be sicker than the patients. The effective urban pastors we encounter in cities around this country, indeed around the world, are not alone in their struggles for integrity and effectiveness in the midst of rapidly changing environments.

It is important to acknowledge that urban ministry preparation broadens the lens. The biblical and denominational functions for pastors may be the same everywhere in the world, but the urban context definitely shapes the functions and informs the priorities for church leadership.

## Two Paradigms of the Church

Bob Bufford, Texas businessman and founder of The Leadership Network, has been hosting pastors of megachurches for the past five years. Recently, he shared his rather succinct perceptions about the church and its pastors in the 1980s.[13] He suggests that the church now operates in the following realities nationally in the USA:

An unchurched culture
Religious and racial pluralism
An information age
Nonbrand name loyalties
Working females and single-parent families
Mobility, individualism and independence

According to Bufford, the result is a shift from a leadership that controls to a leadership that empowers; from the professional pastor to the missionary pastor. Intuitively if not intentionally, most effective urban pastors have already shifted paradigms. The literature on urban churches and pastors has not caught up with the trend, because with very few exceptions, urban pastors are oral; they do not write books.[14]

In 1984 Sam Roberts, from the historic African-American school Virginia Union University and Theological School, and I researched 150 American Baptist "Old First" Baptist Churches in diverse environments. Working from congregational studies rather than libraries, we published our findings in *The Expanded Mission of "Old First" Churches*. We concluded that there were eight critical factors in the revival of old churches, both urban and nonurban. The book fleshed out these principles in a series of chapters:

1. The character and quality of leadership, both lay and clergy.
2. The determination and ability of the congregation to re-energize using sound biblical theology, values, goals, and program commitments.
3. The extent to which the historical uniqueness and identity of churches can become conscious and functional guidelines for contemporary action.
4. Churches' ability to uncover the dynamics and changing nature of their unique context and their willingness to confront it with realism, hope, and congruent models of caring.
5. The willingness of the congregation to inventory God's gifts to them as God's people and to be fired up for their visions and ministries, even if they do not fit the mold of previous programs.
6. The ability to develop and prioritize creative programming that is consistent with mission and not merely maintenance oriented.
7. The ability to change the organizational structure or forms in ways that enable new ministries to emerge and grow.

8. The ability to develop a process for bringing about change in the church, and the development of a caring network of church support systems that provide resources and assistance to help congregations caught in their environmental traumas.[15]

At the Old First Conference in Pittsburgh, where we worked on these issues, participants were asked to profile pastoral leadership for the 1980s and beyond. They grouped their conclusions under two headings: *attitudes* and *abilities*.[16]

### Attitudes

1. A sense of call and commitment to Jesus Christ.
2. A sense of humor and optimism.
3. Flexibility.
4. A strong sense of direction.
5. A biblically oriented vision on the city and the church.
6. A sense of trust in people.
7. A healthy mix of urgency and patience.
8. An informed perspective on the environment.
9. Mature, realistic love—"tough love."
10. Personal discipline.
11. Personal ego security—the freedom to fail.
12. Imagination and innovation.
13. A willingness to live in community.
14. A sense of history.
15. A strong commitment to the gospel as enacted in the local and global perspectives.
16. Personal stamina.

### Abilities

1. To communicate effectively on both a personal and a corporate level.
2. To manage and administer operations effectively.
3. To be able to establish "presence" with people.
4. To know when to delegate responsibilities.
5. To understand the power of symbols and their role in worship and in the life of the congregation.
6. To be able to celebrate corporate life joyously.
7. To be able to study and grow.

8. To be able to find resources for support.
9. To be able to accept people as they are.
10. To serve as a model for the gospel and to enable the congregation to live out the gospel.
11. To be able to live creatively with ambiguity and unfinished tasks.
12. To have the ability to set priorities for oneself.
13. To have an attitude toward ecology that sees the wisdom of recycling.
14. To be able to preach with power.
15. To be able to cope with conflict.
16. To be able to think theologically and biblically about the church's life.
17. To understand and live out the servant role of pastor.
18. To be able to function effectively with multilingual and multiethnic groups.

## Growing Churches in the City

Worship, community, and mission are the three essential ingredients of any urban church that grows, but urban churches often specialize rather radically in one or more of these three features.

A *creative worship* that is biblical, participative, and planned but spontaneous, with a blend of music styles and drama, will reach vast numbers of urban folk who experience the city as a "downer" all week long. For these people, celebration is a key. They are existential.

A *caring community* is the church with many kinds of small groups that provide support systems for people who live in personal or family brokenness, addictions, or dependencies. These people are relational.

A *mission action* congregation calls members to commitments in the market places of vocation and public service as signs of hope and agents of reconciliation in the world. These people are directional. They "scratch the city where it itches" in the name of Jesus.

### The Real Issue

Until now, we have been describing the profiles of effective urban pastors by analogies, metaphors, and the results of case studies. My own long experience as a pastor, my intimate contacts with pastors, and my engagement with pastors in urban consultations on six continents and in more than one hundred large cities have convinced me that effective urban pastors have a unique biblical hermeneutic. They integrate theology and sociology. They have a biblical vision *of* the city and *for* the city. They struggle to be both "Colossian" and "Philippian." Let me explain the last statement:

### The Colossian Vision

These pastors see that Christ dwells in heaven as firstborn of creation, the glue that holds the universe together, the Lord of all systems and structures in the world.

*So,* these pastors know they are chaplains to power and confronters of evil and injustice. They see both creation and redemption as functional mandates. They want to save the people *and* transform the city using the church as the base for kingdom agendas.

### The Philippian Vision

These pastors see that Christ left the power and glory of heaven and came personally to die and rise to give people personal, saving relationships with God and build churches that care for them.

*So,* these pastors do personal evangelism, planting and building churches that, though they are in the city, often are not of it but are like gatherings of pilgrims en route to heaven with Jesus. They feel at home with the powerless of the world.

Two visions of Christ, each with related emphases, but two different kinds of urban spirituality and pastoral styles! Paul had them both. It is not insignificant that these two letters of Paul are close together in the New Testament.

This is a book about discipling the city. Discipling the urban world must include both the spiritual transformation of persons and the social transformation of places.

### The Testimony

The good news is that in the 1990s a growing number of pastors are in fact discipling their cities. As a part of the discipline of writing this chapter, I thought my way around the cities where I have been, and where I met some of you who will read this book. My list grows of maverick urban entrepreneurial pastors who help create unique congregations, set people free for ministry, and balance power with powerlessness, transcendence with immanence, action with devotion, and tradition with transformation. Rejoice! There is hope, for the number of urban disciples is growing!

## Discussion Questions

1. Describe some of the demographic changes occurring in North America and pinpoint a common blunder made by many church and mission leaders.

2. How do college and seminary studies prepare a person for the kind of church leadership described under "The Maverick Developers"? Suggest ways of supplementing school education with other kinds of learning in order to prepare for effective urban pastoring.

3. Describe some of the cross-cultural aspects of urban pastoral ministry, with illustrations if possible.

4. Explain what Bob Bufford means by the "Classical" and the "Contemporary" paradigms of local churches and, from your own experience in various churches, describe concretely how these two different kinds of churches function.

5. Evaluate and explain your own vision for pastoring in an urban environment. Is your vision more "Colossian" or "Philippian"? Describe what you want it to be.

# 10

## DIVERSE WORSHIP TRADITIONS IN THE CITY

*Corean Bakke*

One of my earliest memories as a young girl was the occasional trip to the city with my parents. Come Sunday, we always went to church. In my youthful comparisons, church in the city was bigger and better than church in the small town. The imposing structure, the pipe organ, the stained glass windows, and the countless rows of pews contrasted with the more humdrum accoutrements of worship in our small town. For me, as a small girl, the ultimate in corporate worship was the big-city church, my yardstick by which to measure all other churches.

I now live in Chicago, surrounded by churches. The diversity in worship puts my childhood ideal into perspective as one of many. Measuring one against another now appears unfair and makes my image obsolete for the contemporary reality. An intentional tour of Sunday morning worship in my neighborhood confirmed the inappropriateness of my youthful image and the need for a new one.

## How a Community Worships: A Look at My Neighborhood

The United Church of Christ across the street, a meticulously kept structure, houses a diminutive congregation in which the average age is sixty-four. Within the past month, a Filipino UCC congregation and pastor have come to share the building.

Ebenezer Lutheran is one block farther down the street. When the King and Queen of Sweden visit Chicago, they worship at this church, in the heart of Andersonville. This congregation is becoming less Scandinavian and more ethnically diverse, reflecting the changing complexion of the neighborhood. The pastoral staff includes a woman and a man. Each Sunday a signer interprets for the deaf.

The Evangelical Free Church, two blocks in another direction, has a split congregation. The English-speaking people meet earlier on Sunday morning, the Hispanics later. A lot happens in this building every week. The premises are not as pristine as those of the other two buildings.

In thinking about the diverse traditions of Christian worship in the city, I looked at some of the large and well-known churches. But I also looked closely at churches in my immediate neighborhood on Chicago's north side. In an area marked off by railroad tracks on the west, Wilson Avenue on the south, Hollywood Avenue on the north, and Lake Michigan on the east, I pondered the varieties of Christian worship, looking for things held in common but often observed differently.

### Place for Worship: A Holy, Set-apart Space

The starting point involved the buildings used for worship. Many were visually impressive: large, architecturally beautiful, well kept, obviously the pride of the congregation. The Greek Orthodox Church falls into this category, as it ought, given its theology of the place of worship: the interior of the church represents heaven on earth.

Some churches once were well kept, but members have dropped off. Peeling paint, broken windows, and neglected grounds communicate a general state of decline. Fewer people struggle to carry more responsibility and must set priorities and make choices. The United Methodist Church tenaciously holds onto its building, made of majestic field stones, with a drastically reduced membership. Place is important to its members. They continue to hope that times will get better, that growth will come once again to their congregation.

The small storefront congregations are less visible. Signs in windows distinguish their places of worship from other commercial properties. But small and unpretentious as they may be, storefronts are places where the occupants can settle in and be at home. They can hang their own pictures and symbols on the walls, install their own pulpits and musical instruments, keep their own kitchens. Be it ever so humble, it belongs to them, a place holy and set apart.

Congregations that rent space in church buildings struggle with being perpetual guest tenants. Before each service, they must move their equipment into place; afterward, they must move it back into storage. They must accept less desirable hours for worship, time slots unused by the host church. Their tenants' rights are carefully spelled out. They may or may not use the kitchen. Their presence, while indicated on a bulletin board or sign post, is perceived as subordinate to the host church. They function as a second-class congregation. Their status is regularly reviewed.

The house church is the least visible of all. News of its existence travels by word of mouth. The space is more limited than the storefront, less able to cope with distinctive furnishings desirable in worship, less set apart from secular activities of the week.

The humbler places of worship often serve as nurseries for congregations that grow up and move out. The house church grows into the storefront. The tenant congregation grows into a self-supporting church, able to finance a place of its own.

A place to meet as a congregation is necessary for the growth of a sense of identity and mission. A holy place for worship is a common feature of Christian worship in my neighborhood.

## People: The Participants in Worship

Just as architectural space shapes worship, so do people. Different social classes identify with different worship traditions. Personality types favor traditions compatible with their way of being. In the modern city, which attracts immigrants from all over the globe, numerous ethnic groups further compound the reality of diversity. The ideal of gathering all Christians into a single worship tradition, practically speaking, may be neither possible nor desirable. Not everyone would be satisfied in the same worship environment. The church is much healthier for its variety.

The diversity among people helps to explain the many varieties of worship available in the city. My neighborhood in Chicago is heavily populated with Asians. Cambodian, Laotian, and Vietnamese people have come here as refugees. Koreans, Chinese, and Japanese have come as immigrants. They form worshiping congregations in their own languages, pastored by their own people. The Filipinos are more flexible. Some join English-speaking congregations. Others gather around a Filipino pastor and worship as an ethnic group.

Hispanics gravitate to Spanish-speaking congregations. In Chicago, they are largely divided between Puerto Ricans and Mexicans. Eastern Europeans in my neighborhood who feel more comfortable in their own language and ethnic groups include Romanians, Greeks, and Russians. African groups include Ethiopian congregations and a Nigerian storefront church. Language barriers prevent most of these people from worshiping together even when they are part of the same worship tradition.

More and more churches in my neighborhood accommodate multiple congregations. In some cases they are all part of the same church, and their pastors work together as a team. Periodically they come together by using translators. Totally distinct congregations of the same tradition may use the same building and rarely if ever come together. A single building may house congregations of diverse worship traditions.

In Roman Catholic churches, where small chapels surround the main worship space, ethnic variety can readily be seen. Distinctive flowers, candle holders, and figures of the Virgin Mary and the saints identify these chapels with people from other countries. Protestant churches generally lack places where distinctive cultures can make their own visual contributions. The worship environment may give no indication of their presence.

Diversity occurs within same-language and same-ethnicity congregations. In the United States, youth have a pronounced culture of their own. Elderly people are often isolated from younger ages. The coming together of all ages in worship creates tensions. Multigenerational worship has become a cross-cultural challenge shared by churches in all sizes of communities.

Some worship traditions, like Orthodox, Roman Catholic, African-American, and charismatic groups, expect the full range of family life to come together in worship. They have no parallel programs to accommodate babies and children while their parents and grandparents worship. Their rituals draw people of all ages into worship. Babies and toddlers learn how to worship by watching it happen around them. Small children experiment with the body language of worship: bowing, forming the shape of the cross, lifting their arms, dancing, clapping, playing rhythmic instruments. They grow up singing the liturgy, or the praise choruses.

Many lonely people, looking for a congregation to join, look for personal relationships. They especially value the social interaction connected with worship: greeters at the door when they arrive; get-acquainted time during the service; informal sharing of joys and concerns; testimonies of personal experiences during the past week; light refreshments shared at the end of the service.

The worshiping church is people, many kinds of people, gathered together.

### Baptism: Rite of Initiation

Baptism divides Christians into two camps: those that sprinkle and those that immerse. Baptismal fonts, where used, usually make up part of the worship environment. Baptisteries seldom show. Generally they are covered over or nonexistent. The issue and mode of baptism are encountered infrequently in urban churches during Sunday worship.

### Eucharist or Lord's Supper: Regular, Occasional

My firsthand experiences of varieties of worship in the city have illustrated for me the range of diversity in worship practices. Where Eucharist is the heart of the worship, all parts of the service lead to it. In some of the non-Eucharist services, a table set with chalice and plate remind worshipers of its importance. Worship environments with minimal visual symbols contain no noticeable reminders of the bread and wine.

As to the celebration of the Eucharist, Christendom is divided into several traditions. Some include the sacred meal as part of worship each Sunday, while others include it monthly or quarterly. Some churches baptize infants but postpone communion until more mature years are reached. The Orthodox, on the other hand, both baptize and commune infants, and children eagerly look forward to Eucharist at the conclusion of Divine Liturgy in these churches. Baptists commune all baptized believers.

In theory, Eucharist or Lord's Supper is a common link between all Christians. But in Sunday-by-Sunday practice, it is not common to all occasions of Christian worship. Each tradition has theological arguments to back up its practice.

### Singing: The Praises of All

Mainline Protestant churches tend toward a sedate, formal praise style using pipe organ and hymnals as the mainstays of praise. A more relaxed atmosphere pervades the free churches and those that follow the revivalist patterns of worship. A song leader leads the congregation through the praise portion of the service, freely interspersing comments with the singing.

Many African-American churches cast sedateness aside. In their services, an enthusiastic choir sings, accompanied by drums, tambourines, and electronic organ. The congregation actively participates in the choir music with amens and hallelujahs, hand clapping and dancing.

Roman Catholic worship seems modest and mild in comparison. It intersperses music through its liturgy. The praise is more cognitive, void of exuberant physical demonstration or broad participation. The choice of instruments may include electric guitar and folk instruments, yet the restraint continues.

Going a step farther toward restraint and simplicity, one discovers churches that ban all musical instruments and permit only the human voice in the praise of God. In the Orthodox church, all singing is unaccompanied. Choir and priest together lead the congregation through an elaborate and extensive liturgy.

The Salvation Army adds brass to piano and organ and sings gospel songs. The charismatic churches cast most tradition aside and structure praise in ways understandable to contemporary persons with no church background. Simple choruses and overhead projectors replace hymns and hymnbooks. Electronic keyboards, guitars, drums, and congregational clapping augment or replace organs and pianos.

In storefront churches, doors and windows stand wide open on hot summer days. Cranked-up sound systems provide a barrier between the sacred and the profane, blocking out city noises. Short musical phrases repeated over and over characterize their singing.

House churches operate without the resources available to more developed congregations. When instruments are used, they often have to be portable. A house church in my neighborhood, with seven young adults sitting in a circle, sings Scripture choruses accompanied by classical guitar.

Singing is the most significant corporate activity in worship. It can be grand or simple, loud or soft, accompanied or unaccompanied, traditional or contemporary, Western or Eastern or African. All forms become part of the church's praise.

### Prayer: Traditional, Contemporary

Corporate prayer used to come neatly packaged in two varieties: set prayers and spontaneous prayers. Liturgical churches used traditional, set prayers. Free churches used extemporaneous prayers. The two rarely mixed. But in this day of liturgical renewal, old traditions are breaking down. Roman Catholics are free to use indigenous languages. Charismatics in liturgical churches have introduced extemporaneous prayers for healing and renewal. Some free churches are open to pre-planned prayers. The lines of distinction between the kinds of prayer encountered in various traditions are becoming blurred.

In addition to the liturgical renewal movement and the charismatic movement, the feminist movement has significantly affected the language of worship and prayer in some churches. Efforts to use more inclusive nouns and pronouns have led to significant theological discussions.

Traditional church liturgies stand in solid resistance to change and experimentation. The resonant words of prayer in the Divine Liturgy of the Orthodox church are sung the same today as for many hundreds of years. The quiet, introspective prayers in the Episcopal church, said while kneeling, contrast sharply with the noisy, extemporaneous prayers in expressive African-American churches and charismatic congregations. Litanies, found regularly in the Roman Catholic churches and others as well, offer congregations the more sedate role of responding with short phrases to the prayers of confession and petition. Silent prayers must not be overlooked. They are the mainstay of the Friends' gatherings.

Personal prayer within corporate worship continues in the city. One church in my neighborhood, well attended by lower classes, both street people and welfare people, concludes each morning service with an invitation to come forward for prayer. The multiple staff in that church, plus trained lay persons, pray one-on-one with each person who comes forward. The people in that church have many needs, and they do not hesitate to respond to this invitation.

### Scripture: Read by All, Read by One for All

Wherever Christians gather to praise and pray, they also read from the Holy Scriptures. The amount of Scripture read in each service varies according to the tradition. Those who follow the ecumenical lectionary include three texts in each worship service: one each from Old Testament, Epistles, and Gospels. One of the three serves as the text for the sermon.

In churches where the pastor chooses the text without reference to the lectionary, the sermon text may be the only Scripture included in the service, and that may be as brief as a single verse or portion of a verse.

In the first kind of church, people most frequently come without Bibles. They listen to the Word. In the second kind of church, people bring their own personal Bibles and turn together to the passage. Members do not concentrate on listening to the reading of the Word but follow along in individual Bibles.

The many available translations of Holy Scripture contribute an additional complexity to the diversity of worship. Congregations tend to adopt a favorite, just as people do. Many, if not most, African-American congregations prefer the King James Version. Attempts to use anything else in worship may cause serious problems. Persons committed to ridding worship of excessive and offensive masculine language often choose to use the Inclusive Language Lectionary, published during the last decade. Their attempt to remove from Scripture what they perceive to be "male-oriented" language means removing familiar words like "kingdom of heaven" and "Lord" and substituting "realm of heaven" and "Sovereign."

In the city, where so many people struggle to read because they either are learning English as a second language or are part of an urban culture that does not value reading, some pastors prefer to keep Scripture as simple and understandable as possible and use the Good News Bible.

The King James Version, the Revised Standard Version, the New International Version, the New English Bible, the Jerusalem Bible—the list is long. And these are just the English versions. With all the language groups in the city, the number of translations in use multiplies.

### Proclamation: Sermon, Teaching, Homily

Chicago's churches, like those of any other city, have all kinds of preachers. At least one preacher in Chicago prepares his sermon on Sunday morning, after first reading the Sunday paper. Another spends sixteen hours per sermon. Some of Chicago's churches were built specifically for the delivery of sermons. One example, Moody Memorial Church on the near north side, seats four thousand people. The pulpit is the architectural focus of that church auditorium, a high structure built atop an already high platform. Another church with a high and prominent pulpit, Fourth Presbyterian, stands across from a one-hundred story building on Chicago's Magnificent Mile. In the Presbyterian tradition, pastors are trained as biblical scholars and are expected to produce substantive sermons.

Hyde Park, on the south side, has a large concentration of liberal churches that sprang up around the University of Chicago. Intellectual and philosophical sermons attract students and faculty. Aesthetic priorities appeal to many who take the arts seriously in worship.

The prestigious African-American churches of the city are located farther south and west. People come early to get a seat and expect to be in the worship service at least two hours. Their enthusiastic participation provides a lively and responsive context for preaching.

In the charismatic churches and fellowships, proclamation might more correctly be called teaching than preaching. People in these churches bring their Bibles and pens and paper to take notes. They often have no previous church background, and teaching helps integrate them into the faith.

Chicago has large ethnic churches, like the mother church of the Polish Catholics. Here streams of people walk to Mass and fill the sidewalks and alleys. When pews are filled, people stand in the aisles and several deep in the rear, spilling out into the foyer and onto the front steps. They need the weekly encouragement of sermons filled with words of hope, for they are a people grieving for their native land and relatives left behind.

### Offerings: Money, Time, Talent

Even taking up the collection varies in different church and cultural traditions. The storefront Church of God in Christ prepares for the offering by seating a clerk at a small table in front. As people walk forward and give their money, she writes their names and amounts in her record book. When the offering falls short of the amount hoped for, she announces the exact figures needed to meet the church's needs, and she gets it. Passing the plate down each pew and long-handled baskets held by an usher and thrust in front of each person represent the ways more traditional churches collect offerings.

The concept of giving oneself as well as one's money is necessary for churches to survive and minister effectively. Women often shoulder the heavier part of responsibilities in small urban churches. Committee and board meetings have to be held, broken windows replaced, and new locks installed in the aftermath of burglaries. Flower gardens and small lawns on the premises are often gifts of time and labor by members who feel such things are important and are willing to cope with the vulnerability of such bits of natural beauty in the city.

City churches contain a wide variety of visual art, which is also an offering. In the Covenant Church in my neighborhood, a large, original painting of the head of Christ, done by Warner Sallman, dominates the sanctuary, depicting the humanity of Jesus. At St. Andrew's Greek Orthodox Church, the Christo-Pantocrator, painted on the ceiling of the rounded dome over the front of the church by an iconographer, shows Christ as Creator and Redeemer.

Offerings of time and labor are made every day of the week in the urban church, complementing the Sunday morning offerings. They represent a form of discipleship and help the church stay alive.

## Corporate Worship in the City:
## From Cornerstone to Gemstone

Each congregation in my neighborhood worships in accord with its own views of what worship ought to be. The founders of these churches firmly positioned their worship traditions, and the cornerstones of their buildings witness to decades of commitment to maintaining ethnic identity and worship tradition.

In the city, disciples of Christ are stretched into seeing that the body of Christ is not limited to any one group or tradition. The Christian faith that the apostles spread in all directions gave rise to churches of many kinds, all wrestling to put their unique cornerstones in place. Now, as the movement of people brings groups and traditions into juxtaposition with each other, a new image for the church at worship emerges. It is the gemstone, a stone with many different facets, representing many varieties and reflecting a single universal church.

Worship renewal is coming through interaction between facets of this gemstone. That is one of the beautiful features of worship in the city. Communal groups are expanding the Eucharist into a common meal following worship, sharing it with all. Catholics are becoming expert at providing their congregations with more nourishment in five-minute homilies than is in many a long Protestant sermon. The dedication of ethnic congregations to carry out faithfully their worship services, regardless of external discomforts, contrasts with other Americans' insistence on comfort and convenience and their casual attitude toward the sacred.

This gemstone recalls the precious stones worn by the priests of ancient Israel. It anticipates the building materials of the City of the future, whose foundation consists of precious stones (Rev. 21). The cornerstone laid by the apostles and their successors through the ages has come into exotic brilliance in the city. The press of people against people, disciple against disciple, has produced a gemstone with facets of complementary and indescribable beauty, to the glory and worship of God.

## For Further Reading

John Bentham. *Worship in the City.* Grove Worship Series No. 95; Bramcote, Nottingham: Grove Books, 1986.

Colin Buchanan. *Encountering Charismatic Worship.* Grove Booklet on Ministry and Worship No. 51; Bramcote, Nottingham: Grove Books, 1977.

Anscar J. Chupungco. *Cultural Adaptation of the Liturgy.* New York: Paulist, 1982.

Graham Kendrick. *Worship.* Eastbourne: Kingsway, 1984.

Cheslyn Jones, Geoffrey Wainright, and Edward Yarnold. *The Study of Liturgy.* New York: Oxford University Press, 1978.

M. Francis Mannion. "Liturgy and the Present Crisis of Culture." *Worship* 62, 2 (March 1988): 98–123.

Emmanuel L. McCall, comp. *Black Church Life Styles: Rediscovering the Black Christian Experience.* Nashville: Broadman, 1986.

Gertrud Mueller Nelson. *To Dance with God.* New York: Paulist, 1986.

James J. Stamoolis. *Eastern Orthodox Mission Theology Today.* American Society of Missiology Series, no. 10. Maryknoll, N.Y.: Orbis, 1986.

Bard Thompson. *Liturgies of the Western Church.* New York: William Collins and World Publishing Co., 1962.

Timothy Ware. *The Orthodox Church.* Baltimore: Penguin, 1963.

James F. White. *Protestant Worship: Traditions in Transition.* Louisville: Westminster/John Knox, 1989.

William H. Willimon. *Word, Water, Wine and Bread: How Worship Has Changed Over the Years.* Valley Forge: Judson, 1980.

## Discussion Questions

1. What are the basic elements of Christian worship that all churches can be expected to include in their public worship?
2. Explain why the worship experience of people in a small town is probably quite different from that of Christians in a large city.
3. Discuss the pros and cons of encouraging church members to visit churches that worship in ways that differ from their own tradition.
4. Name some things that you enjoy in worship traditions other than your own, and some that you would not enjoy or accept. Explain your reasons.

# 11

# EMPOWERING LAY LEADERSHIP IN AN AFRICAN-AMERICAN URBAN CHURCH: A CASE STUDY

*Willie Richardson*

Because the church I grew up in as a child did not present a clear message of salvation in Christ, I struggled for several years in spiritual darkness, asking church members what I had to do to be saved. I never received a satisfactory answer. My bewilderment during that time had a lasting impact on my life and future ministries.

After I gave up trying to get the answer from other people and simply surrendered my life to God, I determined to use my life to lead other people out of spiritual uncertainty and into discipleship. I enrolled at the Philadelphia College of the Bible and there came to understand what discipleship was about. I learned that Christian conversion involves the transformation of one's whole life and that discipleship includes thinking, acting, and relating to others in the way Christ wants.

In 1966, with the help of the first man I ever led to Christ and the first backslider I led back to Christ, I started the church I now pastor, Christian Stronghold Baptist Church, in Philadelphia. We began with just six people—three men and their wives. Today this church has over 1,800 active members.

## The Priority of Evangelism

At Stronghold we regard evangelism as the most important ministry of the church. We aim to see people changed into disciples of Christ, and we know that without evangelism such changes do not occur. We regularly see mean, bitter, antisocial people transformed into loving, kind believers in Christ. This does not surprise us, because when people have been regenerated by God's Spirit, there is a clear "before" and "after" evident in their lives.

Every member of our church is trained in a new member's class in how to lead a person to Christ. As a result, we see some new members winning others to Christ within the first few months they are in the church. Nothing matches the excitement of new converts enthusiastically experiencing the joy of the Lord and sharing their faith with other people!

We try to reach everyone in our community with the gospel of Jesus Christ. One of the strengths of the African-American culture is that our churches are generally not developed on the basis of social class. Many White churches are comprised largely of people of the same economic level. There are blue-collar churches, upper-middle-class churches, and churches that mostly the rich and affluent attend. I do not believe Jesus is pleased with socially segregated churches.

In our evangelism plan, we target all classes—poor people, working classes, and professional people. African-Americans in general have no problem belonging to churches that include people of varying economic classes. The current chairman of our deacon board has a doctorate in education. The previous chairman was a high school dropout whom we taught to read in our literacy program. Both men have been excellent leaders.

If a church is to grow, evangelism must be an ongoing ministry, not a now-and-then program. We use our evangelism ministry to develop church leadership. All of our deacons were involved at one time or another in our evangelism ministry.

## Discipling the Members

We believe the church is in the business of helping its members grow into active, fruitful disciples of Christ. Christians do not grow without Bible knowledge, and therefore we place great emphasis on Sunday school attendance. Over the years we have had as high as 80 percent of our membership attending Sunday school. This means that with a growing congregation we have the ongoing problem of finding more classroom space.

In addition, we have our own in-house Bible Institute for members who want more in-depth Bible study. The teaching and preaching are done in ways that help people take the Word of God and apply it to issues in life that are pressing today. One of our teen classes recently studied popular secular music, comparing it to what they believed was biblically moral. They concluded that many of the lyrics of contemporary music are dangerous to their spiritual growth.

## Types of Personal Ministry

Normally, people cannot ask personal questions when a pastor is preaching, although they may have serious questions in their minds. Some questions are too personal to ask even in a Sunday school class; therefore, we believe people need personal spiritual care. Stronghold Church tries to meet this need through four types of ministry: that of the pastoral staff, the discipleship ministry, biblical counseling, and our spiritual brothers/sisters ministry.

The pastor is the most important leader in the church, but he is not the only spiritually gifted person. God never intended the pastor to be the only person caring for the congregation, regardless of its size. According to Romans 12 and 1 Corinthians 12, the body of Christ as a whole has been gifted to carry out ministry. Our goal at Stronghold is to mobilize the entire congregation for ministry (Eph. 4:11–13). Lay people are very much involved in caring for each other. When someone new joins our church, a member is assigned to that person as a spiritual sister or brother, depending on that person's gender. This person will help the newcomer become an integral part of the church family. This often involves leading the new member into a discipleship lifestyle. *The effectiveness of this approach is seen in the fact that more than half of our congregation has never belonged to a church before.*

Sometimes new Christians are the only believers in their households, in which case they may experience persecution. At this point, the personal support of the church family is very much needed.

### Men's Ministry

One of the most exciting aspects of our evangelism and discipleship ministry is our men's ministry. Most churches have more women than men. In some African-American churches, the men can number under 10 percent. Our goal at Stronghold is that 50 percent of our adult members will be men. The closest we have come to this goal so far occurred a few years ago when men accounted for 46 percent. But then single Christian women began to hear about all the single men we had, and they became convinced that God was leading them to join our church! A number of the women are now married to our men. We are thankful for them—even though they brought down our overall percentage of male members! We are still doing well in our outreach to men in the community.

Stronghold Church's men's discipleship groups are among our pools for finding and developing new leaders. One of the men we led to Christ had been an atheist for over thirty-five years. He is now the leader of our community evangelism ministry. Another man, previously a drug dealer and addict, now pastors a church. Among our members we have several ex-offenders and ex-criminals who now love and serve God. We have men who previously spent years in other religions like Buddhism, Islam, and Jehovah's Witnesses; now they are winning other men to Christ. Before their conversion, some of our men fathered children out of wedlock. They lived with the mothers of these children but did not see the need to marry them. Now they have submitted themselves to the Word of God and are married.

### Ministry to Teenagers

We believe it is important to invest in the lives of our youth. A child who is thirteen today will be eighteen in five years. A child who is sixteen today will be twenty-one in five years. Most of our Bible heroes were teenagers when they performed their acts of heroism. David was sixteen when he killed Goliath. Esther was a teenaged queen. Daniel, Shadrach, Meshach, and Abednego were teenagers when they were taken into captivity. Mary, the mother of Jesus, was about sixteen when Jesus was born. This leads us to conclude that we should expect more of teenagers today in spiritual maturity and personal responsibility than most churches do.

Our youth ministry is a vital part of the discipleship program. We expect our youth workers to love, understand, and be patient with teenagers. We spell out what we expect of young people, and we make clear the rewards of obedience to God and responsible Christian living. They learn, too, that there is discipline for inappropriate behavior, such as being excluded from some fun group activity. The church's youth ministry is a parental supplement for some of the single-parent, female-headed homes. We lose very few teenagers at Stronghold, and a third of the church's leaders have come through the youth ministry.

### Seminars for Single Parents

Almost half of all African-American families are single-parent families headed by women. They have special needs. Our single-parent ministry conducts seminars on domestic finances, child care, legal problems, dating, hope in God, and other issues. Families are organized into small, supportive cell groups according to the geographical location of their homes. A few two-parent families "adopt" a single-parent family to provide male role models for the children.

I believe God has called the church not merely to perform marriage ceremonies but to establish Christian families. We feel strongly about this at Stronghold Church; therefore, we will not marry anyone who is not willing to go through our eleven-week training course in Christian marriage. More important, we hold classes for singles, helping them to learn what they ought to be accomplishing as singles. We help them discover areas where they need to grow to maximize their chances of becoming good Christian spouses. In other words, before young people are ready for premarital training, we help them develop a healthy view of themselves, good interpersonal relationships, and a level of spiritual maturity. When they have made progress in these areas, they begin to understand the type of person they want to be, and look for, in marriage.

We counsel singles who want to get married not to be hasty. Far too often young people make verbal commitments, while heart commitments lag behind or are never made. The Christian single should trust God for a spouse and set out to develop good Christian friendships. If, out of these, an intimate friendship evolves, so much the better. Many Christian people today are married but not friends. They have trouble liking each other. Our singles ministry is designed to give opportunity for our singles to meet one another and know each other in a general way before dating each other. We feel this is an important way for the church to build solid marriages.

Because we believe Christians should marry Christians, our evangelism ministry is very important to our singles and family ministries. We have to evangelize single men so our single women will have Christian men to marry! If a married woman in our membership has an unsaved husband, we try to win him to Christ. If a member of our church is the only person in his or her family who is a Christian, our goal is to win the entire family to Christ (Acts 16:31).

## Equipping Leaders

We develop leadership at Stronghold Church from the men, women, and youth in the congregation who are faithful Christians. People who only attend on Sunday mornings cannot be leaders. We give everyone the opportunity for greater ministry involvement through what we call the Vineyard Ministry. This serves as our personnel department. Our goal is to get every member involved in a church ministry. The effectiveness of the Vineyard Ministry shows in the more than 60 percent of the congregation now serving in some specific ministry.

Those who prove to have leadership ability are trained in our Ministry of Management course. In the beginning of each year, we take all our lay leaders and their spouses on a three-day leadership retreat. At this retreat, I share my vision. We discuss church goals for the upcoming year and the next three to ten years. In the middle of the year, we have a two-day, mid-course correction meeting. All leaders are required to train an assistant so that if for some reason they have to drop out, the ministry will go on.

## Opportunities for Partnerships

Years of racism and oppression in America have had an enormously negative effect on life in the city. Education is still the name of the game, yet in America poor education and illiteracy are the norm in many urban communities. Masses of people are untrained for the lucrative jobs available in this technological age. What is most disheartening is that hard-working poor people cannot convince their children that honest labor has its rewards. Young people see that dealing drugs and engaging in crime are more materially rewarding than working hard at low-paying jobs. Even our churches are redlined by banks, making it impossible to get needed loans to expand our ministries.

I know that some of my White sisters and brothers debate the question of social ministry versus evangelism. But we who are ministering in the city cannot afford to engage in that debate, because our people are dying. The life expectancy of Black men is dropping, and there are city neighborhoods where insurance companies will not write life insurance policies on young Black men. There is still not enough affordable housing for the poor. Many people live on the streets or in abandoned houses and temporary shelters.

It is clear in the Bible that Christians ought to be concerned for the poor. We African-American pastors who minister in the city need White sisters and brothers who are willing to enter partnership with us to address some of these areas of human suffering. I do mean *partnership*. White paternalism is not what we want. We know what to do, and we have the leadership. But we are short on technology and resources.

A good example of partnership—sharing technology and resources—is Inner City Impact. Inner City Impact was established by John G. Bennett, Jr., the president of New ERA Philanthropy, Inc. John, a White Christian businessman, observed that, in the African-American community, the churches have the most effective programs addressing community problems. The difficulty is that these churches are limited financially, and as a consequence many people go without the help churches would like to offer. Foundations and corporations do not generally fund churches. But John became a partner with Black pastors, giving them technical assistance. Through Inner City Impact, he trained pastors in what they needed to know and do to make their community programs fundable. In my city, Inner City Impact is sponsored by the Philadelphia Leadership Foundation.

Because so many people are overwhelmed by the unbearable conditions of the inner city, we find as a church that we must build hope in our members. Many, though they are Christians, have lost hope that things will ever get better. But our hope is in God and God's people, Black and White. I believe there are White Christians who care enough about their African-American brothers and sisters to join hands with us to make the changes that will make a difference.

## With Revival Comes Hope

The good news is that revival is taking place in many African-American churches. In that revival, which began about fifteen years ago, old churches are being rejuvenated and new churches planted, and both old and new are growing spiritually and numerically. Evangelism and Christian education are both emphasized. Ministry training is going on, and the preaching of the gospel has never been better.

I believe that this revival was sparked by White conservative Bible institutes, colleges, and seminaries opening their doors to African-Americans during the 1950s and 1960s. Until then, there was a training vacuum in the African-American churches. Unlike many White churches, the Black church generally did not have a problem with false doctrine. Even in the early years, when some of our pastors graduated from liberal schools, they did not move away from preaching Jesus Christ as Savior and Lord. The reason behind this was simple. We African-Americans identified with Israel in Egypt needing a Deliverer. Deep in our hearts we believed that Jesus was our Deliverer from the slavery of sin and death. Instinctively we sensed that any message that ignored the saving lordship of Christ was not worth preaching and surely not worth trusting.

But the vacuum in our churches was because, while we emphasized preaching, we did little teaching. Our preaching was inspirational, which was needed by an oppressed people. But our Sunday schools were weak, and our Christian education programs were underdeveloped. As life in America improves for African-Americans, we are turning our attention to the broader issues of Christian discipleship.

## Strong Preachers, Teachers, and Churches

Nationally known speakers like E. V. Hill, E. K. Bailey, and A. Lewis Patterson have been greatly used by God in the revival of the Black church. Not only have thousands of people come to know Christ because of the evangelistic preaching of Dr. Hill, but he also has given a fresh focus to evangelism in the African-American church. Rev. Bailey, by his teaching on discipleship and his church development institute, has aided in the spiritual renewal of hundreds of churches. As a great expository preacher, Rev. Patterson has motivated pastors all across the nation to work at becoming expository teacher-preachers of the Bible. Many other men have contributed to the revival, including Crawford Loritts, Lloyd C. Blue, and Artis Fletcher.

Strong urban churches all over the country are led by gifted, visionary pastors: Tony Evans in Dallas, John Plummer in Los Angeles, Samuel Pettagrue in Birmingham, Haman Cross, Jr., in Detroit, Billy Baskin in Miami, Timothy Winters and Bishop George McKinney in San Diego, and Earl Stuckey in Berkeley. There are hundreds of others. The same principles of disciple-building and church development guide all these leaders, though the applications differ from place to place.

The revival that has come to Christian Stronghold Baptist Church in Philadelphia is not an isolated thing. It is being repeated all across the cities of North America in African-American churches pastored by men of God who combine great preaching and fervent evangelism with strong discipleship programs that train members to live as Christians. With this revival, praise God, there is new hope for the city and for all God's people in it.

## Discussion Questions

1. Describe the traditional strengths and weaknesses of African-American churches.
2. How does this model—Christian Stronghold Baptist Church in Philadelphia—empower its members to develop into fruitful disciples of Christ? Evaluate the church's program.
3. Where does the author place evangelism among the various tasks of Stronghold Church? How is evangelism linked to other ministries?
4. Briefly describe possible ways in which partnerships might be developed between White churches and African-American churches. What mutual advantages might there be in such partnerships? What should be avoided?

# 12

## CHURCH OF THE POOR

*Viv Grigg*

## A Letter from a Poor Man

For myself I've chosen the way of nondestitute urban poverty, and I form evangelical religious orders of workers among the poor. So why do I take time to write to you, good rich friends, who bought this book about the jewel of the gospel for the poor?

Because I hope that in the process I can call you to the one who is wisdom, who because he was wise chose to leave his glory and dwell among the poor. Perhaps I can impart something of the mind of Christ, who came to preach the gospel to the poor and make them his disciples. And by so doing, I may be able to introduce you to a new way of urban discipleship.

## Squatters—Mission Theme of the Next Decades

The migrant squatter areas are home for about a billion people in the world. Broadly speaking, there are three kinds of poor:

*the unfortunate poor* (typhoons, war, and famine are great contributors to the burgeoning slum populations);

*the oppressed poor* (those made poor because the rich structure society to remain in power and use the poor for their own wealth);

*those who are poor due to their own bad choices* (30 percent of men entering one community in which I lived were there because of vice and immorality).

In some ways these communities are a better home than the rural poverty from which the urban migrants come. Despite unemployment, underemployment, garbage, inadequate water and sewerage, and living six family members per room, they are places that offer a degree of hope. Back in rural poverty there was no hospital, little schooling, insufficient land, no other job, virtual slavery, and no future.

Social research indicates that migrants in upwardly mobile contexts are particularly responsive to religious change. I have found this to be true. Squatter homes contain the most responsive unreached bloc of people in the world. Most squatters share an animistic religious understanding of life. Globally speaking, this animist bloc is as large as Muslim, Hindu, or Chinese blocs, and it is found among them all.

I believe God is calling for missionary movements among the poor in all 6,500 cities of the world, especially the megacities and cities missionaries cannot enter. Megacities, of over 5 million people, each contain about five hundred to one thousand squatter communities. Cities of over 1 million generally have about one hundred squatter communities each. Squatters make up 17 percent of the world and 40 percent of the emerging megacities.[1] If we include other classes of urban poor, people who are less reachable or live in less communal contexts that are not as accessible for establishing churches—the street children, prostitutes, drug addicts, alcoholics, those in decaying inner-city slums, household servants—the figure reaches 25 percent of the world population.

Each movement requires a leader who becomes one with the poor or emerges from among them. Could it be you? Is your role to find and then serve such a one?

## Apostles of Love

Let me tell you a story of an unlikely apostle from one restricted-access city. By this I mean a city missionaries normally cannot enter. There are at least one thousand such cities worldwide. Access is restricted, but not impossible, and we found a way of taking a team into one such place for several years.

Every day for eight months one of the team, the owner of a forest who had chosen singleness and left all to follow Jesus, had visited this small section of the *bustee* (slum). Quietly, daily, he practiced a few new sentences of Bengali on all who would receive him. The only one among these five thousand slum dwellers who could speak English became his good friend.

One day, the language helper refused to pay money into the community fund for the *puja*, the celebration worshiping the goddess Kali. He had learned of the God who hates idols, and he made his choice. Anger swept the community. He fled. At the home of the rich friend, who had chosen to be poor, he knelt and met Jesus.

That night a train smashed into the community. The next night two children died. A fire swept through a house. People said it was the convert's fault. Then the rich man who had chosen to be poor took a basket of fruits and flowers to the homes of survivors, and they wept and embraced each other. The love of God swept the community, and the foreigner became one of them.

The next day an invitation came from the community to the new convert to start a school for the children of the *bustee*. So the church began.

## Incarnational Ministry: Key to Movements That Transform

As a child, reading of that great apostle among the poor, Kagawa of Japan, I learned a principle: the church will not be established among the poor unless it is tended day and night. The biblical principle is that of a grain of wheat. It must be buried. It must die among and for people in order for a new movement to grow up among them.

Incarnation was a *profound sociological act* for Jesus. It is not by chance that the sociological expression of the kingdom—the church—is known as his body. Those who choose to emulate Jesus in this way probably will produce significant societal changes. Such is the impact of the two million Franciscans in the world today, and of those who follow John Wesley and William Booth.

Incarnation was a *profound historical symbol* for Jesus. It is from such symbols of humility, sacrifice, and love that men and women are emboldened to transform the earth.

An evangelist may work from the outside; but if he does, he must find a pastor on the inside to develop the new embryo. A development worker may work as a catalyst from the outside, but the church will be established only if there is a pastor tending this work day and night from within.

Incarnation was a *profound economic act* for Jesus. It reversed values, defined jubilee principles, demonstrated the active intervention of a heavenly Father in providing for his needs. Incarnational ministry among the poor, by which I mean living among them, is the primary step to transforming the economics of an emerging Christian community. And, if it is matched with a kingdom theology, it frequently results in the transformation of the economics of the broader community as well.

In practice, one has to balance the various components of such statements. The wise discern what is appropriate: appropriate response to the cause of poverty in a community, appropriate size of the Christian community, appropriate timing, appropriate group dynamics. . . .

Let us consider the balance of three other factors—evangelism, economic and social uplift, and involvement in class conflicts—that are part of urban church planting and development, part of establishing the kingdom in the slums.

## Holism During the Initial Phase

The following characteristics appear to mark the holism of this phase in an apostolic ministry context:

### *The Primacy of Proclamation*

While affirming theologically the holism of the kingdom, strategically it is the availability of the written Scriptures and the teaching and preaching of the Word that break through the darkness and set the captives free. The commission and training of Jesus were built around commands to go and to *preach, teach, heal, and deliver.*[2]

### *Power Encounter*

Not only is proclamation central, but also these commands of Jesus occur in the midst of miraculous deeds that demonstrate the power of God over common factors of life. These signs are just that—signs. They rarely occur on a regular basis. As the gospel breaks into Satan's territory, the demons cry out and seek to defeat the gospel. When they fail, they depart.

Dramatic healings often occur at this stage. As the initial, apostolic phase gives way to the pastoral phase, healing tends to take place over longer periods—no less by the power of the Spirit, but in a more pastoral way. Signs continue to happen but not as the central element of ministry.

## Deeds of Mercy

Because he loves people and becomes actively involved with their lives, the urban apostle meets physical needs in a personalized, informal, unstructured way.

The most beautiful jewel can be damaged if it is cut wrongly. This applies to mission work. During the early stages it is inappropriate to enter a community with large sums of money and large-scale economic projects. My experience with scores of ministries among the poor has taught me that economic projects, when used as entrees into communities, do not facilitate church planting or growth. In fact, I am hard pressed to mention more than one or two churches that have developed from such an approach. New churches among the poor are established as a result of the preached Word, and this is independent of any provision of financial resources for economic development.

There are several reasons for this. One major reason is that the introduction into a community of significant financial resources causes the evangelist to be viewed primarily as a source of funds, not as a spiritual person who is bringing life. The outcome of Jesus' feeding the five thousand is an example of such assistance gone wrong. There are times when feeding the five thousand is the thing to do, when the goals are not to break into a community and establish a church but simply to deal with destitution or poverty. Famine in Ethiopia, flooding in Bangladesh, and an earthquake in Central America are examples of such situations that call for direct relief. But the two goals—relief and church planting—are different. They are both Christian, and at times compatible. But many times they do not support each other well at all.

A second reason was suggested by Jesus: "Seek first his kingdom and his righteousness and all these things shall be yours as well" (Matt. 6:33). We see here that material blessings are a derivative effect of significant spiritual change. The life of Christ once received creates new life in all areas.

I recall numerous communities of believers with whom I have worked in which, as the natural outworking of the received Word, drunkards stopped their drinking and became better able to work. Gamblers closed their gambling houses and, after a period of struggle and unemployment and with the help of believers, learned new trades and began to earn an honest income. Immorality among the men and prostitution among the women ceased, and with stabilized families they were able to find and sustain decent jobs. At the same time, God miraculously provided work for others in direct answer to prayer.

Putting all these experiences together, I can say that ten to fifteen years after a community receives the gospel one usually can perceive significant economic uplift. This is borne out by several recent studies of the urban poor in Pentecostal churches in Latin America. Rejuvenated economic life is a natural outgrowth of new kingdom life in a community. It may be assisted by outside programs, but these do not generate kingdom life. They only reflect it. It is the Word preached in the power of the Spirit that produces the life. The jewel of the gospel has its own inner life-producing radiance.

It appears that where workers enter a community with a priority to proclaim, many deeds of mercy, acts of justice, and signs of power will occur. From these the church will be established. But when workers enter with a priority of dealing with economic need, they may assist the people economically very well, but they rarely establish a church. There is a time for both, and there are life callings to do both, but they must be distinguished.

## The Nature of Poor People's Churches

What kind of church should the missionary team expect to form in the slums? Churches of the poor do not look like middle-class churches. Middle-class people are often upset by the nature of churches among the poor, and hence they put poorer Christians down. Understanding the culture of the urban poor helps decrease such tensions.[3] What tends to characterize urban poor churches?

### Legalism

The migrant poor are sometimes referred to as *peasants in the city*. Urban peasants are people who grew up in villages where any change in traditional patterns could send the whole village into poverty. Among these people, any deviation from traditional patterns is strongly discouraged. Consequently, the patterns of teaching and behavior introduced at the time the squatter church is first established will probably be maintained for a long, long time.

For example, the missionaries who planted the first Brazilian Assemblies of God churches wore suits and ties and frowned on beards. Today I cannot preach in many of these churches because of my beard. If they do invite me to preach, I must be sure to wear my preaching suit and tie. In the same way, constant repetition of certain doctrines is regarded as important.

### Authoritarianism

The members of a squatter church establish a new community not unlike a peasant village. The pastor is generally regarded as the *padrino*, the middle man between the poor and the middle-class society, and between the *informal sector* where the poor operate and the *formal sector* of government departments. There is group decision making in such communities. But once the consensus is formed, the pastor articulates the decision and it is law.

More than that, coping with all the psychological problems, centuries of life as an oppressed people, and the depths of sin from which many of the converts are emerging requires a strong authoritarian style of leadership. That is why you find few Baptist or Presbyterian churches among the poor. Baptist and Presbyterian church structures are built around leadership patterns that do not work well among the poor.[4]

### Noise

The slums are a noisy place. One would expect noisy worship in a context where people daily face deep emotional traumas because of the external tragedy of their poverty. Worship provides a time of emotional and spiritual release. It involves the expression of centuries of pain.

### Power Encounter

Coupled with this is the extent of demonic activity among the poor. Numerous studies by secular researchers, who do not profess to believe in the reality of demons, indicate that demonic activity is significantly more evident among the lower class. The worldview of the poor contains more about spirits and demons than about the official tenets of Islam, philosophical Brahmanism, or Catholicism. Since they lack the resources of modern medicine, the poor seek healing through spiritual means. On conversion, it is natural for them to go to Jesus for healing, and he responds to such faith.

### Isolationism

Each peasant village is a self-contained entity. Survival seems to require a closed society. Hence there are strong taboos and fears against the next village. A positive aspect of the church in the squatter area is that it creates a social structure that enables the people to feel something of the security of the village they left behind. The negative aspect is the fear and suspicion toward neighboring churches with different names and doctrines.

Part of the role of middle-class Christians is to help bridge the gaps between such churches. Middle-class training and culture can sometimes make us peacemakers among the urban poor.

### Small Size

Some of the above characteristics will tend to keep the poor people's churches small, usually consisting of not more than three extended families. The lack of management skills in the slums also results in pastoral leaders who cannot handle a congregation of more than thirty, fifty, or one hundred members. Sometimes these small fellowships are linked to a megachurch that gives them a sense of broader identity.

## Holism at the Pastoral Phase

These glimpses into squatter church culture raise issues about the nature of holistic ministry in the slums. How do we work within such an imperfect context to form jewels of Christian discipleship?

I was preaching in a church ten years after I had helped bring it into being, and my topic was, "*Ingit, ingit, ipis sa puso*" ("Envy, envy, cockroaches in the heart"). The people listened with rapt attention. It was their language they were hearing. And it was the voice of one who had lived among their cockroaches. As I looked, I saw the transformation of those faces. Ten years had slowly changed the darkness of poverty into light, the hardness of broken families into softness. The kingdom had truly come to this slum. Jewels had been formed, but it had taken ten years.

The healing of the poor is not instantaneous. The church is a gathering of broken people being healed, sometimes over ten or twenty years. This is the work of the Spirit in the context of the preaching of the Word. It is not so dramatic as the initial, apostolic phase. It is, in fact, full of problems. It always looks imperfect.

During this phase, the crucial issue is the development of strong leaders who can function as elders and deacons. The leaders have to emerge out of a context of broken families and immorality.

Let me return to the use of outside economic resources to create a holistic ministry that deals with both the poverty and the spiritual need. It is not inappropriate during this phase to use outside resources to meet the needs of the widows and orphans, construct part of a building, or establish income-generation projects. These are proper activities of a Christian diaconate. They have to be done wisely if they are not to destroy the indigeneity of the church. Yet they are also expressions of the mercy of Christ and of the church universal.

In general, however, there are enough resources accessible to the community of believers for its healthy growth. The main issue is not a lack of resources but the need for a diaconal team that can identify the needs of the community, formulate appropriate responses, and then find and manage the resources that are available. In this process outside help can make a significant contribution.

## How Do the Poor Escape Poverty?

The question is not, "How do we help the poor?" but "How do the poor themselves escape poverty?" If we learn the answer to this question, we can work with them in the processes that lead to transformation.

Surprising as it may seem, the answer to the question is not in terms of economic projects. Throughout history the poor have escaped poverty through *migration*.[5] Where are the Christian international job placement bureaus? General William Booth's strategy to help thousands of poor escape London's poverty included migrant colonies in Canada, South Africa, and Australia. He died before this part of his plan could be implemented. The poor churches that have emerged in the last ten years in the slums of Manila have been funded largely by slum workers who have migrated to Saudi Arabia for employment.

Another poor people's solution is *education*. A poor family will sacrifice all to get one child through college. That child will then bring the next. Money from wealthy churches for vocational scholarships is not wasted.

*Mutual aid associations*, where small amounts are collected from each member and, when amassed, given as capital to one of the group, periodically enable quantum jumps into new levels of business. The obvious solution for poor people's churches is the development by the diaconate of credit cooperatives.

*Middlemen* are a central component in the economic advancement of the informal sector. Pastors with links to rich churches can often function in such a role.[6]

## The Politics of Incarnational Ministry

In writing about holistic kingdom ministry in the slums, I began where most evangelicals begin, with the spiritual and the economic. But the cause of the poverty of the slums has to do not only with the spiritual condition of the slum dweller and the lack of resources among the poor. It has to do also with oppression and the political and economic structures of society that operate in favor of the rich. Holistic ministry cannot avoid confronting the principalities and powers that pervert and corrupt the structures of society in ways that bring abundance to the few and grinding poverty to many.

To walk into the slums may be a nonpolitical act on your part as a simple, sincere disciple of Jesus. But it will likely be perceived by those in power as profoundly political.

In the same way, when Jesus came from the Father's hand into a smelly manger, his act had *profound political implications* for governments through the ages. The Jewish leaders sensed this, and it aroused their opposition to the point of crucifying him, the ultimate political solution (or so they thought).

For you to transfer finances to the poor may seem to be nothing more than a simple act of mercy. But to those in power it may be seen as a political act, because it threatens their control of the poor, the source of much of their wealth.

Do not be surprised, then, at the opposition that comes against you as you walk in the paths of Jesus among the poor. Neither be surprised when you are brought into the presence of kings and they seek your counsel, sometimes in chains and sometimes as a guest (Matt. 10:17–25; John 15:8–25). Unintentionally you are a political person, for you are causing changes that affect the *polis*—the people, the masses.

Learn political savvy from Jesus, the man of the people. Hide when you sense danger, confront evil at times that are appropriate to you, debate issues that extend the kingdom publicly, but do not answer people on issues that are irrelevant to kingdom community development. Be as harmless as a dove and wise as a serpent (Matt. 10:16).

While the issues already mentioned may be acceptable to people holding a conservative, evangelical theology, the next level of political action about which I *must* talk, if I truly care for the poor may be upsetting. For compassion among the poor requires teaching the church how to deal with poverty and its complex causes. While preaching the kingdom, we are to live by and advance kingdom rule to creation and society.

Consider this: If the poverty of your squatter area is caused by oppression, the pastoral response will involve actions that may conflict with the interests of those who oppress. What you set out to accomplish will be viewed as political action. Obtaining water is a political act. So is seeking city help with garbage disposal. These easily become issues of class conflict. *Community organization* is a discipline that has emerged in this century to deal with such conflicts. It is unfortunate that much of its theory was developed from Marxist presuppositions. Marx's analytic tools were inaccurate, and his solutions far worse. But he did deal with real issues, and those issues await the serious attention of evangelical Christians.

Where are the evangelical theologians who, from experience in following Jesus among the poor, are writing about godly patterns in the midst of class conflict? Where are the Christian agendas for transforming the slums? It is pointless to spend time criticizing liberation theologians while failing to come to grips with the agonizing issues those theologians seek to address. Go to Jesus the wise man, who began among the poor.

Helping slum people is sometimes made illegal, for they are illegal, at least until election time. Their only illegal act may be finding a place to sleep in an overcrowded city. It is like healing on the sabbath—illegal. The theological issues of our time are shaped by the fact that half the world consists of landless peasants or illegal squatters. They are dispossessed. It was illegal for a Buddhist woman to set up schools in her slum in Bangkok, until an international award made it politically wise to encourage her. Where are the evangelical theologies of land rights?

And ultimately, the poverty of the poor cannot be changed by that great inertia called the masses. It is the middle classes linked to the educated elite who bring social and economic transformation. In every city we need a movement of the educated elite who follow the economic, social, and political discipleship of Jesus as they work among the poor. Then we may see the poor saved not only eternally, but also from their poverty. Then we may see the kingdom established not only in the future, not only in the establishment of churches, but also in the transformation of many aspects of society. The changes will benefit believer and nonbeliever alike: poverty will be abated, corruption curbed, oppression minimized, and economic security enjoyed by a greater number.

## And What of Our Role?

I have outlined some of the issues of ministry among the migrant poor. I have outlined enough grand themes for several lifetimes of work. They may excite you. But one question is more important. Can you ignore Jesus, the Son of God, who chose to come and dwell among the poor in order to establish a community of disciples? Can you ignore his command to go and do likewise?

Will you take your gifts and become part of a team of urban church planters? Will you pressure your mission board to adopt new strategies for reaching the urban squatter communities? If for health, family, or other reasons you are unable to go yourself, will you commit your resources to backing up other people who will go where you cannot? Will you help create movements among the elite that will lead in tangible ways to the economic and social transformation of the poor?

At the end of your life the question you will have to answer is this: Did you follow the Prince who became a pauper?

## Discussion Questions

1. What did you find to be personally challenging, perhaps even disturbing, as you read this chapter?
2. Explain why many evangelicals prefer to work with the middle class rather than the poor.
3. Give as many reasons as you can why high priority ought to be given to ministry among the urban poor.
4. Describe the kind of ministry the author is calling for—its purposes, participants, and methods. Why was political action included?

# 13

# DISCIPLING WHITE, BLUE-COLLAR WORKERS AND THEIR FAMILIES

*Charles D. Uken*

Blue-collar workers make up a significant part of the mosaic of any large city. The challenge is to disciple the significant number of blue-collar workers who do not attend church regularly and to make the gospel meaningful, vital, and practical to those who do. To disciple people is to lead them to accept Jesus Christ as Savior and Lord and to bring every thought and action into obedience to him (Matt. 28:18–19; 2 Cor. 10:5). Discipleship also involves motivating and equipping workers to lead others to a living relationship with Christ.

My aim in this chapter is to describe the blue-collar world and then to show how relating the gospel to the blue-collar world may affect the structure and program of the church.

## Blue-Collar Demographics

While manufacturing jobs once dominated the urban labor market, providing almost 50 percent of nonfarm jobs,[1] their share of the total American work force now stands at 16.4 percent and is expected to decline still further to 14 percent by the turn of the century. In contrast, service-sector jobs increased by 204.5 percent since 1970.[2]

Technological change, advances in bulk transportation, and a freer world economy have brought about this radical change in the composition of the American work force. Computer technology and robotics have automated repetitive processes and increased the precision of work and the quality of the finished product. In such a work environment, good-paying jobs are difficult to find for those who lack the requisite skill and training. Today, workers unskilled in the new technologies are competing with barely literate first-generation rural-to-urban migrants in Third-World countries. Multinational companies have exported modern production technologies and have found that foreign workers, when adequately trained, can do the same job as Americans. The American factory worker today competes directly in a global labor market where the economy of low Third-World wages offsets the higher cost of transportation.[3]

To be competitive with the global assembly line,[4] companies have had to close unprofitable factories, modernize plants, or move to more favorable labor markets.[5] To compete with foreign imports, many large corporations like General Motors and Ford are outsourcing much of their production to small, nonunionized companies able to find people willing to work for lower wages in saturated labor markets. Sweat shops have reemerged among immigrants to the U.S.,[6] and workers unable or unwilling to upgrade their skills are often forced to seek employment in unskilled, low-paying service jobs. Many younger workers who found a job right out of high school and thought they would have a secure place in the company once they got ten or fifteen years' seniority are now discovering that they will have several "in-on-the-ground-floor" experiences before they reach retirement.

The American labor force, like that in many Third-World countries, is now tending to split into two distinct levels: those following careers in high-status, high-paying professional, technical, and managerial positions, and those working in low-status, low-paying clerical, service, and factory jobs.[7]

## The Blue-Collar World Described

Blue-collar workers and the millions employed in the service sector can only be described as having jobs, whereas those above them have careers.[8] Their work is often dirty and dangerous, repetitive and dull, and they are supervised by others.[9] "For eighty million Americans there is no such thing as an interesting job."[10] Working men definitely prefer leisure to work.[11] They work in order to live (support the family, hunt, fish, remodel the house); they don't live in order to work. Work is something to be endured, not enjoyed, and certainly not something in which to be fulfilled.

Workers carry a prevailing suspicion of management. They feel that managers will invariably use their expertise and knowledge of production techniques for the company's benefit and not for workers' security or well-being.[12]

Advancement in the factory through the various blue-collar ranks is possible, but upper-management positions generally are not open to them. As a result, some of the more entrepreneurial workers will leave the factory to start their own businesses like a bar or a small construction firm, take maintenance jobs, become truck drivers, or enter the ranks of firemen or policemen.[13]

Because many manufacturing processes cannot be shut off after eight hours, factories employ men on shifts. This disrupts family and social life and often affects workers' physical well-being.[14] If both husband and wife work, they may elect to work different shifts to share child care and household chores. In these homes, the only time the couple can enjoy each other's company is on Sunday. The rest of the week they are by themselves or meet only on the run. Men with a mortgage, children, and a nonemployed wife work as much overtime as they can, further limiting their time with the family.[15]

Blue-collar workers live with considerable insecurity. A 1971 University of Michigan survey found 28 percent with no medical or hospital coverage. Thirty-eight percent had no life insurance, while 39 percent were not enrolled in a pension plan. They try to have at least one member of the family work at a company that provides medical insurance. More than other workers, they depend on physical health and strength to perform their duties. Workers are too affluent to receive government subsidies for food, medicine, or day care centers, but not affluent enough to build financial security through savings and investments. They are the first to feel the effects of unemployment during a recession.[16]

Blue-collar workers take two very different approaches to leisure. Some spend a lot of time in an all-male environment at a tavern or in sports, both participant and spectator. Others shun the bars and spend most of their leisure time at home with their families.[17] Besides sports, many men invest almost all of their free time remodeling and improving their homes, which are their chief investments. To do this, workers help each other at specialized jobs, borrow tools, and buy and swap new and used materials.[18]

The "working man" is central to the blue-collar man's image of himself.[19] He does "real" work, with his hands. Others literally do not work. Big businessmen don't work; they hire people who do.[20] People on welfare don't want to work. They are lazy and parasitic.[21] Factory workers describe their work as making "an honest living" rather than "shuffling papers" or earning a living "with your mouth."[22]

Few blue-collar workers did well in school; most were classified as nonacademic. For them, "school was a period when their self-esteem was under continual attack."[23] The most frequent way the men account for their failure in school is to blame teachers and the curriculum, both of which they deem irrelevant to their interests or needs.[24]

Several white-collar professions are viewed with special distrust and hostility: law, medicine, teaching, and union leadership. Lawyers charge exorbitant fees when workers are going through tough situations like divorce or filing accident claims. Doctors charge huge fees, misdiagnose, and park in privileged parking areas. Teachers remind workers of their sad experience in school and are blamed for their children's problems with study. Further, workers see themselves as paying the teachers' salaries through property taxes, hurting their own standard of living.[25] Most workers value the union for the job security it provides, but they bear a cynical distrust of white-collar union leaders, who, they feel, work in collusion with management to workers' detriment.[26]

Housing encompasses trailer homes, older frame houses of pre-World War II construction, apartment complexes or row houses, prefab modular homes, and the more modest suburban homes.

### Family Life and Sexual Mores

David Halle found that among the blue-collar workers he studied, 35 percent were happy to be married and spoke highly of their wives. Many of these credited their wives for rescuing them from a wild lifestyle. Twenty-five percent had mixed feelings, some having been on the verge of divorce. For the remaining 40 percent, relations with their wives were a source of considerable frustration and anger.[27]

Family and marital happiness were directly related to how the men spent their off-work time. Those happily married spent most of it with their families. In her study on the working woman, Ellen Rosen found that her happiness in marriage was not enhanced by her husband's making more money, but by his helping her with household chores.[28] Blue-collar workers who reported a high level of conflict in the home tended to spend a great deal of time with their male buddies at the tavern drinking, gambling, or playing pool, or in sports activities like hunting or fishing. For the wife, the time a working man spends with his buddies is a complete loss, unlike the pattern among white-collar men, where outside time spent with others frequently enhances a career.[29]

A macho self-image lies at the heart of much marital discontent. Except for sex, understood as physical relief of passion rather than an expression of tenderness and love, blue-collar men find women and women's interests dull and uninteresting.[30] For them, the woman's place is in the home with the children, yet most are quite willing to have their wives take outside employment to help with finances, as long as the wife remembers "her place."[31]

Even though the workers want to leave the house and kids to the wife, they still wish to influence their sons to become like themselves. Sons are to learn to defend themselves physically. Any boy who grows up a sissy is a failure. Sons must also learn how to handle women. They should learn how to seduce them, so proving their prowess and domination. If they are resisted, it could mean that they will later be henpecked. Fathers want to get their boys out from under women teachers and into the athletic program of the school. Sons must not become suckers or be spoiled, something wives are often seen as doing to them. Girls learn from their fathers not to trust men. The fact that wives are socializing their sons to assume family roles while husbands are socializing them for occupational, military, and "manly" roles generates substantial conflict and misunderstanding between husbands and wives.[32]

Women are also aware of their options. Outside employment gives them independence, leverage, and power. They know that social welfare is available to mothers of dependent children. These factors make divorce an increasingly real and even attractive possibility to unhappy wives of blue-collar workers.[33]

Another source of dissatisfaction for wives is their blue-collar husbands' gross and profane language.[34] This is especially embarrassing if the wife has more formal education than her husband, works in a white-collar environment, and attends church with the children.

Changing family mores, necessity, or a desire to improve the standard of living have brought increasing numbers of women into the work force, mainly into the service sector, where they dominate the labor force as clerks, secretaries, store attendants, or nurses. Women now make up 44.5 percent of the work force, and 65 percent of women with children under 18 work outside the home.[35] If the wife's job pays more and carries a higher status, the husband can have a serious identity problem, especially if he becomes unemployed from a good-paying job and has to start out again with another company at a level where he must compete with younger, less experienced workers.

When marital problems arise, the husband is generally unwilling to seek counseling, even if the wife wants it. Blue-collar workers have no faith in the ability of psychologists and psychiatrists to serve as counselors either for them or for their children in school. They call these representatives of the educated, white-collar culture "head shrinkers."[36] Because of their mistrust of professional counseling, blue-collar men go through divorce with only the informal counsel and support of male friends who share the same code of ethics and view of marriage.

### How They View Religion

Almost all of the blue-collar workers David Halle studied were Roman Catholics who went to church at least once a month. About half even went every Sunday. Yet, Halle writes, "their religious beliefs are fragmented and full of doubt and avoid many of the important issues in their lives. Their attitude toward the church and clergy falls far short of the respect often associated with religion, and their attitude toward God cannot be described in terms of awe and the sacred."[37] Disrespect for the clergy, God's representatives among them, is widespread among blue-collar workers. They complain about the clergy's financial greed and sexual misbehavior and feel that the church is always asking for money.[38]

In the workplace where Halle conducted his study, conversations about God and theology were rare.[39] Questions about pain, sickness, accident, and misfortune were never answered, and God was often equated with luck. Asked about the afterlife, one worker responded, "I'm too busy to worry about that . . . . That garbage is the kind of thing you do when you're in a wheelchair."[40] Some got the answers to religious questions from television shows. Halle reports that one worker, to show that he believed in life after death, said, "Like there was a movie on television about this woman. Her husband died and the spirit wouldn't leave. It haunted the house."[41] When Halle asked the men what God means and what God does, the question provoked considerable perplexity; the men regarded the question as too difficult to answer. Blue-collar workers generally see no way of drawing on God's power for their personal benefit.[42]

None of the workers Halle studied held to Christianity as a "primary cosmology," "a set of beliefs that a person considers to be true and that explain an aspect of the world that is of central relevance to that person."[43] Matters of primary relevance were who runs America (rich businessmen and crooked politicians), workers' position in society, medical science (for its explanation of physical and mental ills), and the practical knowledge related to their jobs.[44] None of these are integrated into a Christian worldview. "Christian beliefs about life after death are of central relevance but for most workers are uncertain or untrue," while beliefs about the birth and life of Jesus are considered true but largely irrelevant to their lives.[45] When talking about marital problems, no worker ever mentioned the church's position on divorce, while many expressed fear of losing their property because of New Jersey's divorce law.[46]

Many men were content to leave religion to the women and children. They were quite willing to let the church exist so long as it makes no great demand on them. "One cannot imagine any of these men missing the first day of deer hunting because of some religious function, but then it is hard to imagine their missing the first day of deer hunting for any other reason either."[47]

## New Churches for Blue-Collar Workers

If we are faithful church members or belong to the clergy, we must be aware of the cultural gap that separates us from unchurched workers. In their minds, preachers are in the same class as lawyers, politicians, teachers, doctors, and psychiatrists. It should not surprise us if they vent their hostility on us and the church. We are entering a foreign land, and the natives think we are strange. If we come from a middle-class, educated, evangelical Protestant background, experience in cross-cultural ministry will be a big asset. Not only must we cross a church/world barrier, but also we must cross a socioeconomic one.

When I speak of a cross-cultural barrier, I am not thinking of those blue-collar workers who hold steady jobs and have been long-time members of a suburban, middle-class church. The gospel has had its unifying, integrating, and molding effect on all the members so that they can rightly say that they belong to the one family of God and are "just the same as everyone else in church." These workers are not the ones that we have to reach. Our aim is to reach the ones on the outside, the ones who are not "church broke," who do not know how to act in the house of God. I am thinking of the workers who cannot keep a job because of anger, insubordination, or addiction; workers who abuse their wives and children; workers who lie, cheat, and are unfaithful; workers who face bankruptcy because their credit cards deceived them into thinking their means were as big as their wants; workers who are personally acquainted with hospital emergency rooms and food stamps. These are people whose knowledge of Scripture hardly goes beyond John 3:16 and a few vacation Bible school stories. They have some acquaintance with the church, but they heap derogatory remarks on anyone who is a straight-laced Christian.

As we enter this foreign land, it is our goal to preach Christ in such a way that the workers, the bearers of this American subculture, might hear the good news in their own language, be converted from their sin, and become servants of Christ in the fellowship of a Bible-believing, culturally relevant church. In other words, new churches or alternative worship services must be started in which workers will feel comfortable.

Missiologist C. Peter Wagner has discovered that in Third-World countries, the evangelists who have been able to win the lower-class urban masses are the ones who not only give a clear presentation of the gospel but also feature miracles, healings, and deliverance from evil spirits. Power encounters, the display of the power of Jesus over demonic forces, are an integral part of the message.[48] As a result of their findings, Wagner and friend Peter Wilkes have categorized the personal and Christian preferences of the upper and lower classes (see fig. 13.1):[49]

Others have noticed these same emphases in churches popular with blue-collar workers in North America.[50] If these generalizations apply to the blue-collar workers in our area, and if the church we represent gears its program to the needs of the educated middle class, we should seriously

**Figure 13.1**
**Comparison of Personal and Christian Preferences**
(by social class)

| Upper Class | Lower Class |
| --- | --- |
| Personal Preferences | |
| Intellectual | Intuitional |
| Rational | Emotional |
| Scientific | Experiential |
| Deductive | Inductive |
| Literacy essential | Literacy optional |
| You control life | Life controls you |
| Christian Preferences | |
| Faith complex | Faith simple |
| Conversion gentle | Conversion confrontational |
| Holiness gradual | Holiness sudden |
| Biblical criticism | Biblical literalism |
| Systematic theology | Absolute ethics |
| Preaching based on study | Preaching based on prayer |
| Weak demonology | Strong demonology |

consider starting a satellite church or offering separate worship services in which to gather working-class families.

This is the conclusion John Wesley reached during England's industrial revolution. Neither the Anglicans with their reliance on rites of passage nor the Anabaptists who welcomed the converted into their fellowship were reaching the poor and alienated working class. Wesley's method was to awaken people to their lostness and their need for God through open-air field preaching. Those awakened were invited to enroll in a Methodist "class meeting" of twelve or fewer people. Those who continued steadfast and desired to live as Christians and experience a new way of life were enrolled in the "society" three months later.[51] Wesley's field preaching can be compared to a modern "seeker service" or revival meeting led by a dynamic, relevant preacher. Those who manifest interest are enrolled in small discipleship groups. The Wesleyan model is followed by many charismatic preachers in Korea[52] and other Third-World countries.[53]

Wesley instructed Methodists to receive the sacraments and attend the local Anglican parish. He ministered to the growing number of classes and societies through traveling lay preachers whom he discipled and trained. Shortly after his death, the Methodists became a separate denomination. Had the established Church of England seen Wesley's movement as contextualization of the gospel to reach the disenfranchised instead of a threat, it might have made Wesley a bishop with authority to ordain his circuit-rider preachers. Instead it clung to a static parish system and insisted on a clergy trained at a theological school.[54]

Another approach does not start with a mass meeting at all. Agnes Liu of Hong Kong's China Graduate School of Theology and her colleagues reached the conclusion that Christianity in Hong Kong was a middle-class movement. They researched the working-class culture and decided to start lay-led "factory fellowships." After sixteen years of study and outreach, over one hundred fellowships have been started and a dozen churches organized.[55]

What is the road taken by Chinese workers on the way to conversion? "Their pilgrimage typically begins when they relate to and identify with some Christians they like and enjoy. Next, they begin to like church (worship services) and to think of the church as okay. Next, they start 'liking Jesus,' and they become open to learning more about him. Then in time, they become open to commitment to Jesus."[56] During this process, workers typically have one or more experiences of answered prayer. Many also experience the power of Christ to heal, to cast out demons, or to remove a feeling of worthlessness. Finally, they come to know Jesus as the Lord who forgives and saves from the power of sin.[57] Only after their attitudes toward Christians and the church have changed and they have had one or more personal experiences with Christ are workers open to doctrinal training.

## Using Indigenous Methods

Often middle-class churches come into contact with poorer, working-class families through children who come to Sunday school, youth programs, or vacation Bible school. They also meet them through diaconal outreach programs. Sincere Christians try to help them in their material and social needs. With rare exceptions, these families are not gathered into our churches. We demonstrate the unconditional love of Christ, but we seldom see them become responsible members of our churches.

As a missionary in Brazil, I noticed that, among the working-class people where I worked, the Pentecostal churches were growing by leaps and bounds and that all the churches, including the Catholic church, that used a "we-help-you-in-your-need" methodology were not winning the lower, working class. People were helped, but the spiritual direction of their lives did not change. Christ the Servant came and ministered to them, but they never came to know Christ the Lord. Pentecostal churches that lacked financial and earthly resources were filled with poor people, were led by barely literate lay preachers, and made hard demands on their people New members were expected to be faithful tithers, to wear clothes that conformed to a rigid dress code, to carry their Bibles to church, and to dedicate a large amount of time to worship services, healing services, home prayer meetings, street meetings, and outreach visitation. The churches that gave the most and expected the least were not growing, but those that gave the least material benefit and demanded the most were growing the fastest. They demanded conversion from sin and preached that Christ had the power to make it happen, and that this power could be received through faith and prayer.

I believe the key was contextualized discipleship that lives within the constraints of the workers' life experiences. Let us put ourselves in the shoes of a worker who has little money, hasn't gone to college, has no specialized skills, and holds no position of power, authority, or status. Suppose he were to ask, "How can Christ use me to extend his rule in the lives and hearts of others? What are the sources God has given me to bring the good news of salvation to others?" He would be rebuffed if the church demanded an educated, professional staff and lots of money. His puny efforts could do precious little and would only be an irritant to those who had much more capability. But if the church were open to use the gifts God has given, things would be different. The converted worker would realize that God has given him the Word, the Bible. He can read it and tell others about its message. He has learned to pray so that God pours out blessing in his life and in the lives of others. He can obey what God commands. As God changes him, he knows that others will be inspired to turn to God and make changes in their lives. He has talents that can be used in worship and ministry. They may be singing, playing an instrument, leadership, preaching, counseling, helping, cleaning, or others. A church that is serious about winning blue-collar workers will unashamedly rely on them and the gifts God has given them for a large part of its ministry.

As a matter of fact, the lack of financial resources should be seen as an opportunity to design a program within the means of the workers' socioeconomic situation, to rely on the power of the gospel to change lives and motivate converts to dedicate their talents to worship, praise, ministry, and witness. Our eyes should look to the Lord for help and to new converts to fill the needs of the church rather than to the church that sent us to supply all our needs. If we rely on the church that sent us, we most likely will design programs that make sense to the people who sent us and not to the people we are trying to reach. Indigenous church planting methods require that the patterns of the new church fit the workers' style of living and give converted workers decision-making power and ownership.

Special care must be used in conducting adult Bible-study and discussion groups. Because many lack reading skills, they are easily embarrassed when asked to read. Some may be unable to find the passage, or suddenly become terribly self-conscious. In the beginning, Bible studies that put people at ease will resemble sermons that allow for questions and discussion. No one should be expected to pray or read unless he feels comfortable doing so.

A church composed of and ministering to factory workers will have a great deal of difficulty maintaining a neat program schedule because of shift work. If the wife works, and increasingly this is the case, the couple may have very limited time together with their children. The obstacles to regularly scheduled meetings are many; but if the workers can get together for a work bee or meet at the bar after work, they can arrange to get together under the leadership of another worker for Bible study and prayer. Who knows, a group of second shifters might meet midweek from midnight till 1:30 A.M.! Highly structured programs organized from the top down are resisted, but that does not mean that members will not gather to study the Bible together on an informal basis.[58]

To meet the needs of the worker and his family and to train him for ministry outside the church building, the church should have as many services and types of meetings as possible on Sunday. If there is any day that workers have free, it is Sunday. But even then the whole day may not be free. Several services each Sunday both morning and evening would make it possible for them to attend something. A variety of training courses should also be held at various times so that men and women will be prepared to lead meetings with others as their schedules permit.

Finally, for a pastor to train workers for ministry, he must be in living contact with and learn from the workers themselves. The pastor will get to know his blue-collar workers if he can help them *to trust God and draw on Christ's divine power* to solve their problems: problems with drugs and alcohol addiction (Eph. 5:18–20), problems with authority and purpose on the job (Col. 3:22–25), and problems with family relations (Eph. 5:22–33). As new converts step out in faith to obey Christ in each area of life, they will experience God's blessing (Matt. 6:33) and see a radical change in their world. Indeed, everything will be made new (2 Cor. 5:17), and they will become magnets to bring fellow workers to reconciliation with God (2 Cor. 5:18–20). The shepherd-sheep, master-disciple relationship between the pastor and the newly converted worker will enable the discipled worker to bring the gospel to others and enable the pastor to know workers better and enrich his evangelistic effectiveness. If sociologists, like Halle and LeMasters, could cross class barriers and build up a good rapport with workers over a period of time in pursuit of studies to enhance their careers, surely those who minister in the name of Christ can do the same. In doing so, they will not only get to know workers but also impart blessings to them that have eternal value.

## Discussion Questions

1. Describe with as much detail as you can the social and emotional situation of the average blue-collar male worker. How do many of them look upon their wives?
2. Describe the typical blue-collar worker's attitude toward the church, clergy, and religious beliefs and activities.
3. Why is it important to teach a biblical view of work?
4. Explain why churches have found it so difficult to penetrate the blue-collar class, especially men, and identify at least five things the church must do to make vital disciples of blue-collar workers.

# 14

# GETTING TO KNOW YOUR NEW CITY

*Judith Lingenfelter*

As urban Christians, we desire to minister effectively in cities. But we are overwhelmed by the diversity of peoples with whom we come in contact. Especially when we go to a city that is unfamiliar to us, we quickly become overloaded by the myriad stimuli that come our way.

I remember standing in a long line on a corner in Manila during the Lausanne II conference waiting for a bus. Bus after bus passed by. They all bore signs for the destination I was looking for, but they were crammed full and didn't stop. In addition to the buses, jeepneys swung by, and cars shouldered their way through spots where there was no pavement. The whole area was overhung with exhaust fumes, noise, and humidity. The only way I could begin to make sense of this Manila traffic was to focus on only one thing at a time until I felt comfortable, and then move on to something else. In doing that, I was aided by my knowledge of the anthropological technique of participant observation, which helped me sort what I was seeing into manageable categories.

The purpose of this chapter is to suggest the use of that technique, called the ethnographic method, for researching the varieties of people in the city. This approach is readily adaptable to urban ministry for several reasons. First, its learner-centered focus fits well with the principle of thinking more highly of others than yourself (Phil. 2:3–5). As you make others your teachers for a time, you recognize that they are the experts in their particular spheres of knowledge, while you are just the novice.

Second, continuing study of anthropology convinces me increasingly that the ethnographic method, with its emphasis on participant observation, mirrors the kind of efforts good urban missionaries have always made in getting to know people. The problem with the method is that it appears simpler than it is. A few years ago I had a student who wanted to do an independent study with me on urban church planting. I told him he would have to do some ethnographic research, but his final paper rested almost entirely on demographic projections. Yet he insisted that it was ethnographic because he had talked to a few people who lived in the area where the church was proposing to start. I had to inform him that good ethnographic research is not just a haphazard "talking with people."

Third, the method is inexpensive and depends on the researcher's training rather than on expensive computer programs or lengthy questionnaires. Often these questionnaires fail to be very helpful anyway, as they tend to be of the type that certain people would be too scared to answer.

Finally, this approach helps new missionaries learn to feel at home in the city. In my travels working with various mission agencies in cities worldwide, I have come across many people who believe that God has called them to the city but who, when pressed, admit that they don't like cities. My own experience suggests that they feel this way because they don't take the trouble to get to know and enjoy the city. This is especially so if the new missionaries come out of the evangelical subculture with its anti-urban bias. It's fine to quote Jeremiah 29:5–7 at them, which says to settle down, build houses, plant vineyards, marry, and have children in whatever city God has placed you. But as they may point out, they are living in an overcrowded apartment with no visible soil in which to plant anything, and they are single! How can they learn to like the city and its inhabitants? The method below can help.

## Preparing for Arrival in a New City

No urban missionary should arrive in a new city without some idea of what to expect. Fortunately, many published materials are available on specific countries and cities throughout the world. Using standardized reference sources like the United Nations demographic and statistical volumes, the *Europa Yearbook,* the *World of Learning*, the Department of State area handbooks, and many others, a person can learn the population statistics for a city, its major newspapers, diplomatic representation, museums, art galleries, universities, and many other things before ever arriving on the scene. Other specialized sources like *México Hoy y Mañana* or the *Book of World City Rankings* add to this knowledge. Doing one's urban homework in a library or bookstore heightens the anticipation of beginning work in a new city.

## Entering the Scene

In most major cities, new missionaries can begin fieldwork the moment they step off the plane. Marvin K. Mayers suggests that newcomers keep a record of the things that irritate and surprise them within the first few weeks of arrival, and that certainly can include the airport personnel.[1] While most new missionaries arrive weary, recording the frustrations of the arrival experience itself can provide some excellent insights later when they are ready to laugh about them.

My husband and I arrived in Guatemala City on a Sunday morning in the summer of 1989. Only four other passengers disembarked with us. With no guidance, we wandered toward a ramp and were in a waiting room before a harried uniformed guard told us we had taken the wrong ramp. He directed us to immigration, where we were told to go over to another room and fill out a customs declaration because we were bringing in a piece of equipment for another missionary. In the next room, two men were playing ping pong. We asked what we should do. They shrugged and waved us back out. By the time we got back to the immigration window the worker had disappeared, since there was no more business! We finally found a woman who directed us to someone who muttered that we shouldn't be allowed through, but then stamped our passports, directed us to open our luggage, and then deliberately turned his back on us. Surprised, we hastily gathered our belongings and fled. As the only customers in the entire area, we felt conspicuous, especially since our Guatemalan friends and others were watching the proceedings with great interest from a vantage point on the second level.

A few days later we tried to analyze the experience and see what we had missed and what we could learn from it. We generated some questions: Did the man expect a tip when he turned his back on us? Could certain procedures be circumvented if one knew the language well and answered questions in a particular manner? Why were there so few passengers that day when it was the only plane that went to San Salvador and Guatemala City? These questions and others gave us some initial things to explore and made our short stay in Guatemala more interesting as we continued to gather data and revise our hypotheses.

## Finding Out Where People Gather

I have heard Floyd McClung of Youth With a Mission talk about spending the first six months of his time in Amsterdam walking the city and claiming it for God, praying for it as we are commanded to pray in Jeremiah 29 for the peace and prosperity of the city.

Walking the streets and praying for people—these two combined make a good beginning for urban ministry! The first part of any attempt to learn the diversity of the city should be to explore it thoroughly. The year we lived in Pittsburgh, we bought weekend bus passes and went all over the city, wherever the buses went. We learned more about that city in one year than I had ever learned about Philadelphia, where I grew up.

Plan to spend the first few months in solid participant observation. Don't just ride the trains in Calcutta or Hong Kong; learn what train riding behavior entails by observing and asking questions. Find out where people gather. When we were in Hong Kong, a friend took us on a walking tour of downtown on a Sunday afternoon. When we got to Statue Park, he pointed out the hundreds of Filipino women sitting all around. He told us approximately thirty thousand of these women worked as maids for high-class Chinese families, and on Sundays, their day off, they had nowhere to go but the park. This caused a certain amount of friction in crowded Hong Kong, where public space of any kind is at a premium. These women represented one of many ethnic groups in the city, yet because they didn't live all together in an ethnic enclave, they might be overlooked unless a person identified the public places where they gathered.

Once missionaries have identified places, activities, or specific groups of people in the city, they are ready to begin learning more systematically. James Spradley identifies five different observation patterns that reflect a continuum from outsider to insider.[2] The first is nonparticipation, or learning about a culture from watching television or films, reading newspapers, or some other unobtrusive measure. The limits of this approach are obvious for urban missionaries who want to get to know certain groups of people better. However, young mothers often fail to use this source as a culture-learning tool when they are confined to the home with very young or sick children and feel sidelined.

The second type, passive participation, requires one to be present at the scene, but not take part in any way. When language skills prevent other forms of interaction, this still allows observation, note taking, and formulating questions about what is happening.

Moderate participation, the third type, suggests that the outsider becomes involved to a certain extent, as when one goes into an ethnic restaurant to eat for the first time and perhaps interacts with the waiter or waitress.

Active participation allows the outsider to practice doing what the insiders do regularly, like playing basketball or riding the bus.

Finally, complete participation means that the proposed observation centers on something the researcher already does as part of his or her normal routines, like observing in the restaurant where he eats three or four times a week. For a beginning urban ethnographer, Spradley's book is an excellent tool, because it is extremely practical and guides one through the process of participant observation step by step.

## Specific Ethnographic Techniques

### Participant Observation

People who intend to be urban church planters, pastors, or teachers in the city need to spend time learning about the city before they begin any kind of ministry. I would suggest that the first three to six months be set aside for learning the city. Knowing how to use the ethnographic method will make this learning time much more profitable.

The tasks of getting started and analyzing the data collected generally prove to be the hardest parts of the project. At first one doesn't know what to look for, because culture has trained us to shut out extraneous information. That makes participant observation hard work.

A few years ago, I spent a month in Hong Kong. While there, I studied restaurant behavior. We had to eat out daily, and we discovered that most Hong Kong Chinese do, too. As I shared my insights with Chinese friends, they corrected me or added to my knowledge. It was a delightful study, and it made my stay in Hong Kong more profitable because it opened up new ministry approaches in my thinking. But it was also tiring. When it was time to leave Hong Kong and go to Malaysia for a month, I remember sitting on the plane thinking, "I'm exhausted from all the participant observation I did in Hong Kong. How can I begin all over again in Malaysia?"

"What am I supposed to be seeing?" is a common query during the first stage of ethnographic research. This is the stage when the researcher must take detailed notes on everything, *especially* things that seem common.

Spradley suggests a simple ordering of observations by actor, activity, or place. All three parts are necessary to any good participant observation, and the interrelationship of all three should provide some new material. Further, Spradley creates a chart of generic questions centered on what he considers the nine basic questions of observation in any context: space, object, act, activity, event, time, actor, goal, and feeling.[3] Using these questions as a guide, beginning researchers should rewrite them to reflect the context of the specific research they are undertaking.

When a student named Bonnie did her project at a restaurant frequented by senior citizens, her first thought was that the place seemed no different from other restaurants she visited. However, as she began to write down everything she observed, she noticed an interesting pattern: one particular waitress joked a lot with the younger patrons but almost not at all with the older regulars. Surprised at this, she finally asked why. Looking uncomfortable, the waitress replied that she did not want to get friendly with the older people because as soon as she did, they died. Ignoring them was her protection against the pain of losing friends in the restaurant.

Writing down everything in as much detail as possible can give the beginning researcher the data to begin making preliminary hypotheses and trying to reject them. For example, Bonnie looked at her data, counted the number of interactions she had observed up to that point between the waitress and patrons, and then hypothesized that the waitresses in this restaurant all followed the pattern she had observed. Then she began to come in at different times of the day and different days of the week to see if other waitresses reacted the same way. After several weeks of observing these interactions, she concluded that this was a definite pattern of behavior for waitresses in this restaurant. This conclusion generated some new considerations: Did the older people notice this difference? Did other people feel the same way about this population? If so, what kind of ministry strategies might it suggest? Bonnie's research was only preliminary, limited by the demands of the school calendar. Yet the information she accumulated was enough to help her begin thinking about ministry in an entirely different way.

### Mapping

A technique I have encouraged in the beginning of the participant observation process is mapping. When people don't know where to start, the thing to do is to count, quantify, and map! Over the years my students and I have developed some useful kinds of maps to help in this participant observation process.

One kind fixes architectural features, then uses the maps to collect actual data. For example, a student doing a research project in a local park drew a map of such fixed features as trees, swimming pool, and parking lots. He then added a space for date and time of day, duplicated it, and used the maps to track the movement of various people in the park. This is similar to what William Whyte calls "charting spatial relations" in his discussion about observational methods.[4]

A second type of map could use Kevin Lynch's categories of nodes, paths, landmarks, edges, and districts to help determine geographic areas of safety and danger for specific persons.[5] Asking the person to describe to the researcher where friends live and where he or she goes shopping helps to get at native perceptions rather than observers' perceptions. Lincoln Keiser did this in studying gangs in Chicago, where he needed to know the boundaries of their respective territories.[6]

Other types of maps can be drawn by the observer and discussed with an informant. When I observed my first African-American church service, I mapped the sanctuary and the placement and movement of people during the service. At the end, all those in the group I was with were invited to lunch in the church social hall. During that time, I asked the pastor to explain several things I had observed, and he was delighted to do so. Later, I asked others the same questions to see if the meanings described by the pastor were commonly held by others in the church.

Mapping serves several purposes. First, it helps in learning how people use space. Do men and women sit together in church? Does a specific ethnic group monopolize the basketball court at the local park?

Second, mapping builds rapport by asking nonthreatening questions. When I accompanied a Chinese friend to a school graduation, I could not understand a word of Cantonese. However, I had a notebook along, so I mapped the platform and the location and sex of each person up front. Then I mapped where students were seated in the auditorium, how many bowed when receiving their diplomas, and any other items that I could observe. Later, I asked my friend to explain what went on. The questions were nonthreatening, because I was only asking about observable things that were common to him.

Third, mapping helps one to learn indigenous terms, categories, and points of importance. In my restaurant study, I had a Chinese student map the restaurant he went to several times a week. As he noted the location of tables and the behavior of patrons, he pointed out something that made him angry. On Saturday mornings, he said, old Chinese men would come in as soon as the restaurant opened, occupy the largest round tables, and wait for others to come and join them as space got scarce. In exchange for holding the table, these old men expected the newcomers to pay for their breakfast. My friend, as a complete participant, thought it was unfair of the men to do this. But that piece of information could be looked at in a very different way for potential urban ministry. If the old men represented a common phenomenon in Hong Kong restaurants, could not a new urban missionary join one of them at the table on a Saturday morning and begin to learn language and culture? The price of breakfast would be well worth it!

Fourth, mapping can remind the researcher of additional information that should be recorded. When Doug began a study of a Los Angeles park, he mapped the men sitting around on benches. He noticed that occasionally they would go relieve themselves at a specific spot, and once he noticed someone at a different spot. When he asked, he learned that even the urinating places in the park were ranked according to whether they were pickup spots for homosexual action. This led Doug to explore the last purpose of mapping: asking better questions. When Doug began to ask more questions, he realized that a homosexual network operating in the park involved the Anglo men and young illegal-alien Hispanic men. As he said, "It helped me ask better questions, but I wasn't sure I really wanted to know the answers!" As a result of his study, however, he decided that the outreach group he was associated with at a nearby church would need to focus on the young Hispanic men to help them break the dependency cycle. Doug's research provided the impetus for a ministry to people and a problem that the group had not even been aware existed.

### Systematic Observation

Closely related to mapping, systematic observation uses a list of characteristics or behaviors and then observes at specific intervals to record their presence or absence. For example, in my restaurant study I began to try to quantify the various forms that were held in common. Table 14.1 illustrates the chart I created to help me look more carefully at things like napkin use and the procedures for calling for the check. I made many copies of this chart, added a place for the date and restaurant name at the top, and then used each sheet to create a systematic record of the differences and similarities in restaurant behavior. By numbering each of the forms being observed, I was able easily to continue by observations on the back of the sheet when necessary.

## Table 14.1
## Form and Meaning
(as generated through hypotheses)

| Form | Observations | Hypotheses |
|---|---|---|
| 1. size of restaurant (number of rooms and floors) | | |
| 2. waiting for a table | | |
| 3. seating | | |
| 4. size/shape of table | | |
| 5. table setting | | |
| 6. dishes | | |
| 7. glasses/cups | | |
| 8. utensils | | |
| 9. napkins | | |
| 10. ordering | | |
| 11. serving | | |
| 12. service | | |
| 13. calling for check | | |
| 14. placement of check on table | | |

### Interview

Formal and informal interviewing can help us collect comparable data to really understand people. The first problem comes in knowing what kinds of questions to ask. Ray Bakke has many favorite questions like "What do you think I ought to know about this neighborhood?" Another source of questions is Spradley's *Ethnographic Interview*.[7] He suggests recording the questions people ask in everyday life. He also says one can create a hypothetical situation and ask for questions: "If I listened to students going through the cafeteria line at supper time, what questions would I hear them ask the staff working there? What questions might they ask each other?"

Spradley categorizes questions into three types: descriptive, structural, and contrast. The descriptive questions are the easiest to ask and should be used first. Spradley calls the most useful ones "Grand Tour Questions": "Can you tell me all the things that happen when you get arrested for being drunk, from the first moment you encounter the police, through going to court and being sentenced, until you finally get out of jail?" "Can you tell me all the names of your relatives and what each one is like?" "Could you take me on a tour of the park?" "Could you play a hand of cards and explain what you're doing?"

Structural questions form a second category. These include general questions like "What ethnic groups are in Los Angeles?" Or they may be more specific, like "Are Guatemalans, Salvadoreans, and Mexicans all considered Hispanics? Are there any other kinds of Hispanics living in Los Angeles?"

The third type of question Spradley suggests is the contrast question. Contrast questions build on descriptive and structural questions and yield the most comprehensive information. For example, "Can you tell me the difference between a Salvadorean and a Mexican from your perspective?"

In some cases, it is a good idea to have interview questions written out ahead, so that the researcher remembers to ask each person the same questions. There are ethical principles involved in ethnographic interviewing that are outside the scope of this chapter but should be known. Spradley does a good job of discussing these in *Ethnographic Interviewing*.

### Projective Techniques

Projective techniques can range from a simple wish projection like "If you could wish for any one thing, what would it be?" to simulations and psychological tests. For the purposes of urban ministry, the wish question often opens up dialogue.

### Physical Trace

Suppose a researcher wants to study the other apartment dwellers in his or her complex. What kinds of cars do they own? What kinds of things do they throw out each week? Some researchers actually sift through people's garbage, but this is not recommended. What I have in mind here are things that are easily observable and give clues as to people's wants, lifestyles, and interests.

### Analyzing the Data

An urban researcher has collected all kinds of information, but she doesn't know what it means. "Where do I go now?" is a common complaint. One of the things I do in the classroom is to have graduate students talk about their research and what they have learned so far. The other students and I interact, ask questions, and make suggestions. Almost every year students comment that the feedback session is probably the most helpful of the semester.

Searching for themes and patterns is critical to the analysis of qualitative data. Urban research is a social science that has contributed a great deal of information to the study of people in the city. Beginning researchers need to become informed about the literature and read widely in it to tie their own research in with the results of other people's study and analysis.

## Putting It All Together

Ethnographic research has great potential for application to urban ministry. Using the six stages outlined below, people in urban ministry can begin targeting specific groups of people for ministry and discipling.

1. Contacting the population—where are the public places where people gather?
2. Defining population divisions and characteristics through mapping, observation, and interviewing.
3. Assessing population routines and opportunities for witness by observing such things as time, space, activity, event, actors, goals, and feelings.
4. Learning the experiential and linguistic context for witness through grand tour questions, structural questions, and contrast interviewing.
5. Analyzing social organization and leadership patterns through networks, associations, and groups to target people of influence and develop witness strategies for them.
6. Analyzing values and features of worldviews that provide obstacles and opportunities for response to the gospel. (Often urban ministry *begins* here and ignores the other five stages!)

The ethnographic research approach described in this chapter is not a true ethnography in the professional sense because it is designed for application, not mere description. But as people committed to doing urban ministry, we want to see the practical applications of the research we conduct, or else the project is not worth our time and effort. The practical value of ethnographic research is clear because students using it have been able to identify ministry opportunities and needs of which they were previously unaware. On the basis of applied research and analysis, students are equipped to do things of importance for the extension of God's kingdom in the city.

There are, in addition, a number of side benefits. The ethnographic method can involve the entire family or team in a common task. This helps new people enjoy their settling-in experiences rather than simply enduring them. It also helps them to know how to pray more effectively for the peace and prosperity of the city and how the Word of God should be brought to bear on urban society. Communicating the gospel message well and building an appropriate mission strategy depend, far more than we often have recognized, on the use of research like this.

## Discussion Questions

1. What things bewilder you most about big cities? Tell about some experience you had in a city that confused or frightened you. Try to analyze what caused you to feel uneasy.
2. What features of the research methods suggested in this chapter do you think will be most useful? Are there some things you feel will not help?
3. Distinguish and explain grand tour questions, structural questions, and contrast questions. Give an example of each type. What good does it do the missionary to be so curious and ask so many questions?
4. Apply the participant observation technique to some area within your present environment as a student (e.g., the cafeteria) or the general community and, like Bonnie, analyze your data, make preliminary hypotheses and test them, and try to suggest ministry possibilities drawn from your feelings.

# 15

# DISCIPLING CITY KIDS

*Edna C. Greenway*

When summer comes and kids are on the street, city neighborhoods can become desperate for ways to prevent trouble and do something productive with the kids' time. A few years ago, at the beginning of summer, flyers appeared on the windshields of cars in church parking lots throughout our neighborhood.[1] Mothers placed them there—mothers concerned that their kids stay out of trouble during the coming summer. Their message was simple:

PLEASE PLAN ACTIVITIES FOR OUR KIDS.
KEEP THEM OFF THE STREETS.
TEACH THEM.
HELP THEM MAKE THIS SUMMER A GOOD TIME IN THEIR LIVES.

The message was addressed to churches, community groups, and individuals concerned for the welfare of the neighborhood.

Our church responded by organizing a Kids' Club that met one morning a week, much like a Vacation Bible School but continuing throughout the summer. We also showed a movie in the church parking lot one evening each week. The movies were suitable for family viewing, and we served ice cream for everyone who came. We coordinated our program with others in the neighborhood. The effect was a message from all the churches to the neighborhood: "We care, and God cares, about kids." Yet it was just the beginning of many new things that needed to be done.

## A Complex Challenge

How do churches in racially and culturally changing neighborhoods provide social and religious activities that are meaningful for children and youth? For decades city churches have struggled with that question. Most churches' educational programs are geared to the youth of the traditional membership, generally middle-class, white, and English-speaking. But when the population changes, churches are caught without an effective outreach in the neighborhood. Churches that cannot or will not respond to this new challenge face serious difficulties.

Over the years, churches have developed a variety of responses to their changing neighborhoods. Tutoring programs, sports activities, summer camps, and learning clubs that combine Bible studies with other activities are examples. They aim to stimulate young minds, channel energies, and keep kids out of trouble. Behind these programs is the basic commitment of Christian people to serve Christ by introducing children and youth to God's Word and training them to be the Lord's disciples.

The complexity of the challenge stems from the fact that city children often represent a variety of social, cultural, and religious backgrounds. Add to this the divers competitors for the children's interest and attention, many seriously detrimental, and the extent of the challenge is clear.

Sooner or later almost all city churches in the Euro-American tradition will have to decide whether they will change and adapt their educational programs to meet the needs of children of other races and cultures, or watch their memberships dwindle and their ministries gradually die. Asian and Hispanic churches will also face the issue, though in a different way. As children of the congregations learn English and adopt the ways of North American culture, church leaders must decide whether to persist in using the language of their origin and the educational methods of the past, or employ teachers who speak English and use a curriculum that reflects North American culture.

## An Experiment: A Two-Track Sunday School

In the 1970s, the city church I attended began to face the reality of our changing neighborhood, but it took us several years to decide how to respond. As we studied the surrounding neighborhood, we began to realize that we had a major problem educating children. The old neighborhood, entirely Euro-American, middle-class, and characterized by strong two-parent families, was disappearing. The new neighborhood consisted of many single-parent homes riddled with social and economic problems. An increasing percentage was African-American families. While the neighborhood was changing, our educational program wasn't. The curriculum reflected the culture and goals of the old neighborhood, not the new. No wonder so few neighborhood children attended!

What could we do? We had a continuing obligation to educate the children of traditional members, most of whom now attended schools far from the neighborhood with high educational standards and expectations of strong parental support of the learning process. We understood these children and how to develop their faith and life. But now, all around us, there were children who did not fit the church's traditional educational mode. What changes could we make to meet their needs?

For several years we experimented with a two-track Sunday school that offered different curricula based on the needs of children from different parts of the neighborhood. We allowed the children or their parents to choose which track they wished to take. Most of the neighborhood children attending Sunday school were in elementary school, so we laid out the two-track program to go from kindergarten through fourth grade. Whenever we could, we explained the two tracks to the parents and invited new children to observe both to see which they preferred.

The regular track assumed higher reading ability and prior knowledge of basic Bible stories. The neighborhood track was designed for children with a wider range of reading levels. It offered different types of class activities and assumed less Bible knowledge. Since each track followed a different curriculum, teachers taught classes in the track that best suited their skills.

Theoretically, the two-track approach made sense. But in practice, it ran into difficulties. Staffing the different classes with their variety of students became a serious problem. Assigning the children to the proper groups proved complicated. Worst of all, outside observers judged the system discriminatory. They were sensitive to any form of segregation. After several years of struggling, the church reverted to a single-track program of a traditional kind, and most of the neighborhood children stopped attending.

## Kid Power and How It Functions

The challenge of developing a religious education program that met the needs and attracted the interest of inner-city children forced us to experiment further. The next attempt proved successful. A neighboring city church had developed a community children's program called Kid Power. It proved effective, so our church decided to try something similar.

Kid Power meets once a week, from late afternoon to early evening. It opens with singing, prayer, and Scripture reading. Then the children enjoy a simple, nourishing meal. Afterward come serious Bible study and a brief time of crafts or a game.

A seminarian employed part-time by the church for community ministry serves as the director of Kid Power. Adult members volunteer for a host of Kid Power tasks. Some drive the church bus to transport children who live too far away to walk. Some prepare and serve the meal, while others clean up afterward. Others provide cookies and desserts or teach classes.

Two local Christian colleges also provide a number of the teachers. Often these are students participating in a student volunteer organization that assists inner-city ministries. Some are going into education, and by teaching in the Kid Power program they gain valuable practical experience.

Kid Power has proven an effective way to reach inner-city African-American children and youth, using the facilities and staff of an existing Euro-American church. Some of the youth who attended for several years eventually became Kid Power teachers themselves. Recently, an African-American church moved in across the street from us and agreed to take over the present Kid Power program. We hope it will be able to draw Kid Power youth into regular church membership; we could not.

Our church now plans to begin a Spanish Kid Power program aimed at the growing Hispanic population in our neighborhood. One difference will be that Spanish Kid Power will be administered through the Spanish congregation that now shares our church facilities. We believe that for consistent disciple making to take place, the youth program must be closely linked to the church as a whole, including Sunday worship. For this to happen, the same social and cultural adaptations that characterize Kid Power during the week must be present on Sunday. Otherwise the youth will sense the difference and the relationship will end.

## City Curriculum for City Kids

Many city children have limited Bible knowledge and church backgrounds. They often do not attend church education programs regularly because their families move frequently. The time gap between settling into a new neighborhood and finding a church with a children's program causes discontinuity in biblical instruction.

This instability also means that there is often a lack of biblical instruction in the homes of urban children. Many urban children are left to fend for themselves; they must ready themselves for day school, Sunday school, and Bible club. Many parents do not attend church and feel no responsibility for Christian nurture in the home. Sometimes even parents who do attend church leave their children's spiritual training to the teachers of the kids' clubs or Sunday schools in the church. As a result, the education children receive in the church is not balanced with biblical instruction at home.

A further problem is that children in city schools often do not acquire the basic reading and problem-solving skills most available church curricula assume for their grade level. When teachers find that a curriculum's grade level is above the children's comprehension, they must use materials from a lower level. Though these materials may fit the children better academically, they do not always fit them psychologically and socially.

Meanwhile, publishing companies report that the market for urban curriculum is not large enough to warrant producing and publishing such specialized materials. Teachers in the urban church continue to devise their own materials—putting together Bible lessons from files of traditional Sunday school ideas, Bible story books, and visual resources collected over the years.

Nonetheless, at least two publishers have produced materials for urban children.[2] One—Urban Ministries, Inc., in Chicago—has done a great deal to enable African-American churches to reach urban children. Along with producing curriculum, it periodically organizes Christian education conferences at which consultants assist members of local churches in organizing and carrying out educational ministries.

Kid Power used Urban Ministries' materials in its midweek program. Even though most were African-American, children from other culture groups enjoyed the materials, too. In Kid Power, the younger children received the most benefit from the urban curriculum. They were introduced to biblical background and stories and were able to understand the basic truths of the lessons. For older children who did not have an extensive biblical background, the material was too difficult. Extra time had to be spent explaining terminology and concepts. When the younger children become older, having experienced the program for several years, the problem will no doubt be solved. However, in the urban situation teachers will continue to deal with students coming in at every level.

Urban curriculum needs to be culturally and academically relevant not only in content but also in presentation: layout, design, and graphics. At first glance, the graphics in the Urban Ministries' curriculum may shock Euro-American viewers, since biblical characters are pictured as African people. For years, African-American churches have used materials picturing Christ and his disciples as Nordic people. Now we see what happens when the African-American church prepares graphics for its own curriculum. Curriculum preparers should be careful to portray biblical characters honestly, realizing that neither the Nordic nor the African expression is historically correct.

David C. Cook recently published culturally relevant urban materials called "Echoes." They are highly recommended by noted African-American church leaders as Bible-based, ethnically identifiable, easy to teach, and economical.

## A Proposed Curriculum: What Makes It Unique?

My suggestion for curriculum for Sunday schools or Bible clubs comes from the struggle of my own city church to find suitable curriculum for Kid Power. The curriculum I will describe is different because it is designed to meet the needs of a part of urban society that most churches in the past have not addressed.

First, it is designed for youth with limited Bible knowledge and church backgrounds. The lessons are arranged to help learners understand redemptive history progressively, the way the Bible reveals it. They begin with the story of creation and end with the second coming of Christ.

Second, the curriculum is flexible. This is important because of the diversity of skills and levels of Bible knowledge among the learners. In the Kid Power program, some third graders could read better than some sixth graders. A teacher who teaches well-skilled third graders must present the lesson in a different way from the teacher of less-skilled sixth graders. Similarly, children in the program will have varied degrees of Bible knowledge. The proposed curriculum allows teachers to adjust the material so that each learner in the class experiences a meaningful lesson.

Third, the curriculum includes topics that convey biblical truths in a concrete fashion. Theological terms are not avoided altogether but are explained in simple language. Since even upper-elementary students in the urban church may have an immature understanding of fundamental teachings of Scripture, ideas about God, sin, and salvation have to be made understandable to all the learners.

Fourth, the curriculum includes stories from every part of Scripture. One of the greatest challenges for all children is understanding how all the stories and events in the Bible fit together. This is especially true for Kid Power learners. Earlier curricula took a thematic approach, using Bible stories to illustrate themes like love, honor, or obedience. But a thematic approach does not readily encourage children to understand Scripture as redemptive history. The proposed curriculum, therefore, incorporates Bible stories from Genesis to Revelation in historical sequence.

## How Does the Proposed Curriculum Work?

There are twenty lesson plans in the curriculum, ten from each Testament. They progress in chronological order, beginning in the fall and ending when the school year is finished. The midpoint comes at Christmas time.

Each lesson focuses on a particular topic from Scripture, with each teacher having a choice of stories to teach from under this topic. An example of this is lesson 14, shown in the lesson plan on page 203. This lesson focuses on the parables of Christ. Each teacher is limited to teaching one parable but has the freedom to choose any of them.

When one teaches a lesson to a group of children with diverse cognitive development levels, Bible stories constitute the best lesson material. Teachers can use them to convey a variety of truths appropriate to the individual comprehension levels. Besides the truths found in the stories, learners become acquainted with the progressive redemptive history of Scripture. They begin to see how God worked through Israel in the Old Testament and the promised Messiah in the New Testament and continues to work today through his people until Christ returns at the last day.

Children in urban church programs are not unique in their lack of understanding of Bible stories and redemptive history. Yet because of irregular church attendance, they are especially vulnerable to it. Bible stories, presented in chronological fashion, do much to overcome this problem.

The most significant benefit of the curriculum is its repetition of each lesson on a year-to-year basis. Beginning with kindergarten and continuing through eighth grade, children have similar lessons each year. The lessons are not identical, but the setting, background, and main characters are the same. This helps the children to recall and reinforce lessons from past years. As their thought processes mature, their teachers can add details to the lessons. "What if?", "Why?", and "How?" questions can be added to the more content-oriented "Who?" and "What?" questions. Class discussions, role plays, problem solving, and drama all can help to teach abstract theological concepts.

# What Does the Proposed Curriculum Look Like?

Twenty stories from Scripture are the core of the curriculum. If a church's program is year-long, other stories, such as additional accounts of parables and miracles, will need to be added. If a program continues through the summer, a series on the life of Paul would be ideal.

Since many children come with little or no Bible knowledge, the year must begin with the teacher explaining a few fundamental truths regarding the Bible: the Bible is the Word of God, it records events that took place in history, it reveals how God saves sinners through Jesus Christ, and it shows us how we must live. The teacher can explain that the lessons throughout the year will follow in chronological order. A time line on a bulletin board is an excellent tool.

What follows is a list of the Bible stories for a twenty-week program:

## Old Testament

Lesson 1:  **Creation and Fall**
Story 1.    God the Creator and the perfect creation
Story 2.    The fall and its consequences

Lesson 2:  **Noah and the Ark**
Story 1.    Building the ark, gathering the animals and the people
Story 2.    The flood
Story 3.    God blesses faithful Noah

Lesson 3:  **Abraham, Isaac, and Jacob**
Story 1.    Abraham's early years
Story 2.    The sacrifice of Isaac
Story 3.    Jacob and Esau

Lesson 4:  **Joseph**
Story 1.    Joseph's coat of many colors; Joseph sold as a slave
Story 2.    Joseph in prison
Story 3.    Joseph saves Egypt from famine

Lesson 5:  **Moses**
Story 1.    The beginning of Moses' life in Egypt
Story 2.    Moses and the burning bush
Story 3.    Moses/Pharaoh and the plagues
Story 4.    The Passover
Story 5.    The parting of the Red Sea

Lesson 6:  **Israel in the Wilderness**
Story 1.    The manna and the quail

Story 2.   Water from the rock

Story 3.   Mount Sinai: the covenant, the Ten Commandments

Story 4.   The building and meaning of the ark and the tabernacle

**Lesson 7:   Israel in Canaan**

Story 1.   Rahab and the spies

Story 2.   The battle of Jericho

**Lesson 8:   The Judges**

Story 1.   Any story of Samson

**Lesson 9:   The Kings**

Story 1.   Saul, the disobedient king

Story 2.   David and Goliath

Story 3.   David and Bathsheba

Story 4.   Solomon's wisdom

**Lesson 10:   The Prophets and the Exile**

Story 1.   Daniel in the lions' den

Story 2.   Shadrach, Meshach, and Abednego

Story 3.   Isaiah's prophesies of the Messiah

## New Testament

**Lesson 11:   Christ's Birth, Early Life**

Story 1.   The birth of Jesus

Story 2.   Jesus at the temple

Story 3.   John the Baptist

**Lesson 12:   Sermon on the Mount**

Story 1.   The Beatitudes

Story 2.   Teachings of salt and light

**Lesson 13:   Miracles of Jesus**

Story 1.   Any miracle account

Story 2.   Raising Lazarus from the dead

**Lesson 14:   Parables of Jesus**

Story 1.   Any parable

**Lesson 15:   The Betrayal and Death of Jesus**

Story 1.   The Last Supper

Story 2.   Gethsemane

Story 3.   Jesus before Pilate

Story 4.   Jesus on the cross

**Lesson 16:   The Resurrection of Jesus**

Story 1.   Mary and Mary Magdalene at the tomb

Story 2.    Jesus appears before the eleven disciples

**Lesson 17:    Ascension of Christ**
Story 1.    On the Mount of the Ascension
Story 2.    The Great Commission

**Lesson 18:    The New Testament Church**
Story 1.    Pentecost
Story 2.    Persecution of the apostles
Story 3.    Peter's deliverance from priso

**Lesson 19:    Paul the Missionary**
Story 1.    The Damascus road conversion
Story 2.    One of the missionary journeys
Story 3.    Letters of Paul to the churches

**Lesson 20:    The Second Coming of Christ**
Story 1.    The last things
Story 2.    Saint John's vision

As the list shows, the curriculum moves quickly through the Scriptures. This fast-paced style makes it imperative for the teacher to link the stories week to week, reiterating the theme of the history of redemption.

For example, two Old Testament lessons can be linked this way: "This week's lesson is about Moses and the children of Israel in Egypt. Do any of you remember how the Israelites came to live in Egypt?" (children's responses). "That's right. It was because many, many years earlier Joseph and his brothers had come to Egypt. Do you remember that we talked about this last week? How did Joseph get to Egypt? What was God's plan in this?"

## What about Crafts?

Crafts for each class need to be planned and prepared by a craft director or the teacher. One suggestion is to have each student make a book out of construction paper. Each week a new looseleaf page is added to the book. Younger children can draw a picture appropriate to the lesson. Older students may be encouraged to write a response to the lesson in the form of art work, poetry, or prose.

Old Testament lessons may be put together in one book and New Testament lessons in another. When the books are complete, the children can take them home and share the message of the lessons with their parents and friends. Children learn to treasure the books because in their classes they have learned the tremendous impact of how God works with and leads his people.

## Learning Centers

Public schools have used learning centers for several years, and church education can use them effectively, too. Children enjoy moving around actively during lesson time, and learning centers facilitate this while providing diversity in structuring each lesson's activities.

Three or four learning centers work best to provide variety. Each center is set up in a corner of an all-purpose room. If such a large room is not available, the centers can be put in individual classrooms.

Themes for the learning centers can be as varied as the imaginations of the teachers. There can be a Memory Verse Center, a Puppet Center, a Music Center, an Art Center, or a Drama Center. The themes can vary from week to week, depending on which part of the lesson teachers wish to reinforce.

Classes can be consolidated if learning centers are used. To begin, all the classes (kindergarten through sixth grade) meet together. The full class then divides into as many groups as there are learning centers. Each group is allotted about seven minutes for the activities of each center.

The usual opening exercise takes place with all the children seated on a large rug in the middle of an all-purpose room. If such a room is not available, plan the opening exercise in a chapel area or hallway. After the opening prayer and a song, a twenty-minute Bible story is presented. Next, the children move with their groups from one learning center to another. Seven minutes in each of the four centers, with time allotted for moving around, allows for an hour for the entire lesson. Afterward, the children come together for a closing act of worship. Table 15.1 presents a model schedule for moving students through four learning centers.

**Table 15.1**
**Model Schedule for Learning Centers**

| Time allotted | A Group | B Group | C Group | D Group |
|---|---|---|---|---|
| 20 min. | All groups together for opening and Bible story | | | |
| 7 min. | Memory Center | Drama Center | Art Center | Music Center |
| 7 min. | Music Center | Art Center | Drama Center | Memory Center |
| 7 min. | Art Center | Memory Center | Music Center | Drama Center |
| 7 min. | Drama Center | Music Center | Memory Center | Art Center |
| 3 min. | All groups together for closing worship | | | |

## Is This the Right Curriculum for City Kids?

This curriculum can be used for children in many different contexts. What makes it ideal for city kids is the manner in which the Bible stories are sequenced historically. Each year the children will receive the same basic Bible stories. New children will be taught the same sequence of stories. The children who remain in the program year after year will gain a strong Bible background to establish them in the Christian faith as they grow into adulthood.

Teachers play a major role in making this program a success. They should take time to build relationships with their students. As they gain an understanding of their backgrounds, they will tell the Bible stories and plan the lessons to apply to their day-to-day needs.

A host of urban themes emerges from the biblical accounts. Old Testament stories show how the heroes and heroines of faith endured loneliness, homelessness, and poverty. The parables of Christ are natural springboards to such lessons as fair play and justice. The miracles manifest God's power over evil spirits and his ability and desire to fill spiritual and physical needs.

With God's help, the twenty-lesson curriculum, faithfully taught and crafted, will help the urban child to grow in grace and love for Jesus Christ. The goal of church education for city children is developing and training urban disciples who in turn will disciple the next generation of city kids.

## Urban Church Education Resources

Carney, Glandion. *Creative Urban Youth Ministry*. Elgin, Ill.: David C. Cook, 1984.

Davis, Billie. *Teaching to Meet Crisis Needs*. Springfield, Mo.: Gospel Publishing House, 1978.

Educaid Series. Division for Life and Mission in the Congregation, American Lutheran Church, 422 South Fifth Street, Minneapolis, Minnesota 55415.

Everist, Norma J. *Education Ministry in the Congregation*. Minneapolis: Augsburg, 1983.

Hunter, Lea Anne, and Magdalen Sienkiewicz. *Learning Clubs for the Poor*. New York: Paulist, 1984.

Roehlkepartain, Eugene C. *Youth Ministry in City Churches*. Loveland, Colo.: Thom Schultz Publications, 1989.

Rogers, Donald B., ed. *Urban Church Education.* Birmingham, Ala.: Religious Education Press, 1989.

## Discussion Questions

1. Why do city churches often find it difficult to provide an adequate educational program for their youth?
2. What did the two-track Sunday school try to achieve? Why was it discontinued?
3. Explain what is different about the curriculum proposed in this chapter. How important do you feel the differences are?
4. What do you like, or dislike, about the proposed curriculum? How would it fit the needs of the children of your church?

# 16

## THE LIFESTYLE OF URBAN DISCIPLE-MAKERS

### Roger S. Greenway

In May 1959, my wife and I and our three-month-old daughter arrived in Colombo, Ceylon (now Sri Lanka). We had to wait nearly four months for our baggage because a dock workers' strike completely paralyzed the port. No cargo of any kind was loaded or unloaded. During those four months, we made our initial adjustment to the island and its people and to Nugegoda, which was part of metropolitan Colombo. There, in a lower- to middle-class area, the national church had rented a house for us.

We set up housekeeping, purchasing everything we needed in Colombo stores. Our furniture was made by local carpenters. The only imported items we purchased were a few fans, a small stove, and a refrigerator. Mechanical items like these were not manufactured in the island but came from England. From America we had only what we had brought in our four suitcases. To our surprise, we got along fine.

Four months later, word came that our baggage had finally been unloaded from the ship. The ship's captain, tired of waiting at anchor in the Colombo harbor, had taken the vessel to the former British navy base at Trincomalee on the opposite side of the island. There the cargo was unloaded. Our baggage went by rail to the customs office near the Colombo docks and, after clearing customs, was loaded into five bullock carts for delivery to our home.

I well remember the sight of the bullock carts coming up the street with our baggage from America! The combined load consisted of no less than eighteen steel barrels and two big crates. On the one hand we were excited. It seemed like Christmas in August, with bullocks instead of reindeer bringing wonderful things from the north! On the other hand, we were disturbed. We kept asking ourselves, "Why do we need all this stuff? Why did we buy it in the first place?"

Our neighbors, some poor and none well-to-do, turned out in force to see what the Americans were getting. As we opened the crates and barrels by the side of the house, the neighbors stared in wonderment. How rich and important this young American couple must be to afford five cart-loads of wonderful things! They didn't know, of course, that we had friends who sold to us wholesale—saving us money, we persuaded ourselves. They didn't realize that as tall Americans, getting the right size clothing (especially size 14 shoes) was a concern to us. They just stared in amazement as we emptied barrel after barrel, envying us for all the marvelous items we had brought from America.

Unpacking our baggage, carefully observed by our neighbors, remains in my mind one of life's most awkward and embarrassing moments. For four months my wife and I had been building relationships and seeking to identify with the community. Our blond baby daughter provided a natural opener for conversation and a jump start toward new relationships. Though we were foreigners, our neighbors could see that we were not altogether different from other young parents. We were concerned about raising our child, about solving everyday problems and meeting basic needs. They went out of their way to help us, for they could see that we had the same needs as everyone else.

Now, suddenly, they saw that we were what some probably suspected we were all along: rich Americans who could fill their home with every conceivable comfort and adornment. A thousand sermons could not undo the damage done that day. It would have been better for our ministry if the ship had dropped our barrels and crates in the Indian Ocean.

We had made our first major mistake before sailing out of New York. We had listened to advice concerning all the things we surely needed in order to be properly outfitted for the mission field. But a more serious problem was not yet apparent to us, and it took years before we recognized it. It had to do with the very message of Jesus Christ that we had come to Asia to proclaim and how certain aspects of our lifestyle subtly undermined it. Only time and a deeper understanding of the gospel and how it is communicated would prepare us to deal with that problem.

The subject of this chapter is a delicate one, because it touches on the personal lifestyle of city workers and missionaries and how lifestyle affects ministry. To avoid making myself appear overly judgmental, I will begin by raising certain questions, questions based on my own observations and those of others. These are designed to challenge our thinking—mine as well as yours—and to provoke discussion.

When I write about lifestyle, I refer to how missionaries spend money, how they live, the housing they choose, the vehicles they drive, and the kind of recreation and entertainment they spend money on. In short, I am addressing the general lifestyle of city workers, particularly expatriate missionaries, and how it affects the ministry of multiplying disciples of Jesus Christ.

When we speak of discipling the city, we have in mind first of all the essential missionary goal: filling the world and all its great cities with the knowledge of God and salvation in Jesus Christ, and increasing the number and influence of those who in all areas of the city live by God's grace under Christ's lordship. That is what urban mission is all about. The missionary enterprise, with its organizations, administrations, schools, budgets, policies, and strategies, is simply the means the church uses to pursue the goal of discipling people.

Hovering in the background as we probe these issues is the disturbing question of our primary commitment. As God's servants in the city, is our primary commitment really to multiplying and enhancing urban discipleship in the most efficient and effective manner? Or does our deepest loyalty lie in some other area, perhaps in our personal goals and ambitions, or in the expansion of our missionary organization? Or do we dream of a huge and powerful church under one great leader, where all city dwellers can have their needs met like birds flocking to one tall, wonderful tree?

## Question 1: Do Our Belongings Deter Our Bonding?

Most of us are familiar with bonding, the process by which outsiders like missionaries come to feel at home in a second culture. Bonding is extremely important for all missionaries, in cities and rural places alike. Failing to understand bonding and the steps that make it effective means risking never feeling at home in a second culture and never building close relationships with local people.

Through their writing and teaching, Elizabeth Brewster and her late husband, Tom, have done a great service to Christian missions by helping us understand how important it is for new missionaries to bond effectively with nationals as soon as possible after arriving in the new culture. Effective bonding entails becoming both bilingual and bicultural and thereby becoming truly at home with people of another land.

In one of their most important articles on the subject, "Bonding and the Missionary Task: Establishing a Sense of Belonging," the Brewsters observe that after a decade of working with missionaries in almost seventy countries, observing firsthand missionary activities and relationships with nationals, "only a small percentage of these missionaries manifest the kinds of relationships with local people that would demonstrate that bonding had occurred."[1] Then follows a paragraph that struck me especially because of our own embarrassing experience with our eighteen barrels:

> Happiness is belonging, not belongings. Yet the life-style of the majority of Western missionaries is a major deterrent to bonding. It is hard to devote time to pursuing the meaningful relationships with local people when concerned about getting barrels of stuff through customs and unpacked and settled. This sense of belonging to one's belongings is a bonding of the worst kind—bondage. Unfortunately, it is a subtle bondage that is difficult to throw off.[2]

Every time I read that I feel the sting in what it says. I know what the Brewsters say is true, because *bondage to belongings* damaged the relationship-building process my wife and I sought to establish with our neighbors in Sri Lanka. Because of purchases made months before arriving on the field, we found ourselves surrounded by material possessions that aroused the envy of our neighbors and insulated us from belonging relationships with them.

In consulting with urban missionaries, the number-one problem I have discovered has to do with relationships. Many missionaries, even those who have been in a country for many years, are not effectively bonded with nationals. This leads me to wonder how honest and straightforward mission leaders are with candidates, and how candid they are with missionaries on the field, about bonding. Many missionaries' effectiveness is quietly undermined every day because their relationships with local people, including Christians, are not intimate but merely professional. Yet this subject is seldom talked about.

Serious damage is done to the spread of the gospel when its conveyors are themselves in bondage to belongings. In the missionary enterprise, we spend a great deal of money sending new personnel to language schools where, we hope, they will become bilingual. We generally expose them to a good amount of information about becoming bicultural and adapting to the ways of local people. But we offer very little material that addresses forthrightly the danger of excessive attachment to possessions and a lifestyle that prevents missionaries from developing close relationships with local people.

Do we avoid this issue because we know how deeply attached Westerners are to material advantages and so fear scaring off new missionaries and hampering recruitment? In developing our urban strategies and selecting target populations within the city, are we turned in the direction of the upper class because we fear that we might have to lay aside our affluent lifestyle if we sought to bond with poorer people?

## Question 2: Is Western Affluence a Deterrent to Urban Evangelization?

In his 1991 book, *Missions and Money: Affluence as a Western Missionary Problem*, Jonathan J. Bonk, professor of missions at Winnipeg Bible College and Seminary, offers a disturbing critique of Western missions. He carefully lays out the pros and cons of money and its role in missionary life and activity. He examines the historic and contemporary contexts of what he calls missionary affluence, and he honestly analyzes the main arguments in defense of missionaries living in relative wealth compared to the people around them. Most of the arguments defending material discrepancies stem from an earlier era when mission work was largely in rural areas.

Bonk examines the consequences of the disparate living standards of Western missionaries and nationals. In exchange for the comforts and securities they enjoy, missionaries sacrifice effectiveness and credibility, Bonk claims. While they purport to represent a Lord who became poor for our sakes, they project the image of persons who love worldly possessions a great deal. "Failure to counter wealth's insidious effects upon its missionary endeavors will ensure the continued ebb of the Western churches as a Kingdom force," Bonk argues.[3]

The relative wealth of the Western missionary, Bonk points out, almost inevitably affects interpersonal relationships in a number of ways, each antithetical to all that Christ modeled for his followers. To begin with, the living standards most Western missionaries maintain insulate them from the harsh realities experienced by the people to whom they minister. While making life more bearable for the missionaries, this severely limits their ability to understand and communicate with people who don't enjoy the same privileges.

Furthermore, relative affluence isolates missionaries socially. Such isolation can be seen in its grossest form in mission compounds and protected residential areas nestled in the city. These are places protected by walls and fences, armed guards, and surveillance systems. In one Asian city that I visited, a sprawling interdenominational missionary compound occupies several city blocks with a wall around it so high that from the outside you can see only the roofs of the large, American-style houses.

Since biblical faith is a relational faith, it is not only sad but sinful, says Bonk, when protecting personal possessions and privileges prevents, distorts, or destroys close relationships between missionaries and the common people. But this is almost inevitably the price of affluence.

Bonk writes about the wide and painful social gulf between missionaries and nationals, a gulf put in place and maintained by their differing economic levels. Along with economic advantage inevitably comes the illusion of superiority. We may say we're equal, but who drives the car? Then there is the mistrust that eventually develops between many national church leaders and missionaries due to economic disparity. Whereas missionaries may regard themselves as making sacrifices, and compared to the lifestyle of their friends and relatives back home they are, in the eyes of national workers the missionaries are enormously wealthy, and every time they come back from furlough the number and quality of their possessions seems to increase.

Wealth brings isolation, Bonk reminds us. It breaks down communication, trust, and relationships. Western missionaries pay a staggeringly high price for their relative comfort, security, and possessions. In communicating the gospel, both medium and message are significantly affected by the relationship of the missionary to the convert or would-be convert. If world evangelization consisted merely of announcing a series of theologically correct statements, we could get the whole job done quickly and easily. "But the Word must always be made flesh, and dwell among men. And the Way has always been shown by those who can be accompanied by would-be pilgrims. A missionary is above all a Way-shower . . . whose life must be imitable by his converts. The missionary is not simply a voice box, but a pilgrim who invites others to join him on the narrow way."[4]

Schools that train missionaries generally miss the main point of disciple making. "Contrary to the emphases embedded in most North American mission curriculums," says Bonk, "not communication theory, but communicator living, is the key to incarnational communication."[5] Tragically, however, this is a subject that training courses hardly touch on, and social and economic differences between missionaries and nationals continue to wreak havoc on urban ministries.

When gospel communication and, hence, disciple making are seriously hindered because of the economic disparity between speakers and hearers, something is terribly wrong and must be addressed. Bonk concludes that the strategic costs of missionary affluence are so high that the entire missionary enterprise is in jeopardy. He calls for new directions at the following levels:

a. Individual missionaries should voluntarily follow a simpler lifestyle, defining needs not by Western standards but by local conditions.

b. Missionary families where children are raised at home should inculcate in their children an appreciation for kingdom values and a lifestyle built on those values. Where missionary children are regularly exposed at school to Western materialism and its values, parents need to do everything possible to help them avoid adopting the attitudes and standards of the rich and privileged.

c. Mission agencies should provide a milieu in which member missionaries who voluntarily choose to lower their standard of living overseas are given understanding, encouragement, and protection from the criticism of others within the organization.

d. Training institutions and sending churches should consider the "crucified mind" strategy, so repugnant to the Western, materialistic outlook, in matters of personal and institutional lifestyle, because "only a community of believers who themselves have chosen to reject the materialist spirit of the age can stir its members to pursue genuine self-sacrifice abroad."[6]

The issue Bonk raises has direct bearing on urban ministry, because nearly half of the population in the world's largest cities is poor, or near-poor, and in many instances they are also more receptive to the gospel than ever before. If by adopting a simpler lifestyle urban workers can become more effective disciple makers, the issue is clear even though it will not be easy. The problems related to Western missionary affluence are as difficult as they are undeniable. But if we are serious about discipling cities, we must try our best to resolve them.

## Question 3: Is There a Cheaper Way to Disciple Cities?

While the previous questions had to do with the *effectiveness* of Western missionaries, the third question addresses their relative *efficiency*. By *efficiency* I mean the financial cost of achieving intended results. The most efficient mission strategy is the one that achieves what you want at the lowest cost. When we consider, on the one hand, the billions of urbanites who need to be evangelized and discipled, and, on the other hand, the limitations of Western missionary resources, we recognize efficiency as an extremely important matter.

Is it good stewardship to continue sending thousands of high-cost Western missionaries when national missionaries coming from the Two-Thirds World can be supported on much less money and achieve the same or better results? If in the past mission professors and agency executives have avoided that question, we had better start examining it now, because younger church members are looking into it. They are aware of the growth of mission sending agencies in the Two-Thirds World, and some are already shifting their support to such agencies as a matter of responsible stewardship.

My wife and I are loyal supporters of Western missionary organizations, and we foresee a continuing role for such agencies far into the twenty-first century. But the vastness of the urban challenge and a realistic assessment of both costs and resources make us realize that a great deal of the work of discipling the world's great cities is going to be done not by Western-based agencies but by the new, emerging Third-World missions that operate at a much lower cost.

An insight based on my family's situation and experience can clarify the point. My wife and I have two daughters serving with their husbands in foreign countries. One is married to a North American, and together they have served for ten years in Santo Domingo, capital of the Dominican Republic, under our denominational mission agency. Their support package is in excess of $35,000 annually. The other is married to a Latin American, a man who by virtue of his gifts, training, and high level of commitment has become an effective evangelist and church planter with a Pentecostal denomination in Mexico. He is currently developing a new church, the third he has started in the past twelve years, in Ciudad Juarez. During most of his ministry he has supported his family and borne a share of the cost of his ministry by working forty hours per week as a technician in various factories.

I regard both of my sons-in-law as effective missionaries. But I also recognize the enormous difference between them in the economic support they require from their sending churches. When I reflect on the thousands and thousands of evangelists, pastors, and other Christian workers needed in this rapidly urbanizing world, and when I consider what it would cost if all of them had to be supported at $35,000 per year, it becomes very clear that the number of "tentmaking" missionaries must be greatly increased.

K. P. Yohannan raises some disturbing questions regarding the efficiency of traditional Western missionaries in his book *Why the World Waits: Exposing the Reality of Modern Missions.* President and founder of the Indian mission organization Gospel for Asia, Yohannan has written and published over forty books in India. He is best known in North America for *The Coming Revolution in World Missions.*[7]

Yohannan argues that if we are sincere about our professed intention to evangelize the world, then "mission leaders and sending churches must start asking the tough questions about their financial stewardship." For example:

How much did it cost to present the gospel to each hearer last year as a mission overall, as a field, as an individual missionary?

How much would it have cost to support a native missionary to do the same evangelistic work? Would it be more efficient and effective for us to support native missionaries?

How much was the average cost to start up a new church last year as a mission overall, as a field, as an individual missionary?

How much would it have cost to support a native missionary to do the same church-planting work?

In your mission program, how are both foreign and native missionaries accountable for the funds entrusted to them? Are results measured in terms of return on investment, or does financial accountability end with only a financial audit in the U.S. offices?

What about conference attendance, missionary consultations, and other strategy sessions? How does your mission program attach numbers and measure results from these meetings in terms of converts, new churches planted, and missions launched to unreached people groups? Are we getting benefit out of these meetings equal to their cost?

As we look toward (the unfinished task) . . . how much is it going to cost using Western personnel and methods? How much is it going to cost using indigenous personnel and methods?[8]

Yohannan acknowledges that not all fields are alike. Some ministries are more expensive than others. Start-up costs may be higher in large cities than in rural areas. But there is no excuse for ignoring stewardship questions, and when it comes to missionary personnel, one of the burning questions in this decade will be whether mission agencies should continue sending mostly Western personnel or consider alternatives in light of the gigantic challenges of world evangelization. As Two-Thirds World mission agencies grow in number and strength, I think it is clear where the pressures for change will come from. The more Western missions train and equip Third-World Christians for ministries in the city, the greater will be the urban harvest in the decades ahead.

## A Dilemma for Western Evangelical Missionaries

Western evangelical missionaries face a serious dilemma rooted in our culture's pervasive materialism. The worst aspect of this dilemma is the refusal by some of us to admit that a problem exists. Western society in recent years has been swept from one end to the other by the spirit of practical materialism, often called consumerism. Not only the world at large, outside the church, demonstrates an intense infatuation with possessions, comforts, and entertainment, but also the evangelical community—the support base of our missionary endeavor—reflects many of our culture's materialistic values. By and large we want the best we can get for ourselves and our children.

We talk and write about discipleship, but the dimensions of discipleship that mean substantially downgrading our lifestyle are seldom mentioned, not even for the sake of mission. Our lifestyles are close reflections of the culture around us, and we defend our practical materialism so carefully that few evangelical leaders dare challenge it head on. Most leaders long ago resigned themselves to popular demands and expectations. In scores of ways, our churches, schools, and mission organizations have accommodated to the values, standards, lifestyles, and, consequently, budgets that people living in a materialistic society cherish and expect.

The high living standards enjoyed by a large share of the evangelical community in North America have from childhood taught most missionaries we recruit and send out to take for granted a very high level of physical comfort and an array of gadgets designed both to entertain and to make life easier. To be deprived of even some of these is regarded as entailing great sacrifice.

Here enters a temptation that has a peculiarly urban twist. Third-World cities offer all the comforts and accommodations found in Western society if one has the money to pay for them, and there exists in every city a small portion of the population that can afford to enjoy a Western lifestyle. The temptation for missionaries is to identify with that small fraction of the population. It begins by locating the missionary residence where the familiar comforts can be enjoyed and where the neighbors share the Westerner's materialistic values. It proceeds by developing a ministry strategy that protects an affluent lifestyle.

When missionaries yield to this temptation, two things happen: their support becomes very expensive, raising legitimate questions regarding efficiency and stewardship; and their ability to disciple people from large and receptive portions of the city population is drastically diminished.

Even if financial support were not the problem that in many cases it currently is, and Western missionaries could raise their support with ease, the question would still arise: what unspoken messages do the Western values translated into missionary lifestyles convey? Or, to put it personally and concretely: What message did our eighteen barrels and two large crates communicate to our Buddhist and Hindu neighbors? Did that message contribute to the fact that in the years that followed none of our converts came from our immediate neighborhood, but all from some distance away?

We needed time, my wife and I, before we became aware of it, but gradually the truth dawned on us. When on the one hand you adopt the consumerism of Western society, and on the other hand you meet the challenge and requirements of world evangelization, you see the clash of two opposing value systems and the worldviews behind them. You must choose one or the other. Try as you may, you cannot have both. Each conveys its own message, and the messages are worlds apart.

When Jesus said to the crowd, "Watch out! Be on your guard against all kinds of greed; a man's life does not consist in the abundance of his possessions" (Luke 12:15), he issued a warning and addressed a basic question: What should be our relationship to material possessions? Jesus said that material possessions should never become major concerns for his disciples. When Christian people whose basic needs have been met continue to accumulate possessions and add to their physical comforts and pleasures in sight of people who are suffering and in need, they are making a statement. They are communicating a message about their values, their priorities, and the deep affections of their hearts. And that message contradicts the gospel.

Whether they are rich, middle-class, or poor, materialistic people always operate on the principle that whatever you can afford or legally get your hands on, you have the right to keep and enjoy. Materialists who have a veneer of religion may put it this way: "If God makes it possible for me to get something, clearly he approves my acquiring it and enjoying it." Sheer secularists with no religious pretensions simply argue: "This world is the only world we're sure there is, so let's enjoy all we can." The materialist's philosophy of life is summed up in the bumper sticker, "He who dies with the most toys wins."

One day Jesus was confronted by a man of great wealth who was torn between a desire to inherit eternal life and an ingrained affection for his wealth. The man was saddened by Jesus' demand that he give his wealth to the poor. Then Jesus made this telling statement: "How hard it is for the rich to enter the kingdom of God!" (Luke 18:25).

Why was Jesus disturbed over wealth and so skeptical about the spiritual chances of those who possess it? Because, you see, Jesus understood the *idolatry of possessions*. He was addressing an evil that cuts to the very core of religion, to our souls and to our very being. Whom do we really serve, God or material possessions? Where is our citizenship—the allegiance of our hearts—in this world, or in the next? Do we genuinely believe in the resurrection and the life to come, or do we hedge our bets by talking about the resurrection while pursuing as much of this world as we possibly can?

An illuminating story is told about Samuel Zwemer, the "apostle to Islam" in the first half of this century. On furlough, Zwemer was attending a reunion of his college classmates on the beautiful estate that one of them owned, overlooking Lake Michigan. An old friend said to Zwemer, "Do you realize what you're missing by spending your life out there in the Middle East?" "Yes, I think I do," replied Zwemer. Then gesturing toward the beautiful estate, he said: "I too would enjoy having a place like this. But there is another world!"

Zwemer put his finger right on it: the fundamental transforming truth of the resurrection. It ought to be for Christians much more than merely a statement of doctrine. The resurrection is the value-shaping, direction-setting truth of the gospel upon which the whole witness of Jesus Christ rests. Jesus arose, and because he arose we who believe in him are made children of God and heirs of eternal life.

This is the gospel that missionaries dedicate their lives and labors to announce. This truth alone gives sense and purpose to urban mission and discipleship. Our worldview is fundamentally changed because we accept the reality of the world to come, and this change should be visibly demonstrated in our values and behavior.

## What Message Does Our Lifestyle Convey?

I want to conclude by getting back to a theme that I introduced earlier: the message our lifestyle conveys.

How do Western evangelicals explain why we need to live in fine houses, in many cases houses that only the upper 5 or 10 percent of an overseas population can afford? How do we explain the difference between the lifestyle of Jesus and the apostles, and the lifestyle we maintain and protect when we go overseas to obey Christ's commission? When it is shown to us that an affluent lifestyle probably hinders the effectiveness of our work, why do we feel incensed, as though some brute had stepped on our toes, and rush to defend our right to possessions, comforts, and security?

In view of Scripture's severe condemnation of greed in every form, do we not perceive the dissonance between the affluent lifestyles many of us maintain—at home and on the mission field—and the message of Jesus, who for our sakes became poor and ministered most among the common people of his day? The largest unevangelized segment of the world's population today is people just like those with whom Jesus spent most of his time, the "little people," the common folk, villagers and urban poor. Most people in the cities of the world cannot afford the material conveniences or benefits of the West. Yet by the possessions with which we surround ourselves and by our lifestyles, we distance ourselves from them. In some instances, in my case by the eighteen barrels and two big crates, we provoke them to greed and envy.

Has the demon of materialism taken tight hold of us? What will it require to set us free? Maybe the bicentennial of the commencement of the modern missionary movement from the West will motivate us to read again the personal accounts of men like Carey, Judson, and Taylor, and of women like Amy Carmichael, who spent most of her life in India rescuing and discipling girls destined for temple prostitution. In *Gold Cord*, there is a short poem that every Western Christian, especially missionaries and prospective missionaries, should read and ponder:

> Hast thou no scar?
> No hidden scar on foot, or side, or hand?
> I hear thee sung as mighty in the land,
> I hear them hail thy bright ascendant star,
> Hast thou no scar?
>
> Hast thou no wound?
> Yet I was wounded by the archers, spent,

Leaned me against a tree to die; and rent
By ravening beasts that compassed me, I swooned:
Hast thou no wound?

No wound? no scar?
Yet, as the Master shall the servant be,
And pierced are the feet that follow Me;
But thine are whole: can he have followed far
Who has nor wound nor scar?[9]

There is a price to pay for disciple making in the city. Wounds and scars as well as joy await the workers, just as they did our Master and every fruitful disciple maker since him.

## Discussion Questions

1. Explain why missionaries should limit the amount of things they take with them to another country.
2. If mission agencies push the idea that missionaries should downscale their lifestyle so as to bond with the common people, what repercussions are likely to occur?
3. Why was Jesus so disturbed about wealth and the chances of the rich entering heaven? How does this apply to a society where a high percentage of professing Christians is comparatively wealthy?
4. If the major responsibility for discipling Third-World cities were turned over to Third-World mission agencies and the number of Western missionaries were to decrease, what effects do you think it would have on Western churches, Third-World Christians, and the advance of the gospel worldwide?
5. Bonk maintains that missionaries above all are "Way-showers" and that their lives must be "imitable" by their converts. Explain how this is essential to effective disciple making. How did Jesus and the apostle Paul apply this principle in their ministries?

Material contained in this chapter first appeared in "Eighteen Barrels and Two Big Crates," *Evangelical Missions Quarterly* (April 1992).

# 17

# THEOLOGICAL EDUCATION FOR URBAN MISSION

*Sidney H. Rooy*

Why should we concern ourselves with theological education for urban mission? Seminaries have always produced ministers who could enter many fields of specialization—pastorates either in rural villages or in cities; home missions; inner-city missions; foreign missions as evangelists or teachers; chaplaincies in hospitals or the armed forces; teaching in elementary or higher education; ministries in literature distribution, radio, or television. But traditional theological education has leaned toward mass-market approaches. Therefore its theological premise needs serious re-evaluation.

To describe the theological education needed for urban mission, a preliminary analysis must be made of what *urban mission* means. There are nearly as many theories of right, biblical, and sane methodologies and goals as there are evangelical urbanologists. This chapter considers briefly the theology of the city that determines the approach to theological education for urban mission. Part 1 presents the definition and objectives of urban mission, part 2 the theological premises that determine the content and method of preparation for urban mission, and part 3 some models for theological education. These models are not definitive, however, and quality of theological education must be determined by faithfulness to biblical and other historical guidelines.

# Definition and Objectives of Urban Mission

Urban has to do with cities, especially where growing concentrations of population are found. *Civitas* comes from *co-ire*, which means "live together." Living together can be understood in spacial, statistical, and quantitative terms, but that hardly does justice to the concept. It points rather to a sociological and qualitative relationship. Lewis Mumford gathers this quality into his definition of the city as "the point of greatest concentration of power and culture of an entire community; it is the form and symbol of an integrated social relationship."[1]

In describing man as an "animal of the city," Aristotle correctly implied that man is a social creature and that, in more than one sense, it "was not good for [him] to be alone." Man has his social relationships in various contexts. For many millennia, the human community was relatively small, familial, tribal, and based on strong personal relationships and traditions. But as man shifts from rural to urban areas, qualitative changes in his way of living occur. As some contemporary sociologists have pointed out, secondary relationships become dominant (business done through agencies and offices rather than directly); mores and customs become relativized; new groups based on special interests form; work becomes mechanized and specialized, often with little possibility of creativity; family and larger group ties are broken; and life patterns accent individual initiative and action. The severity of the adjustment is confirmed by the unending list of social and psychological problems: anonymity and solitude, anxiety, social and economic segregation in ghettos, contamination and noise, technocracy and manipulation, rootlessness and insecurity, corruption and deterioration.[2]

These evils, however, do not imply that the city is inherently worse than the country or altogether void of benefits.[3] First, egotism, passion, pride, miserliness, and hate find their outlets no matter where the stage of human action is set. Second, the city has its own values and rewards. The city offers broad human companionship, opportunities for stimulating interchange of opinions, the expression and exercise of diverse artistic and human interest, and the enjoyment of human liberty without restrictive local mores.[4]

The gradual trend from rural to urban living is not simply a geographical, quantitative matter. It is also a social, qualitative trend. Man was made a social, communicative creature. In this sense, the city—where man "lives together"—is part of his essence. And the trend continues. Whereas in 1970 one-third of the world's population lived in cities, by the year 2000 two-thirds will. But we ought not to view this as necessarily evil. Living in the city forces man to face up to some easily neglected aspects of life and offers new possibilities for enrichment.

As noted, rural living is rooted in primary relationships of family, tribe, and narrowly defined social groups. Here personal and societal arrangements are made directly and are mediated through a personalized form of justice. Urban life cannot be coordinated by such structures. In larger human groupings, secondary (bureaucratic) relationships are necessary, relationships that depend on orders of justice and reach beyond the personal and direct dimensions of human love. Many people, consequently, still prefer the personal and tend to resist responsibilities on the broader levels.[5]

Obviously, cities bring a flood of challenges: growing populations, underdevelopment, racial integration, work ethics, free time, family integration, rich and poor neighborhoods, education, and community relations. What should the church do about these? Christians have responded in two contrasting ways: as little as possible, for there are more urgent questions, or as much as possible, for these *are* urgent questions! The approach chosen determines whether special theological education is needed for urban mission. That the second alternative is better, I intend to substantiate before going on to discuss theological education for urban mission.

Cain, Babel, and Babylon have prejudiced the Christian mind against cities. Ancient peoples projected their conceptions of man and the world in building their cities. They placed their temples and altars on the central and highest parts of the city. If there were no natural hill, they constructed a pyramid as the central site for religious and community rites. More than that, the pagan city claimed to be the navel of the universe. For example, Babylon means "the cornerstone of heaven and earth."[6] Through her umbilical cord flowed life and culture to the nation and the world. Furthermore, building the pagan city not only was an act of idolatry but also signified man's attitude of self-sufficiency and the exploitation of weaker tribes and peoples. Sacred cities were built by the slave labor of conquered peoples, as the history of Israel in Egypt exemplifies. Although promising liberty and opportunity, the cities only intensified the enslavement of the human spirit. Cities were erected to fulfill the great hopes of man; instead, they became huge centers of oppression.[7]

In the Old Testament, with the notable exceptions of Nineveh and Jerusalem, building cities frequently was construed as distrust of God's protection and often represented the incorporation of idol worship into Israel's national life (Hos. 8:14). Perhaps in contrast to the idolatrous life connected with the pagan temple cities, Israel was called to be a desert people. The initial destruction of the Canaanite cities, related in Joshua, was complete and merciless. When villages and towns were not destroyed, as in Judges, they frequently contributed to Israel's idolatry. Israel as a particular people, a holy nation with her sacred city (Jerusalem), stood in stark contrast against the pagan cities. Jonah's reluctance to preach to a profane city must be seen in this light. Blinded by provincialism, he lacked the prophetic vision to recognize universal light rays emanating from God's gracious promises to Israel.

The New Testament era, however, introduces a change, advancing beyond the confrontation pedagogy found in the Old Testament. Now the accented relationship between the sacred people and the secular community is dialectical. God's people are no longer a desert (separate) community, but a sent community. They are called upon to live not apart from but integrated into the city (of the world). They do not identify with the city but become a sign of the presence of God's kingdom in it. The community of believers is henceforth called the church of Jesus Christ within great cities like Corinth, Rome, Jerusalem, or Ephesus.

The New Testament church is born of Israel and surpasses her; the church fulfills Israel and excels her. The community of the Word, of the promise, and of the covenant maintains its own human identity distinct from the structures of the city. While the church is not absorbed into the city, it takes its place and realizes its function inside the structures of the city. Flight from the city, the place of heightened human encounter, is no longer allowable, unless it is to go to another city to teach all things commanded by the Lord. The church is still a stranger and a pilgrim looking for the Eternal City, the place of perfect communion with God and man. But the new Israel does not abandon the secular city. Instead, it becomes salt and light within urban life.

Humanity was and is created to celebrate its glorious diversity in unity with the Creator and itself. It is made for unity. Promoting the human community must be the purpose and calling of the city. Man was made of one blood and one family. The city multiplied human relationships. A person in the modern city may enter into more relationships in one day than a *paisano* in Bolivia during the whole of his short life. The city is a center of opportunity and responsibility, often assuming a corporate personality either as good or as bad as its citizens.

With good reason Jacques Ellul deplores the evil of the city, where the human tendency to egoism and pride concentrates: "The city is an almost indistinguishable mixture of spiritual power and man's work. . . . Only

God's decisive action is sufficient."[8] Yet, in Christ all things are gathered together: laborious inventions, technological failures, stumbling advances of history, and tentative social structures. To the extent that due to Jesus Christ the city is not satanic, it is destined to be transformed in a glorious way unknown to us. The redeemed community has work to do in the city, for the opportunity of human interrelationships is as much a gift from the Creator's hand as are the mountains and seas.

The mission of the church in the city is, after all, an intermediate one. It prepares men and nature for the final and eternal city whose builder and maker is God. It furthers "man's conscious participation in the cosmic and historic process."[9] It gives testimony to the plan of salvation in the city; it offers true community between men and between man and God; it anticipates the New Jerusalem. In God's plan, the church is indispensable for the salvation of the city. Thus the mission of the church (including the whole of the body of Christ in that city) is to comprise the people of God who belong to the city, to pervade the structures of the city so that it may repent and the rule of God in anticipatory form may be established.

Pope Paul VI aptly expressed the Christian presence and task in the city:

> To build the city, place of being of men and of their widespread communities, is to create new modes of proximity and of relationships, to perceive a new application of social justice; to face this collective future which is proclaimed difficult, is a task in which Christians ought to participate. To these people piled on top of each other in an urban promiscuity which is rendered intolerable, must be given a message of hope by means of a living brotherhood and a concrete justice.[10]

On the basis of this discussion, consider the following theses:

1. The city is the center and structure of a qualitative and integrated social relationship.
2. The city as such is neither more evil nor more holy than the country. However, the city provides an intensification of human relationships that gives opportunity for greater human sin and an enlarged Christian witness as well.
3. Because urban life depends on multiple secondary relationships, the church must emphasize political justice as the exercise of Christian love.

4. The confrontation of the sacred city (Israel, as a particular separate people in the desert and in the Promised Land) with the profane city (the pagan, secular peoples) was the divine pedagogy for Old Testament times.
5. Through the mediation of Christ, the new pedagogy is incorporation: the sacred city lives as a community within the secular city, sufficiently separate from it to keep from being syncretized by it yet sufficiently integrated into it to convert the city to the divine purpose.
6. The vocation and ministries of the Christian community serve to prepare and transform men and their field of relationships (society) for the coming of the Eternal City, which is the goal and end of history. The preparation of Christians for this task is the goal of theological education for urban mission.

## Theological Premises for Urban Mission

The first question to ask in preparing an educational program is, Education for what? There are other questions, such as: Education of whom? Where must we educate? At what level is the person to be educated? Where does he stand now? What methodology should be used? Some of the latter will be considered in the last section. Here we concentrate on the first question: What are the specific objectives in theological education for urban mission?

Let no one quarrel about words. It is God, through his Word and Spirit, who creates and transforms human hearts and dispositions to do his will. Those who say that we must only preach the gospel and God will do the transforming oversimplify the problems and do not escape the dilemma at all. The gospel truth is that we are colaborers with God. Men are active agents in history, and God holds us to a measure of responsibility for the quality of human life available to our neighbors and ourselves.

*To reach its goal of transformation, urban theological education should prepare and challenge Christians to create a spiritual-corporal community that gives body and life to the reconciliation offered by God in Jesus Christ.*

Reconciliation of men with God and with one another is the primary task of the church. A community, though claiming to be religious, cannot claim to be Christian if it does not embody reconciliation. Church divisions and sectarianism are too easily excused by appeals to correct interpretations of the truth, people's natural desire to be with their own kind, and God's providential approval. Reconciliation is claimed to be only spiritual; the separate denominations on earth will be united in heaven. It takes a good deal of rationalization to explain away John 17:18b, 21: "Even so I sent them into the world (substitute *city*) . . . that they may all be one; even as thou, Father, art in me, and I in thee, that they also may be in us: that the world (*city*) may believe that thou didst send me." The church of Christ in Corinth or Rome or Jerusalem was precisely that—the reconciled body of believers called to be saints in their city. Paul vigorously reprimanded the Corinthian church for not living up to its calling (1 Cor. 1:10–17). The visible unity was not to be invisible, for its very visibility was to motivate the world to believe.

The Western world has slowly come to take visible separation for granted. The great tragedy of disunity, however, is evidenced by the number of denominations in the Third World and the pathetic weakness of the churches in their encounter with other world religions. Out of the 5.3 billion world population, 3 billion people remain relatively untouched by the Christian faith. This shows the need for a united witness.

But educating for reconciliation has a still more painful aspect that directly affects the mission to the city. Paul was scandalized by Peter's making racial distinctions between Jews and Gentiles at the Lord's table: ". . . I opposed him to his face, because he stood condemned" (Gal. 2:11). And again, when the rich ate at a full table and the poor nibbled crusts, Paul was astonished at their lack of sharing. "What!" he asks, "Do you despise the church of God and humiliate those who have nothing?" (1 Cor. 11:22). The gift of reconciliation received in Christ signified and sealed a sacred reality: there is no more Jew nor Greek, male nor female, bond nor free, rich nor poor; all are one in Christ Jesus.

But reconciliation is not a reality in most churches. Though there is a theoretical openness to the rich and the poor, few of either find their way into the church. Mainline churches in Western nations have stuck solidly with the middle class: economically, socially, and culturally. Particularly is this true in their rejection of the great mass of the laboring class, the so-called blue-collar workers largely from the inner city. Protestant church growth in the United States closely parallels the growth of the middle class. Gibson Winter maintains that if these churches had been open to the changing constituency of their neighborhoods, they would now be double their size. He points out two characteristics of the central cities: they tend to be areas of residence for the lower classes; and they tend to be heterogeneous in social composition.[11] Both violate the "life principle" of the major denominations: effectively incorporating middle-class people and keeping heterogeneous classes apart. "Fellowship by likeness" and "mission by friendly contact" form the "iron cage of American denominational religion."[12]

This analysis is confirmed by Larry Krause, although he accepts the status quo mentality as inevitable, whereas Winter strenuously objects to it. Krause emphasizes two lessons that the "successful" congregation must learn:

> The first lesson is that, because the identity of individuals is socially and culturally fashioned, most persons will not voluntarily join a religious fellowship unless that fellowship affirms their personal and social identity. The second lesson is that most people join a congregation *primarily* to have their own personal needs met; and unless their needs are met, they are not likely to commit themselves to serving others.[13]

Krause goes on to say that, although theology defines the church as a prophetic community, experience teaches that it will never be such. Although theology teaches that the church is a brotherhood that overcomes all socio-cultural barriers, experience teaches that it will never be an agency for social change and that few of its members will transcend their provincial identity. He concludes that the local church should basically limit its activity to its own congregation and social, cultural, or economic level.[14]

No doubt the analyses by these men reflect reality. But this does not excuse the church. The church, like Israel of old, has returned to the desert, the ghetto. It has retreated into enclaves of exclusive membership, it presents an arrested form of the body of Christ to the world, and it denies by its life the reconciliation it preaches.

Theological education for urban mission is of little value and can expect little blessing unless it is based on the solid rock of God's reconciliation with man and his demand that man be reconciled with his brother. Because of the complexity of our present church structures, historical traditions, and doctrinal loyalties, it is difficult to prescribe the type of theological education needed in urban mission. Recent studies of the Roman Catholic Church in Argentina show that only 2 percent of the laboring class (which is about 70 percent of the population) in the urban centers is related to the church in a meaningful way, and that most of these are women. Though not as drastic, similar trends are characteristic of urban sectors generally. What this means for theological education will be discussed in the last part of this chapter.

*To fulfill its goal of reconciliation, urban theological education should prepare Christians to carry out a shared ministry that incorporates members according to their gifts into the preaching, conversion, and healing service, both within the local spiritual fellowship and in the broader community of which it is a part.*

The church organization too frequently gets in the way of itself, and church ministries tend to be directed inwardly. The weekly bulletin of many average middle-class churches may carry thirty to thirty-five announcements, with one or two referring to the broader ministry in the secular community. (It would be a good exercise for the reader to evaluate the last ten bulletins of a local church.) Though the whole church basically is a servant community that ministers salvation in God's name to a broken and dying world, its efforts are largely dedicated to itself. Undoubtedly the temptation will remain with us to create new Abrahamic communities, earthly Jerusalems, and social-spiritual enclaves.

The early church reveals a broad use of spiritual gifts. Paul's lists in Romans 12 and 1 Corinthians 12 are indicative. By the second century, the church of Christ in Rome was caring for fifteen hundred poor people. Pagan philosophers like Celsus were lamenting that his fellows did not concern themselves with the lower classes as did the Christians. The Middle Ages were a disaster in many ways, especially during the so-called Dark Ages. It was the church, however, that kept education, care for the poor and sick, general culture, and social organization alive. We may not always appreciate how it did it, but the invaluable character of its work and testimony cannot be denied.

Most of this work was done by special religious communities and generally not encouraged by the regular priests, for the "laity" was severely depreciated in those centuries. Lewis Mumford points out that the medieval cities anticipated the problems of modern urbanism, especially in reference to social and physical conditions. From the Renaissance onward, cities often became disorganized conglomerates perpetuating misery and filth.[15]

But the cities of the Renaissance made a positive contribution in bringing to reality one dimension of human character that had always been held cheap—human liberty. People were free to do as they pleased (in the Occidental world, at least), and many did just that. But in spite of these excesses, people came to the cities. For the first time, according to Max Weber, a man was treated on the basis not of family lines or social class but of his participation in the city. By joining one or more of the city's various associations, he became a part of it. The city retained its magnetic power.

According to José Comblin, the Calvinistic churches renewed the ideal of the early Christian community. They rejected the monastic model in favor of a community-life experience among the members of the church.[16]

This emphasis continues today in the Presbyterian and Reformed traditions, as well as in the Methodist and the so-called free churches. The modern emphasis stresses small community groups with more specific but limited functions of worship and service. The danger remains that the cellular groups tend to become exclusive, autonomous, self-perverting, and self-destroying. As such, they simply mark a return to the medieval monastic pattern that, because of the disintegrating forces of modern society, has even less relevance and purpose today than it had in the past.

The community pattern of the church has significance in the divine pedagogy only when its members actively enter the fabric of urban life. The new Israel fights battles with the "Philistines" and often endures the bitter suffering of exile right within the spiritual wastelands of industrial society. That is her calling, to pass through the earthly city. She cannot know the Eternal City without entering the corporeality of this one and taking its burning needs into her bosom. The parable of the sheep and goats (Matt. 25) makes this clear.

God's way of teaching is long and arduous at times. But the Word does not return void. It accomplishes the divine purpose. It was a long journey from the early church's small groups, to the medieval specialized religious communities, and on to the Reformation's insistence that every member partake of the spiritual ministry. The basic question that confronts the church today is: What is the pedagogical significance of urbanization for the Christian mission? The answer is, More than a constant mending and patching of old structures! Rather, Christians must confess that God is leading through this new reality as a significant step forward in the fulfillment of his promise of the Eternal City. The urban incorporation of men into closer and tighter societal patterns of interdependence may be God's way of bringing mankind to break once and for all its Cain-like egomania. Man was made to be his brother's keeper.

Urban theological education must take the present stage of divine pedagogy into account. It must prepare Christians to minister meaningfully within the structures and challenges of complex urban centers.

*To fulfill its goal of a relevant ministry, urban theological education must prepare Christians for the painful process of re-evaluating their life and ministry in the light of their immediate and broader context. For this task a serious study of the social, economic, and anthropological sciences in interrelation with theology is imperative.*

Padre Seumois, counselor of the Congregation for the Propagation of the Faith, suggests three characteristics of evangelization (*kerygma*): communicate only the essentials of the Christian message, communicate it as good news, and do not add anything more except at a rate that permits the essential to maintain itself.[17]

What is essential? Many would respond with John 3:16, the Apostles' Creed, or a summary of the catechism. For the early church the summary of the faith was "Jesus is Lord." But that statement had political and social, as well as spiritual, overtones. It meant Jesus had priority over Caesar, and that was what the Roman persecution was all about. It meant Jesus was the same Lord for the various social classes, which explains Paul's anger in 1 Corinthians 11 and Galatians 3. It meant that a new lifestyle appropriate to new situations had to be developed.

That confession remains essential today. But what does it mean concretely in today's political situation in which some men give lip service to Jesus as Lord? What does it mean in churches where Christians have turned their backs on inner-city problems? What does it mean when traditional organizational, liturgical, and ethical church patterns are repeated rigidly in new situations?

What really is good news for the abandoned mother who does not know where to get food or medicine for her children? What is the gospel for those who are illiterate or victims of malnutrition? What is our answer? Suppose we begin by saying: "God raised Jesus from the dead." That is true, but it does not respond to immediate needs. One could add twenty statements of Christian doctrine, but that is not the first step. Rather, we begin by listening and then responding to the need that is real and urgent to that person at that moment. We say to the woman, "God knows you love your children; that love is terribly important. In Jesus no real love is lost." She may respond, "And how is that possible?" or, "But how can I show my love when I can't even feed my child?" At that moment the way is open to a tangible expression of what God's love means for her in that concrete situation.

In a rural context, problems can often be worked out on a personal level. However, in an urban context, where whole levels of the population are affected, the situation becomes unbelievably complex. Ministering adequately in Christ's name to urban populations requires the aid of the various social sciences. It is the duty of the community of Christians to minister effectively to the causes of human suffering and human alienation.

The Christian's task is to represent Christ in the heart of the city.[18] This requires especially the use of all God's people with their diverse specialties of work and gifts. These include anthropology, sociology, psychology, economics, urban planning, demography, medicine, law, education, and many more. That does not mean that the organized church is responsible for training in such professions. Rather it means that Christians in these professions have a sacred calling to exercise their gifts in the battle to solve inner-city problems (a calling that is as holy and sacred as that of the missionary, evangelist, or pastor), and that the church has a clear duty to prepare Christians for a prophetic, diaconal, and community ministry in the secular city. This last point means that the church will prepare its members by preaching and teaching the heart and spirit of the gospel, by providing necessary resources for human needs (indicating where needed help is available in the broader community), and by living a true model of community with all the Christians of its neighborhood in a lively interaction with the structures of the city.

These considerations demonstrate that theological education cannot be limited to the professional clergy. Ministry is the task given to the whole church to bring the gospel to bear on all of human life. No discipline or profession remains outside its scope. For that reason the common distinction between Christian education and theological education implies a dichotomy between the laity and the clergy that is unacceptable in biblical theology. Theological education is certainly Christian (though it may be sub-Christian in both method and content), just as Christian education is theological (though it is sometimes moralistic and lacking in theological roots).

The confusion is compounded in certain areas. For example, where full-time pastors are an economic impossibility, as is frequently the case in inner-city missions, laymen can fulfill the functions of administration, preaching, pastoring, evangelizing, giving diaconal help, and administering sacraments. This creates a church-order problem for the historic churches, and as a result the problem is often resolved by abandoning the area. But if the church decides to stay, all the functions of church life fall on the shoulders of the regular members. In such cases, theological training is urgently needed by laymen who under "normal" circumstances would not be pressed into so wide a variety of ministries.

Even if a full-time pastor is present, the full concept of ministry means the capacitation of the members not in abstract concepts but in terms of theological education for mission. Many missionaries fail in the inner city because of their ignorance of sociological, economic, and cultural factors, and Christian laymen are uniquely equipped to cope with these factors.

Other examples of the dichotomy between Christian and theological education could be given, such as areas where education by extension is consequently considered to be of lower caliber, or where there is on-the-job training without formal seminary theological education.

The point is that urban theological education is a learning process for Christians individually and as a community in interaction with the different disciplines. Multiple-ministry orientation and the freedom to adapt to changing situations are essential in preparing for urban mission.

*To fulfill its goal of critical theological education in interdisciplinary self-examination, urban theological education should prepare men and women to define and put into action programs of love and justice on local, national, and world levels.*

In past years, the church too often has expected a promising ministerial candidate to assume total leadership in the Christian community after training in a seminary isolated from the harsh realities of modern society. Few questioned how much the medieval monastic model was cross-bred with modern specialized professional attitudes to somehow produce the orchestra-director leader immediately capable of teaching, pastoring, and administering any variety of congregation—small or large, rural or urban. Few realized that this approach was unrelated to the apprenticeship models of the Bible or to the disciple-oriented models of the early church.

Two aspects ought to be underlined: the need for understanding theology contextually and the necessity of doing theology (to borrow a phrase from José Míguez-Bonino).[19]

Theological education must be contextual. The church and its ministry are not defined on a different level from the world. Although the church is called out of the world, it is not to be abstracted from it. The world is not to be considered the enemy of the church, as it is in certain ascetic and pietistic circles. The church and the world do not form separate spheres of the Spirit's working for the progress of the kingdom. Rather, the world is the sphere of the church. Enemy powers do indeed occupy the world, but the church is called to transform the world. Viewed this way, "worldliness" is a necessary condition for an authentic relationship between man and nature, between man and man, and between man and God. Gustavo Gutiérrez uses *worldliness* in the sense of being meaningfully related to the earth and to history. He goes on to comment that rather than defining the world in relation to the religious phenomenon, "religion should be defined in relation to the profane."[20] God is active in the world and its history in a redeeming and restoring way. The Bible describes God's words and actions in concrete human situations.

Theologies are formed in specific contexts. Innate differences between Occidental and Oriental Christianity come not from different rational and intellectual conclusions drawn from the Bible but from the different contexts in which they developed. The contrasts between Negro spirituals and Welsh hymns stem largely from social and cultural factors. The contrasts between Pentecostal and Reformed or Anglican forms of worship depend on factors other than different modes of exegesis. Theological expression reflects its contextual roots.

This leads to the second aspect, the necessity of doing theology. Theologians must "faithfully translate the meaning of biblical faith into the language of a particular age and particular people."[21] This task requires far more than formulating intellectual propositions. It also requires interpreting the church's obedience to the gospel in concrete human realities.

New insights come most often on the cutting edge of the church's encounter with the world. For example, the lack of a genuine indigenous theology in the Third World has been due partly to the church-versus-world concept imported from the West. Where no genuine church-world interaction takes place, no real theology is born.

What does this mean for theological education? A theology for urban mission, and consequently theological education for urban mission, will be relevant to the extent that the church relates fully to the life of the world society. That is to say, orthopraxis (correct practice) is the sine qua non for orthodoxy (correct theological reflection). Both are born of biblical revelation and human existence. Neither correct life nor correct doctrine is possible without experiential knowing. Doing theology, in the sense in which Míguez-Bonino uses it, and doing the truth, in John's sense (John 3:21; 1 John 1:6), amount to the same thing: he who does not love his brother whom he has seen cannot love God whom he has not seen. Theological education for urban mission must equip Christians to make their faith a lived-out reality. This requires an education that is contextually aware and a theology of the city that moves beyond pietistic retreat. When Christians enter into a responsible relation with their fellow city dwellers, show what it means to be obedient disciples of Christ, and give a living testimony of faith in him, urban mission will take on new relevance.

## Models and Organization of Training for Urban Mission

The disparate situations in which urban missions must function complicate the search for concrete models. As Juan Luis Segundo illustrates this, a person in the Third World moving from an Indian village to the big city makes in five days a journey through history of five thousand years, comparable to bridging culturally the Egypt of the Pharaohs and a twentieth-century neighborhood of New York City.[22] In the northern Atlantic region another situation exists. For example, Musselman estimates that 100 million North Americans are unchurched, the great majority in the city. He judges that one of the great problems of the churches is their fostering a "temple religion in a tabernacle time."[23] Enormous sums are invested in suburban buildings, as though they were being built for eternity. The lesson of the downtown churches is forgotten, for within a few decades the middle class will be on the move again and the same problem will have to be faced. The "suburban advance" of the churches is as much a retreat and withdrawal—not for strategic and tactical reasons, but permanently— from areas once claimed by the love of Christ. As Hoekendijk sums it up:

> The English statesman Disraeli keenly perceived the situation when among the one population he distinguished "two nations," which stood alongside each other and opposed to each other. On the one hand the "respectables," grouped around throne and altar, and on the other hand, the "poor" (it was thought that there was every reason to designate them immediately as the "irreligious poor"), held together in the magic realm of the factory. When a bishop uttered the suspicion that "the church would probably lose the city," Disraeli at once put the matter straight: "Don't be mistaken, my Lord, the church has nothing to lose, for she has never had the city."[24]

The question now is how to prepare a leader who can stem the tide of this retreat. Many groups have faced this problem before. Serious efforts were begun in Europe during the nineteenth century as the age of industrialization dawned. City missions began in Glasgow (1826), London (1835), Hamburg (1848), and Berlin (1858). In 1885, thirty-nine city missions were present in Europe, and in 1899, seventy-one. Leaders were people like William and Catherine Booth, J. H. Wickern, Rev. Couveé, Dwight L. Moody, and Ira Sankey.[25]

In recent times many Christian groups have been studying the problems of urban missions and experimenting with pilot projects. The National Council of Churches, the Division of Urban-Industrial Church World of the Episcopal Church, and Urban Church Planning of the National Lutheran Council are just a few. Most denominations are studying the problem and doing experimental work. Also, specialized independent projects have

claimed public attention, like the Detroit Industrial Mission, the East
Harlem Community Parish, the Urban Theology Unit of Sheffield, the
Centro Urbano-Nueva Parroquia-Lanús in Buenos Aires, and hundreds
more. Many theological seminaries have added special courses and seminars to alert leaders to new demands in changing city environments. They
have also set up special consultations with the use of experts and have put
into operation short- or long-term workshops. McCormick Theological
Seminary in Chicago, for example, set up two programs.[26] One was developed in cooperation with nearby universities to prepare seminary students to
meet "Church and Community" problems. Emphasis is placed particularly
on community planning and organization, social welfare, and urban renewal.
The other program stresses "Church and Industry" and provides training
in the theoretical aspects of industrialization and technological change on the
one hand, and firsthand experience in industrial situations on the other.
Two programs function on two levels: for seminarians, and for pastors,
parish workers, and social workers on an in-service training basis.

But where do we go from here? The following are some practical guidelines, offered more as food for thought than as solutions to existing problems.

*Training for multiple ministries: Who should be taught?* The sacred city
(the church) lives as a community within the secular city. The New Testament way is that of incorporation into the life and structures of the city.
Although there is a danger in adopting syncretistically the spirit of the city,
at the same time integration into the city's life is essential for effective mission. The way to enter the city is through the members of the believing
community. Forays from the outside by those who do not live in the neighborhood may serve as a catalyst to help the believers who live there but
these alone may have little abiding value.

These two premises have a number of implications for theological
education:

a. Theological training must be given to the whole church. Here it
   would be well to cite what is called the Strachan theorem: "The
   expansion of any movement is in direct proportion to its success in
   mobilizing its total membership in continuous propagation of its
   beliefs."[27] No professional does for the church what is really part of
   its life. All members participate in the corporate ministry by fulfilling
   their particular ministries.

b. Theological training should be diversified and specialized. The training must be directed to specific needs and functions of the church in

its community. The community of believers together should define the functions that correspond to their life in the city. Then they should determine what training is necessary to assist them in fulfilling these roles and design courses accordingly.

c. Theological training should develop the creative capacity of the person to relate ideas, evaluate, and draw conclusions; it should not simply transfer content about a variety of subjects. For example, a programmed study of the Gospel of Mark was completed by an adult group in Argentina. The members of the group were lifetime members of the church. Some commented that by concentrating on one book of the Bible they had learned for the first time how to study its other books.

d. Congregations and pastors must be trained to eliminate the elite, professional concept of the full-time ministry.[28] All members of the church community have a sacred function. The members of the community should assume some pastoral functions of calling, preaching, evangelizing, taking part in the liturgy, serving as president of the church board or consistory, and administrating. This relates especially to urban mission where groups are small and no full-time pastors are available. In principle, there are no biblical or historical reasons why these ministries should not be shared.

Reformed churches in Argentina nearly disappeared between 1890 and 1950 from failure to recognize the prerogative and duty of the local communities of believers. They likely would have died had it not been for one layman, A. Sonneveldt, who lacked formal theological training but nevertheless was ordained and valiantly ministered (preached, pastored, baptized, and much more) for forty-five years to a number of groups scattered over two thousand miles. As it was, several of the groups and thousands of believers disappeared from the rolls. Someone may observe that Sonneveldt was exceptional, yet history reveals that it is the man and his God-given gifts that count and not the years of theological education. Churches have many people who can fulfill one, two, or many of the ministries that Sonneveldt assumed.

The experience of Father Myers in New York City appropriately concludes this section:

> Among those who have testified in moving language to the effectiveness of thoughtful and searching theological study by congregational groups is

Father Kilmer Myers, formerly of St. Augustine's Parish on the Lower East Side of Manhattan and presently of the Chapel of the Intercession in Harlem. He has written of his work in the densely populated, lower-income neighborhood in Lower Manhattan, which has become a home for all kinds of minority groups and today includes thousands and thousands of Puerto Ricans and Negroes. Out of this and earlier experience (in Jersey City) he pleads that the Protestant church place its hope for inner-city work in something other than gimmicks, techniques, or programs. That "something other" should be, he contends, solid theological study groups conducted within the core membership (the most committed members) of the congregation, so that they should know what the doctrines they profess to believe actually mean. Once this group has grasped the true nature, purpose, and mission of the church, it can go out into the community to teach others what it has been taught, and thus become a "leaven" in the community. This leavening process includes not only person-to-person contacts but also a recognition by the church of the various power structures in the community and an exertion of the influence of the representatives of the church of Jesus Christ upon these community structures and programs.[29]

*Training for integral ministries: What should be taught?* When people migrated from the rural to the urban context, there occurred a shift from *who* they were to *what* they were. Like a machine, their value came to be estimated by how much they could produce. Who they were and what their home relations were seemed lost and forgotten.

This loss of personal worth is becoming more and more acute in the urban world. A genuine spiritual community is therefore essential for the salvation of man and his city. This is the goal of the earthly city and the final character of the Eternal City. The credibility of the gospel in the urban society depends not so much on what Christians may claim, or on the minister's office, or on sacred liturgies and sacraments, as on the quality of life, the interpersonal relations, and the service that the believing community demonstrates. Its whole ministry is dependent on and closely integrated into the lived-out reality of individual worth inherent in the gospel.

The church is called to be a prophet in the city. It is not to prepare new urban plans for cities, or to administer the funds of the city, or to conceive political programs, or to make sociological studies in the name of the city. Rather, it is to provide the divine energies of the Spirit for these tasks. It is what Bergson called the supplement of the soul that the city lacks and without which it can never live. Many beautiful projects are conceived, but envy, misuse of public funds, demagoguery, vanity, speculation, misery, and selfishness (sin goes by many names) frustrate them. Ultimately, only the power of God and the love of Christ assure progress on the road to the Eternal City.

What training will prepare the church to communicate this message, and who are called upon to proclaim it? We must train men and women to give thoughtful biblical answers to specific questions and so help people find the right answers to their own questions. We continue to alienate people and treat them as things rather than as persons when we give prescription answers to masses of individuals. Eugene Nida warns against a mass message:

> The mass message is simply a depersonalized panacea, which fails to recognize people as people and treats them largely as statistics. Such mass production of the message denies fundamental differences in people's backgrounds and problems and ends up institutionalizing faith as a popular technique for getting something from God, rather than a personal encounter with Jesus Christ and a decision to take up one's cross as a follower of the Crucified.[30]

Being a prophet of the community does not require formal theological education in the traditional sense. Indeed, such education may often become an obstacle to effective prophecy. Some theologians claim to know all the answers, considering themselves the "experts." Theologians can quote the views of Catholics, Pentecostals, liberals, and Jehovah's Witnesses, but this knowledge does not lead men to the fountain of truth—Christ. What is needed is the kind of training that will equip men and women to confess the truth of the gospel in words and experience and deep conviction.

The objective of theological training is to convert or transform the city. Although emphasis here is on the city rather than on individuals, the false conclusion should not be drawn that the meaning of conversion is reduced to a broad socializing effect. Nothing could be farther from the truth. But neither should it be concluded that conversion has nothing to do with social relationships. When Zacchaeus restored what he had wrongfully taken, Jesus said salvation had come to his house. Although what Zacchaeus did was not the reason for his salvation (rather, it was faith in Jesus), neither would his salvation have been real if his life and relationships had remained unchanged. Converting the city, like converting individuals, is a both-and affair.

In the city Christians encounter both individuals and groups. Training, therefore, must prepare members of the believing community for these encounters. These encounters are on every level of the life of the city, whether in education, social clubs, recreation, labor unions, politics, professional associations, or coffee circles. Two things need to be emphasized: conversion should not call individuals or groups out of the city into spiritual clubs that exist as islands in or alongside the city, and the variety of levels of encounter accentuate the necessity that every believer be trained for mission.

The believing community has a healing function in the city. Jesus sent his disciples out to fulfill his mission, joining together both preaching and healing. The form of healing God chooses changes in different periods of history, but the substance of the divine concern and command remains true today as always.

In the urban situation, the believing community should channel its forces through various subgroups. The old rural familial and parochial groupings may serve on occasion, but urban structures call for different approaches. The city substructures should be reflected in Christian microcommunities where Christians together can discuss mutual problems: groups of doctors, lawyers, factory workers, social workers, young parents, university students, the elderly, or singles. These become natural centers for problem solving, mutual theological education, and strategy planning. The success of organizations like the Christian Businessmen's Association comes from its true reflection of urban structures. It also points out a grave danger—forgetting the personal dimension of the microcommunity and its basic mission to the area of the city it is called to serve.

The disunity of the people of God makes it difficult to mobilize the subcommunities for effective prophetic, converting, and healing roles in the city. These groups, to fulfill the church's ministry to the city, must cooperate if the city is to find the Christian witness credible.

*Training for informed ministries: How we should teach.* It will not be useful to list possible techniques. Rather, it is more helpful to focus on three or four basic concepts: resources, methods, interdisciplinary cross-fertilization, and practice-orientation.

The resources should be appropriate to the environment of the mission. This has various implications. First, the economic resources are determinative. A basic option has to be taken: Is the urban mission to be self-sustaining, or is it to be dependent on outside funding? The former is ideal, although at the beginning or at difficult moments some help may be necessary. Basically the work will be carried out by lay leaders whose training will occur at night and on weekends. If the core group of Christians has the resources for a part- or full-time coordinator or pastor, the conviction has to be present that all members constitute the staff of workers, for each person can represent the community to the city at a different level.

Cultural resources are important. Leaders to be trained should live in the area of their ministry and on a comparable living standard. In these respects, preparation of inner-city workers closely resembles preparation of pastors for impoverished areas in Third-World countries. Every effort should be made not to decontextualize the natural Christian leaders of a neighborhood. Harold Brown comments, "The theological seminary is in many respects a derivative of the monastery, in which the principle of withdrawal and concentration is not life-long but is applied for a limited time to enable the graduates to minister effectively in later life."[31]

Because the cultural environment in the inner city is so different from that of typical middle-class Protestantism, leaders for the city should (if possible) be selected from and trained in that situation. The facilities in which leaders are trained and the tools with which they work should also be on the level of the people of the community.

The method most appropriate is on-the-job training. The natural leaders chosen will each dedicate the amount of study time that is available. The leaders should have strong convictions about their calling and be accepted by the churches for the functions they are to fill.

The seminary-by-extension method likely is the most useful for this kind of training. TEE (Theological Education by Extension) began over twenty years ago and has reached tens of thousands of students throughout the world.[32] Latin America accounts for a major portion of the total. The TEE concept is easily adaptable to the inner-city situation. Courses are planned according to the specific need of the area and the person(s) who seek training. Programmed texts, fieldwork assignments, theological books and question guides, and other elements enter into the course programs. A problem-solving, practice-oriented procedure often brings together the interplay of history, Bible, theology, sociology, law, ideologies, and politics. Study programs are not necessarily divided among the different fields of theology. The philosophy of education that supports TEE maintains that the student is motivated because he or she is preparing for concrete and immediate needs, the process of education is adapted to the function for which it is required, meaningful incorporation into the student's own context is made (avoids de-contextualization), education becomes available to natural leaders of the group regardless of age or economic situation (avoids elitism and professionalism), and it follows the biblical pattern of Ephesians 4 in the preparation of the saints for the building up of the body of Christ.

This is not the place to discuss TEE at great length. Theological seminaries, however, should study possibilities of ministering more contextually to other than middle-class segments of the population by experimenting in extension education on different cultural and economic levels. This is essential to any effective training program for urban mission.

Interdisciplinary input is another essential ingredient to an integrated preparation of urban leaders. To prepare inner-city leaders without serious interaction with sociology, economics, and psychology is to handicap their future work significantly. In most situations, the first course in theological education should be dedicated to the contextual situation in which the church is called to minister. This, however, requires a supportive community of believers, mutual interaction in biblical study and worship, a deep conviction of calling, and a natural leader of the group. John Omans says, "From three sources men's lives are made better or worse. First, there is the influence of their surroundings; second, the effect of their actions; third, the power of their beliefs."[33] Of the three elements, it is likely that the first needs urgent attention. It is essential that each situation and its leader(s) develop the program of study with whatever technical help is available.

True leaders cannot be made, they can only be helped along the road. The first and most vital concern is to allow leaders to be and truly become themselves. Real community is possible only when men and women are ready to open themselves to each other. The function of the local community of believers should be to help each other to be open both to people and to God. Until the believing community attains this goal, it finds it difficult to open itself to its broader community. All members should be trained to achieve this goal—the pastor, the psychologist, the understanding mother, and the factory foreman. All can help, but Christ's healing presence through the power of the Holy Spirit is indispensable. In this process of achieving true community, it will become evident who the natural leaders are and what special gifts are present for fulfilling the functions required.

The second goal has to do with doing the truth—seeking the reality of love and justice in the city. Love is being open to a fellow worker, a neighbor, the elderly person who comes to the door, the doctor, and the garbage man. They will sense immediately if Christians are genuine in their love, their reaching out, their caring, their planning, and their fighting. Testimony to the love of God in Christ stands or falls with doing the truth.

Love is related to justice. On structural levels, justice and righteousness must prevail to make love a reality. For a Christian, doing the truth means he must be open and honest with himself, his fellows, and his Lord.

This is urgently related to the urban mission. The conditions in which the poor, the foreigner, the persecuted minority, and the unemployed find themselves arise not entirely from personal sin or laziness. The Christian who lives openly with his deprived neighbors will become one with them. He will pray, eat, and play with them until they say: Truly he is one of us! But he will also speak for them, cry for them, and fight for them, because he loves them and asks for them what God intends. A well-trained leader for urban mission may not be entirely acceptable to the professionals who trained him, for to them he will belong to another world. But he will be effective, for he will not only have found himself, but by the grace of Christ he will also have found his brother for whom Christ died, and together they will work for the coming of the Eternal City.

## Discussion Questions

1. Explain the author's definition of urban mission and the goals he sets forth.
2. The author states that the objective of theological education is to convert or transform the city. Discuss the concept of urban transformation and the role of theological education in preparing Christians for dynamic witness to Christ and the gospel on all fronts in the city.
3. Explain how personal conversion and social relationships are both included in the idea of transformation.
4. Show how various social sciences contribute to our understanding of urban discipleship.
5. After reflecting on this chapter, what changes would you suggest in the theological curriculum of the school you attend, or the school you know best?

# 18

# THE KINGDOM OF GOD AND THE CITY OF MAN: A HISTORY OF THE CITY/CHURCH DIALOGUE

### Harvie M. Conn

In A.D. 374, Saint Jerome, "scolding a monk for having abandoned the desert" for the city, wrote, "O wasteland bright with the spring flowers of Christ! O solitude out of which come these stones that build the city of the great King in the Apocalypse! O desolate desert rejoicing in God's familiar presence! What keeps you in the world, O brother? You are above and beyond the world. How long is the shade of the house going to conceal you? How long shall the grimy prisons of those cities intern you?"[1]

Jerome's words highlight the dialogue of this chapter—the church and the city-dominated world. What is the relation between the kingdom of God and the city of mankind? Jerome's own anti-urban solution to that relationship is the prototype for one contemporary answer. What other solutions does history offer?

## The Church in the Cosmopolis

At the heart of Jerome's response to the city was the ancient recognition, shared by Christians and pagans, of religion as the integrating core of the city. The utopian dream of a world order integrated by religion and focused on the city arose long before Jerome. The classical heritage exemplified it.

The ancient Greek city-state was a religious community in the official sense. Its citizens were those who could trace their roots back to the god or gods responsible for the city. Citizenship carried with it the right and obligation to worship at civic shrines. To be ostracized was to be forbidden to enter the city walls. To live outside the city walls was to live outside of civilized life. The terms *pagan* and *heathen* originally meant those who lived outside those city walls.

The cities of Olympia and Delphi, among others, modeled that interconnection of religion and urban life.[2] Olympia stood for the body as the active physical expression of the human soul. And, for Olympia, physical exercise was disciplined play of a religious sort. Until the fourth century B.C., when prize winning became an end in itself, the games that took on the name of that city every four years were to establish "a state of political peace in which inhabitants of all cities could travel freely under protection of Zeus . . . [and] to violate any such pilgrim was an act of sacrilege."[3]

From Delphi and its twin gods, Apollo and Dionysius, came the theater as both an urban institution and a religious festival, the priests from the temple occupying the front row of the "orchestra." Attic comedy had grown out of old fertility rites; Delphic tragedy wrestled with the religious problems of human development opened up by the new urban order: fate, chance, free will. As time wore on, these religious dimensions shriveled. Tragedy lost its cosmic dimensions and provided a symbol of the new course of urban development. The real religion of the fifth century became "a devotion to the city itself."[4]

Against this stream of theopolitical trivialization, Plato flung his dreamplan for a new city-state, *The Republic.* As a quest for social justice, it represented an attempt to recover the religious dimensions of ideal justice, a cosmopolis constructed by the Good, "religion within the limits of human reason." But as an urbane vision of the city, it had come too late. The city-state had passed its peak.

### Hellenization and the First Urban Wave

Aristotle's pupil, Alexander the Great, found another purpose for the city. It became a tool for the colonization of his conquered world, a world that by 323 B.C. included the Persian empire, stretching from Macedonia on the Balkan Peninsula across Asia Minor, Mesopotamia, and Persia into India and encompassing Palestine and Egypt. At strategic points, Alexander built Greek cities to serve as administrative centers. Through these cities a new cultural vision began to penetrate the alien world of the East: "urbanization became the means of hellenization."[5] For six and a half centuries, from Alexander to Constantine, the city was the leading instrument in social, political, and cultural movement.

In the process, the gods abandoned their place as religious center to the city. The city itself became the holy sanctuary, a sacred enclosure around an altar.[6] Stoic cosmopolitanism won the day, rejecting Plato's idealization of the city-state. Combined with the hellenistic social humanitarianism of openness and tolerance, it promoted a universal community, a world ruled, said Zeno, its architect, by a single universal divine law. "Men, through their unique gift of reason, could learn and obey the cosmic will. With the gods, they constituted a spiritual world-city."[7] Rome, for the Stoics, became the political embodiment of their cosmopolitan theology.

### The Church and the Roman City

Against this backdrop, the church began its dialogue with the city-religion. Whether from the right or from the left, the early champions of the gospel in the city were aware that the good news of Jesus Christ and his redemptive work meant a de-divinization of the ancient city.[8] The conflicts of the second-century church over emperor worship were not because Christianity was antipolitical, as were the mystery religions. They flowed from Christianity's radical break with the notion of the city as the meeting place of the gods and humanity. How was the church to be in the city but not of it? How was the church to function as an "alien citizen"?[9]

The historical context demanded an answer. With few exceptions, Christian groups in the second century were found in cities where Judaism was strong. To the outsider the church was an illegal association, an opposition urban cult. Its emerging system of government, with bishops and clergy as apparent heads of an urban community, had a city flair. Not till the last twenty years of the third century, in fact, did Christianity begin to impact some important rural areas of the empire.[10]

To the right and what might be called a Christ-against-the-city posture was Tertullian. For Tertullian's Christian, life was an urgent attempt to escape the pollution and idolatrous decay of urban life surrounding us. Christians are to be found everywhere in urban society, he responded to those who saw a disengaged church. "We sail with you, and fight with you, and till the ground with you; and in like manner we unite with you in your traffickings—even in the various arts we make public property of our works for your benefit" (*Apology* xliii). But ultimately the only city that matters for the Christian is the heavenly Jerusalem. The alien character of Christianity was to dominate.[11]

From the left was the Christ-of-the-city perspective of the Gnostics with their efforts to naturalize Christ into the cosmopolis. The movement was molded by an individualism that saw the knowledge of Christ as a severely spiritual (amaterial) experience that had its place in the life of the city as the very pinnacle of human achievement. It saw the church not as the new people of God but as an association of "the enlightened who could live in culture as those who sought a destiny beyond it but were not in strife with it."[12] Participation in the life of the city was now a matter of indifference; it involved no great problems.

## The Church in the Theopolis

With the acceptance of Christianity by Emperor Constantine and the securing for Christianity of the privileges of a licensed cult by the Edict of Milan in 313, the Christian approach to the city began its march from cosmopolis to theopolis. "During the first three centuries the tendency of events had been, on the whole, to accentuate the elements of opposition between the Church and the world."[13] Now a synthesis began to emerge in which the Roman concept of cosmic harmony in the city of reason and order was fused with the Christian concept of God as emperor to form a *corpus Christianum*, the Christian body politic.

Eusebius of Caesarea, the church historian of this era, celebrates the era of Constantine as "nothing less than the realization of the secular hope of men, the dream of universal and perpetual peace which classical Rome had made her own, but of which the *Pax Romana* was merely a faint and imperfect anticipation."[14] Lactantius, the Christian philosopher, sees in the New Republic a new concept of the city built on the Roman vision of life as a continuous process of self-development and founded on the respect for humanity imperfectly realized in the classical cosmopolis. This, thinks Lactantius, is the *ratio mundi*, the law of nature that he identifies with the law of God.[15]

This Christian celebration of the city was far too optimistic and ill-timed in light of the ensuing decline of urban history. The empire's commonwealth of self-governing cities was already crumbling under the onslaught of Vandal invasions. In 410 Alaric's Visigoth army sacked Rome, the symbol of Eusebius's urban dream. The first great urban theologian, Augustine (354–430), took pen in hand to demythologize that dream.

## *Augustine and the City*

Augustine's majestic evaluation of the fall of Rome, *De Civitate Dei*, proclaimed a new model for understanding the city: Christ, the transformer of the city, or Christ-for-the-city. As a systematic rejection of the Eusebian picture of the urban empire, Augustine's model argues that the working out of God's purposes does not stand or fall with the fate of Rome, or indeed with the fate of any human society. He sees all humanity divided into two urban commonwealths: the terrestrial and the heavenly. It is a division, he contends, created before the foundation of the earth to be sealed at the judgment of the last day. The whole of history, therefore, is an eschatological movement toward the constitution of the heavenly city as it will finally emerge.[16]

In that movement, Christ is the transformer of the city. He redirects, reinvigorates, and regenerates that life of humanity, expressed in all human works, that actually is the perverted and corrupted exercise of a fundamentally good nature.[17] Augustine sees the reality of the present *civitas* as abnormal, the good nature of creation corrupted by the root of sin. Flowing from that abnormality he sees what Niebuhr calls "the social sinfulness of mankind," a disorder extending to every phase of urban culture.[18]

Jesus Christ comes to this disorder to heal and renew what sin has infected, to restore and redirect what has been perverted. The culture of the city is not discarded by this work of regeneration; it is redirected by the power of the kingdom of God. "The Christian life can and must make use not only of these cultural activities but of 'the convenient and necessary arrangements of men with men'—conventions regarding dress and rank, weights and measures, coinage and the like. Everything, and not least the political life, is subject to the great conversion that ensued when God makes a new beginning for man by causing man to begin with God."[19]

In all this, Augustine insisted, we are restrained from slipping into a "culture Christianity" by our awareness of the antithesis that operates in history through the conflict of the two cities. "Two loves have built the two cities: self-love and contempt of God the earthly city, love of God and contempt of self the heavenly. The first seeks to glory in itself, the second in God" (*De Civitate Dei* 14.28).

In any empirical city, the two loves are inevitably interwoven. A city is only the sum of its members, the two cities inevitably present in any historical city. No commonwealth, even that ruled by Christian emperors like Constantine, can be identified with the city of God. The Christian church as an organized institution is the threshing floor on which Christ separates the wheat from the chaff, always containing both until the day of judgment.

Augustine's model had its tragic flaws, though they were not found in the antithetic dualism of the two cities.[20] These flaws were rooted in the favored place he gave the church and his frequent reduction of faith to obedient assent to the church as an authoritative, cultural institution.

In the immediate centuries that followed, these flaws became more noticeable as the cities lost ground and the church grew dominant. The disintegration of Rome, the incursions of the Germanic peoples, the rise of Islam and its conquest of the Mediterranean basin—everything moved toward a catastrophic decline of the city as a model for the world.[21] By the end of the fifth century, the western half of the empire had slipped into chaos, nearly all its cities stunted by decline. In Britain only a few major places, like London and the legionary camps of York, Lincoln, and Chester, remained inhabited. By the end of the seventh century, the once busy port of Genoa had become a fishing village. The concept of the city as an independent political entity, as a symbol for the world, vanished entirely in the Dark Ages.

### The Second Urban Wave

Its reemergence, beginning perhaps in the tenth century, now found a new model for its center—the church. In spite of such anti-urban aspects of Christianity as its opposition to the pagan way of life embodied in municipalities, its withdrawal from the secular world of the city into the desert or monasteries, its neo-Augustinian substitution of the heavenly for the earthly city, the church's form and organization began to lend its shape to the re-creation of the city. The second great urban wave was born, and the church was its midwife.

Strangely enough, the earliest model for this theopolis came from one of the very reasons for the city's downfall, the monastery. Plato's vision found realization in the Benedictine order, the monastery as the link between the classical city and the medieval city. "It was in the monastery that the ideal purposes of the city were sorted out, kept alive and eventually renewed. It was here too that the practical value of restraint, order, regularity, honesty, inner discipline were established, before these qualities were passed over to the medieval town and post-medieval capitalism, in the form of inventions and business practices: the clock, the account book, the ordered day."[22] The image of the heavenly city and the Roman cosmopolis were fused and kept alive by the monasteries.

Following the tenth century, when the new urban communities were re-forming, this Roman inheritance began to take concrete shape in an architectural emphasis on enclosure, protection, security, durability, and continuity. As the barbarian populations of northern and central Europe swung over to Christianity, the role of the city/church began to grow. After the fall of the Roman empire, the church became the one powerful and universal association in western Europe. The fundamental political divisions of society, the parish and the diocese, took their forms from a church that had once taken them from the empire. "From the smallest village with its parish church to the greatest city with its Cathedral, its many churches, its monasteries and shrines, the Church was visibly present in every community: its spires were the first object the traveller saw on the horizon and its cross was the last symbol held before the eyes of the dying."[23]

### Aquinas and the City

The great systematizer of this theopolitical synthesis was the thirteenth-century theologian Thomas Aquinas.[24] Aquinas sought to answer the question about Christ and the city with a "both-and." Yet, as Niebuhr indicated, Aquinas's Christ is far above the city, and the gap between Christ and the city is never taken seriously enough.[25] He seeks to represent a model sometimes designated as a nature-grace dualism. Christ and the city, grace and nature, are not hostile worlds but complementary ones. "Since, therefore, grace does not destroy nature, but perfects it, natural reason should minister to faith as the natural inclination of the will ministers to charity."[26]

So, Aquinas need not seek a rule for human social life in the Gospels. These urban rules must be found by reason. "They constitute in their broad principles a natural law which all reasonable men living human lives under the given conditions of common human existence can discern, and which is based ultimately on the eternal law in the mind of God, the creator and ruler of all. . . . Culture discerns the rules for culture, because culture is the work of God-given reason in God-given nature."[27]

But there is another law for the city—the law revealed by God through his prophets and ultimately in his Son. This law is partly coincident with the natural law and partly transcends it. The city provides humanity as a social being with direction in accordance with natural law. The church not only directs us to our supernatural end but also, as custodian of the divine law, assists in the ordering of our temporal life. The urban man or woman of reason sometimes falls short of that goal and requires the gracious assistance of revelation.

# The Collapse of the Theopolis

Aquinas's synthesis left the world of the city relatively autonomous of the kingdom of God, except in a supplementary way. It was to set up a schizophrenic two-realm a priori, leaving open the possibility of reasonable people building a utopian vision for the city with a minimization of the disruptive, city-destroying power of sin. The seeds of the secularized city, the modern megalopolis, were sown by Aquinas and harvested in the more consistent efforts of the Renaissance and Enlightenment minds.

From the thirteenth to the eighteenth centuries, the transition from theopolis to megalopolis was achieved. A new pattern for the city was to spring out of a new economy—mercantilist capitalism. A new political framework, the centralized despotism or oligarchy, was to be embodied in urban culture. A growing skepticism moved from the secularist isolation of nature and grace, hinted at in Aquinas, through the progressive isolation of nature from grace, trumpeted by Duns Scotus (1270–1308), to the humanistic abandonment of grace by the Renaissance and the Enlightenment.

In the political realm, this growing secularization finds expression in the new vision of the city nurtured by Dante Alighiere's *De Monarchia* (1310–1313). Dante called for a divine dual appointment for the governing of humanity. The pope was to rule in the spiritual realm and the emperor in the secular, each absolutely sovereign in his own realm.

The vision received an even more secular twist with Machiavelli's fifteenth-century treatise *The Prince*. This work signaled the beginning of the radical transfer of absolute authority from God and the church to the national state. The divine attributes of sovereignty and power were denied to God and attributed to the *civitas*. The ancient Roman dream of a world order whose object was to promote the public good and not private interests was in the process of being re-divinized under a new sign, the sign of the prince.

This growing vision, however, was still transitional, still linked to the Christian past of earlier days. Francis Bacon (1561–1626), in his utopian novel *New Atlantis*, sketches an idyllic island community revolving around what he calls the house of Solomon, "a house of science and technique, a laboratory, a bureau of planning and a workshop. Upon this complex scheme was built his hope of a perfect society."[28] Built into Bacon's ideal community is a vision of science that has since controlled people's minds. But it is still not fully divorced from Christianity. The community Bacon describes had earlier received a book containing the Old and New Testaments and, with it, a letter promising the inhabitants of the island peace and goodwill from God. Christianity and the humanism of the emerging science are still interwoven at this stage of the transition to megalopolis.

The effect of the process, however, was wearing away more and more at the interaction of Christianity and the city in the fourteenth and fifteenth centuries. In the cities, the medieval ideal of the Christian knight and the Christian prince was being replaced by a new urban image, the commercial merchant. Cities were changing while the church, represented by its clergy, seemed tied to another world, outsiders to the city and its citizens.

Late medieval Flanders, for example, was a city of only external, formalized religiosity among laypeople, a significant number of its citizens never darkening the door of the confessional for years on end.[29] Late medieval Germany was in a similar state. Although a form of piety was evident in the city, it was flawed and unsatisfying. On the eve of the Reformation the medieval model was failing, especially on the city level.

> Rome's extensive ecclesiastical bureaucracy, which had been the unity of Europe during the Middle Ages, was disintegrating in many areas, hurried along by a growing regional sense of identity and administrative competence. The well-entrenched benefice system of the church, the muscle of patronage, which had permitted important ecclesiastical offices to be sold to the highest bidders and residency requirements either to go unenforced or to be fulfilled by poorly qualified substitutes, revealed its deleterious effects especially on the local level. Bishops were traditionally appointed from the nobility and not always known to have either a shepherd's heart or a theologian's mind. Cities were very sensitive to their lack of firsthand knowledge of and sympathy with local urban problems.[30]

The focus of this tension became increasingly the freedom of the city from the church.

> There was constant quarrelling in town councils about the bishops' right to intervene, about the rights of patronage, and thus about authority over parishes and parish clergy and about the extension or restriction of ecclesiastical jurisdiction. Corporations and councils tried to guard against attempts by the clergy to separate itself from the laity by claiming privileges such as immunity from taxes, jurisdiction and civic obligations. Town councils tried to control the administration of ecclesiastical and monastic property and to take over ecclesiastical functions which had civic consequences, such as schooling, provision for the poor and sick, oversight of social morality.[31]

The free-city concept was finding roots in some of Europe's urban centers. Cities like Augsburg, Nurnberg, and Lubeck were seeing themselves as organic parts of a cosmopolitan order of civil rights and freedoms. In this concept, the religious embraced the secular; sin and salvation had strong social and political connotations. One chronicler of the free-city apologetic wrote: "God has become a citizen of Bern, and who can fight against God?"[32]

## The Reformation Interlude

In this transition from theopolis to megalopolis came the interruption of the sixteenth-century Reformation, uniquely an urban event. Contradicting at its core the disintegrating effect of nominalistic secularism on the city and the then emerging Renaissance call for a return to a new cosmopolis, it rediscovered a sovereign God unleashed by an open Bible in the life of the city.[33]

In the course of the century, fifty of the sixty-five imperial cities subject to the emperor officially recognized the Reformation either permanently or periodically and as either a majority or a minority movement. Of Germany's almost two hundred cities and towns with populations exceeding one thousand, most witnessed Protestant movements. Some of the largest— Nurnberg, Strasbourg, Lubeck, Augsburg, and Ulm, all with populations in excess of twenty-five thousand—became overwhelmingly Protestant.

The Reformation cannot be understood as reinforcing the iconoclasm of the late medieval age. Its attractiveness was the heart of its proposals for the religious life of cities and towns. "Protestant preachers pointed out what many laymen had evidently also come to suspect—that the church and her clergy would first have to undergo a major redefinition before they could be integrated as good citizens into society. The root of the problem, I am suggesting, was not the privileges of a special clerical class or even its administrative and moral failings but the most basic beliefs and practices of the church it represented."[34]

The need was for a religious transformation. Calvin supplied that transformation when he spoke for the Reformers in defining the ultimate purpose of the city, whatever its form, as God's righteousness. God's law, engraved by him on our conscience, was the origin of all our ideas of right and wrong, not the cosmopolis or the theopolis. The most basic political institution was to be the covenant instituted by God between himself and the magistrates and people of a city.[35]

The Reformation call involved a new social ethic for the city. The Protestant concept of the clerical ministry as an activity, not a passive sacramental state, appealed to burghers who had fought to curtail clerical privileges and immunities. The Reformation slogan of the priesthood of all believers stratified urban society in the pragmatic and ethical terms of who could best serve his fellow citizens. Being lord over all was no longer incompatible with being servant to all. The importance of secular life and vocations was confirmed, sanctifying as it did the laity. Conversely, it also worked to secularize the clergy. The citizen saw the Reformation as inner freedom from religious superstition and nominalist uncertainty, as a new ethic of urban service. "The Reformation appears as an enlightenment. The special religious works and ceremonies of the medieval church are criticized as psychologically burdensome and socially useless in contrast to Reformation sponsorship of natural and useful service to one's neighbor through ordinary lay vocations."[36] The Protestant movement was seen as an unprecedented religious flattering of secular life, but without the medieval separation of the sacred from the secular.

### Reformation Models for the City

Three models divided the Reformation perspective on the city. From Luther came the two-kingdom theory, a dualism of Christ and the city in paradox. Unlike the Thomistic synthesis, built on a concept of the city in need of divine amplification and development, Luther sees the culture of the city as cracked and madly askew, a kingdom of wrath and severity. The reasonable institution rests on a great irrationality.

Yet, unlike the radical notions of Tertullian, Luther knows that he belongs to that culture and cannot get out of it, that God indeed sustains him in it and by it. "This is the basis of Luther's dualism. Christ deals with the fundamental problems of the moral life. But by the same token he does not directly govern the external actions or construct the immediate community in which man carries on his work."[37] In the city of humanity, the Christian is ruled by both divinely bestowed reason and humanity's natural wisdom, "a fair and glorious instrument and work of God." Living in paradox between Christ and the city, "the freedom of the Christian man," for Luther, becomes "autonomy in all the special spheres of culture."[38] It is precisely here that Luther may be in danger of encouraging the modern process of secularization in the city. He frees humanity for responsibility under God, but he does it by creating two worlds where there had been one.

The second Reformation model flowed from a deep sensitivity of the failure of Luther and Calvin to construct a view of the church that would repudiate the theopolitical heritage of Constantinianism. Anabaptism, the radical Reformation, called for a restitution of a "confessional church based on personal faith." Any church that allowed itself to become identified with the *civitas* was to the Anabaptists fallen.

In many respects, Anabaptism sounds like a Reformation return to the Christ-against-the-city model of earlier days. It saw the city's culture as "not simply an amorphous conglomerate of evil impulses but a structured reality taking concrete form in the demonic dimensions of economic and political life."[39] For some this might resemble Luther's two-kingdom theory. But against him, the movement saw the kingdom of God incarnated in the believing community of disciples and hostile to *Kultur*, humanity's autonomous creation and setting of values. The insistence on the separation of the church from the Constantinian world had structured a concept of a world intolerant of the practice of true Christian principles in the urban society. The society of the city would always be the partner of the flesh and the devil. But the church must walk another road, exemplifying in her fellowship the living and suffering and dying of the Lord Jesus.

Thus, though both Lutherans and Anabaptists were pessimistic about the world of the city, the Lutheran was willing to make a paradoxical compromise by participation in a world order that remained sinful. The Anabaptist would not. "He must consequently withdraw from the worldly order and create a Christian social order within the fellowship of the church brotherhood. Extension of this Christian order by the conversion of individuals and their transfer out of the world into the church is the only way by which progress can be made in Christianizing the social order."[40] To use the language of Roland Bainton, Anabaptism symbolized "the church withdrawn."

Calvin provided the third model from the Reformation: Christ as transformer of the city. Drawing his strengths (and some of his weaknesses) from Augustine, he looked for the present permeation of all life in the city by the gospel. Dominated by the cosmic dimensions of the sovereignty of God, Calvin saw the city as God's minister, not only in a negative fashion as a restrainer of evil, but also positively as a promoter of human welfare.

Even in the radical ruins of the fall, Calvin discerned the splendor of the image of God in human nature. He looked at the vocations of humanity as activities in which they may express their faith and love, glorifying God in their calling as they were faithful to the demands of the law of God.

His understanding of human depravity allowed for no optimistic hope in "the transformation of mankind in all its nature and culture into a kingdom of God. . . ."[41] At the same time, Calvin's perspective was theocentric enough to work for the manifestation of the rule of the kingdom of God in the city through the application of evangelical laws in the body politic. He refused to allow even this sphere to be ruled by natural law or the benevolence of humanitarian reasonableness. Here, too, the law of God was to govern the entirety of life.[42]

The Reformation ultimately offered no brake on the increasing pressure for the secularization of the city. Anabaptism called for a new model of the kingdom of God structured against the city. Luther left the city to the dictates of natural law and reasonableness. Calvin compromised his call for reforming by not breaking entirely with the Constantinian ecclesiology in which the church embraced all in a given locality.[43]

The old vision of the city as a theopolis collapsed under the blows of the Reformation.[44] But it was the Renaissance spirit of humanity as the measure of all things that carried away the pieces for a new construction. Christopher Wren's plan for the reconstruction of London after the Great Fire of 1666 recognized this new ordering of city life. He did not give the dominating site to St. Paul's. He planned the new avenues so as to give this honor to the Royal Stock Exchange.

## The Church in the Megalopolis

With the collapse of the medieval theopolis, a new vision of the city began to emerge. A growing isolation of the sacred from the *saeculum* found modern humanity now searching for a new religious way to see the city without having to find God at its center. The Greco-Roman world had integrated religion and city by asking, "Am I a good man?" The Reformation question, rejected by the growing consensus, asked, "Am I a Christian man?" The modern question became, "Am I a happy man?"[45] The pursuit of individual happiness became an inalienable right for the modern urban dweller.

Seventeenth- and eighteenth-century humanity had not lost its medieval passion for religious comprehensiveness and order. It was still animated by what the French call *l'esprit de systeme*, a religious yearning for total explanation. Only now that yearning was sought not in God, but in the secularity of humanity itself; not in theopolis but in megalopolis. At the heart of the change was a profound revolution in consciousness, the religious mindset of secularization.[46]

Thomism's natural order had finally overpowered grace. In the process, even the understanding of that natural order had been transformed. The accommodating mentality of the theopolis (a nature-grace consciousness) shifted to an emancipating mentality (a nature-freedom consciousness). "Grace disappeared in the religious thinking of modern man and its place was taken by the category of freedom. Man was to be reborn as a completely free and autonomous personality and released from all controls over his thinking. And, in this spirit, even the category of nature, still retained from the medieval synthesis, was transformed. Nature became a 'macrocosmic sphere within which human personality could exercise its autonomy.'"[47]

In the centuries immediately after the Reformation, this new mentality began to manifest itself in many areas of urban life. The choir, which once chanted hymns to God, was removed to the concert hall. Drama, leaving the porches of the church, was turned over to professional actors under the patronage of the nobility. The nave, the bare assembly place of the church, became the bourse. The merchant, not the minister, became the spokesperson for power in the city. Not God, but the individual, was celebrated as the builder of the new city of humanity. Bacon's utopian *New Atlantis* became the *Leviathan* of Thomas Hobbes (1588–1679). Societies and cities were heralded as mechanical contrivances created by individuals to serve their mutual interests. Hobbes's designation of the body politic as the "mortal God" shocked his world with its irreverent adjective, *mortal*, but it signaled as well the beginning of a new era in the history of urban mythology.

### The Third Urban Wave

Anchored in the emerging Enlightenment exaltation of humanity, pressured by an accelerating population growth, encouraged by eighteenth-century inventions like a usable steam engine (1767), the Western city, already infatuated with capitalism,[48] embraced the machine. The medieval city represented protection and security. The industrial city represented the priority of the individual and the calculated risks that promoted the individual. Cities exploded with vitality and problems.

In 1800, not a city in that Western world had even a million people. About 3 percent of the world's 906 million people are believed to have lived in the mere 750 places of larger than 5,000 population. But by 1850, the picture was changing radically. London, the biggest of the Western world's cities, grew from 959,310 in 1800 to over 2 million. By 1901, the figure was well over 4 million. In one century she had grown by 3.5 million people.

In the United States, the pattern was similar. In 1850, 85 percent of the population was still classified as rural, but by 1900 there were three cities of over 1 million people and an additional thirty-five between 100,000 and

1 million. In the century between 1790 and 1890, the total U.S. population grew 16 fold, but urban population grew 139 fold. By 1920, the urban population had passed 50 percent. Limited transportation found workers living near factories in densely packed tenements. Pathetic living conditions, poverty, and squalor increased as waves of new immigrant workers from southern Europe poured into American cities during the last quarter of the nineteenth century.

In the face of the urban manufacturing world's pain and squalor, some people turned away from hope in the individual. Individualism in the city, they cried, brought only "brutal indifference." "The unfeeling isolation of each in his private interest becomes the more repellant and offensive, the more these individuals are crowded together. . . . This isolation of the individual, this narrow self-seeking is the fundamental principle of our society everywhere, [but] it is nowhere so shamelessly barefaced, so self-conscious as just here in the crowding of the great city."[49] With these words, Friedrich Engels (1820–1895) looked at industrialized Manchester, England, and saw there "the marvels of civilization" for the few linked to the "nameless misery" for the many. With Karl Marx (1818–1883), an observer of London's growing gap between rich and poor, he joined in calling for the inevitable downfall of capitalism and the bringing of the working class to power. Hope of the future for them lay in the inevitability of the class struggle.

### Revival of the Christ-of-the-City Model

Marxism, however, was not yet to have its day. The optimistic idealism of the individual, triumphing in the brotherhood of mankind, was a more cheerful solution to urban pain.

Albrecht Ritschl (1822–1899) provided much of the theological underpinnings for that response. He promoted the idea of the kingdom of God shorn of its supernaturalism—the kingdom of ends. In that kingdom was to be found the true form of a world ethical society. "The Christian idea of the kingdom of God," he wrote, "denotes the association of mankind—an association both extensively and intensively the most comprehensive possible—through the reciprocal moral action of its members, action which transcends all merely natural and particular considerations."[50] Closely related to Thomas Jefferson's hope for a mankind gathered into one family "under the bonds of charity, peace, common wants and common aids," Ritschl's vision of the megalopolis under God becomes a synthesis "of the great values esteemed by democratic culture: the freedom and intrinsic worth of individuals, social cooperation and universal peace."[51] Ritschl becomes the midwife of classic theological liberalism, and Jesus is delivered as the Christ of culture.

In England, Ritschl's vision, touched with a hint of Marx, was part of the impetus for the incarnation of the Christian Socialist movement of 1848–1854 under the leadership of F. D. Maurice (1805–1872). Like Ritschl's, Maurice's vision of the kingdom was a teleological, universal one in conflict with what he termed "unsocial Christians" and "unchristian socialists." He spurned the desire of the evangelicals of Germany and England "to make sin the ground of all theology" and with it their views of hell and eternal punishment. His answer was that Christ is the head of all humanity and the kingdom of God would be realized through the participation of the organizations of humanity in a new, universal society for all.

In line with this social model for his humanitarianism, Maurice attacked the whole *laissez faire*, competitive, commercialist outlook in the name of Jesus. According to him, the true law of the universe is that we are made to live in community as children of God. Writing with his associates in the short-lived journal *Politics for the People*, he pressed with caution his theme of liberty, fraternity, and unity as God's intention for every people under heaven.

From that theme flowed a measure of reform movements in English urban life. In a day when higher education for women was a distrusted novelty, Maurice founded Queens College for women (1848). To prepare working men to manage in the industrial revolution, he founded the Workingmen's College and became its first president. Though the spin-off projects made some small impact, his wider vision was what made its deeper influence in the church.

This same humanitarian liberalism spawned the social gospel movement in the United States at the end of the nineteenth century and the dawn of the twentieth. Would we ever see an end to the urban face of crime, poverty, congestion, racial polarity, and pollution?

In 1887 appeared Edward Bellamy's utopian, social-gospel answer to that question, *Looking Backward*. The most influential novel in America since *Uncle Tom's Cabin* (1852), it quickly sold a million copies. Endeavoring to picture a future "'City of God, to shame . . . the imperfections of the City of Man,' he limned a social order of welfare programs, garden cities and public works, mechanization of labor, vast educational resources, women freed of household drudgery—recognizable features, in great measure, of contemporary industrial society—and, greatest blessing of all (this still to be achieved), people living together as loving brothers."[52] In this society, the fatherhood of God had become the brotherhood of mankind.

Bellamy's vision was shared by men like Washington Gladden (1836–1918), Shailer Mathews (1863–1941), and Walter Rauschenbusch (1861–1918), who appeared to give it more theological teeth. Calling for an alliance between the church and the working class, Rauschenbusch, like Ritschl before him, retooled the biblical formula of the kingdom of God into the reformation of society as Christianity's only true task. Sin became injustice; redemption, social morality; heaven, a just society; and hell, a slum. As a pastor of the Second German Baptist Church in New York's "Hell's Kitchen" area, Rauschenbusch's experiences created a liberal revision of the gospel into a socialist solution for overcoming the evils of industrial society.[53]

### Evangelical Responses to the City

The evangelicals of these centuries were not silent. The Wesleyan revival of eighteenth-century England produced the Clapham Sect of wealthy politicians and businessmen. Led by men like William Wilberforce, they became an influential center of urban and social reform. Under the inspiration of their parish rector, John Venn, founder of the Church Missionary Society and father of its illustrious secretary, Henry Venn, the group led in the abolition of slavery in the British Empire and a wide program of prison reform.

In the nineteenth century their tradition was carried on by Lord Shaftesbury. His career achievements included better treatment of the mentally ill, improved housing, better health, sanitation, and recreation facilities, better schools, labor legislation, improved mining conditions, and opposition to the opium and liquor traffic.[54] Shaftesbury's support of the Society for Improving the Conditions of Labouring Classes and his report to Parliament of housing conditions in St. George's Hanover Square, London, prompted the erection of model lodging houses.

But, unlike the Ritschlian response, the evangelical response harbored no illusions of building the kingdom of God on earth. The manifesto of the Clapham Sect was Wilberforce's 1797 work *A Practical View of the Prevailing Religious System of Professed Christians in the Higher and Middle Classes in this Country Contrasted with Real Christianity*. The social services of the English upper and middle classes were a product of religion, not an end. What Maurice was later to reject, Wilberforce endorsed. The religion of the upper classes did not recognize, he wrote, the primacy of Christianity in life, the temporal nature of the present, the coming judgment at death, and the folly of attempting good works without faith in Christ.

The temptation to place this model in Niebuhr's typology of "Christ the transformer of culture" (Christ for the city), however, must be resisted. For along with a ringing affirmation of the biblical supernatural was a deadening insensitivity to the secularism of the period's capitalism.

Borrowing from the voluntarism characteristic of an earlier Anabaptism and the introspective concern over the individual reinforced by Calvinistic Puritanism, the evangelical of these times did not fully acknowledge the processes of industrialization and modernization as secular voluntarism. As a result, voluntarism's focus on the individual did not lose its hold on the evangelical even in his or her deep commitment to social amelioration. The religious roots of urban individualism were not acknowledged, and unregulated economic activity (the productive assets of the individual) remained unquestioned by the reformers.

As the nineteenth century moved into the twentieth, that lack of sensitivity on the part of the evangelical led to other growing problems. The evangelical moved from social amelioration to social reinforcement, from change agent to defender of the status quo. The voluntarist concept of institutions (embodied in its views on the church) increasingly left the evangelical without the theoretical capabilities to deal radically with the structural enormity of the problems of industrialization and urbanization.

In the United States, for example, the motivating compassion of Christ, coupled with acculturated, secularized individualism, produced large-scale religious philanthropy and organized charity programs for the city.[55] But the drag of secular accommodation could not manifest Christian justice for the city.

Reinforcing this perspective was a new way of defining poverty that was gaining popularity. A distinction was growing between the "worthy poor" and the "unworthy poor." This combined with a racist social polarization that identified the poor with the foreign-born immigrant poor.[56]

All these factors combined to build an anti-urban mentality among America's evangelicals.

> Urban problems, like substandard housing, poverty, unemployment, disease and crime were too much for the churches with their limited resources to cope with effectively. Many of the faithful shook their heads in despair and concluded there was little they could do about the wretched social conditions except pray and try to evangelize their neighbors. Added to this was the

retreat from the inner city by established Protestant congregations, leaving many slum areas virtually devoid of churches.[57]

As the American evangelical moved into the first half of the twentieth century, other historical developments reinforced these tendencies. An increased reaction among the evangelicals began to build up against the impact of the social gospel movement on two fronts. The identification of that movement with theological liberalism created animosity toward it. In addition, its identification of systemic, environmental structures as the root of urban dislocation and its espousal of socialistically oriented methods for social reform were also menacing to the evangelical.

The combination of all these elements led not simply to a rejection of the social gospel movement but to a vigorous rejection of social reform with it. In the aftermath, the pietist focus of earlier years on individual piety and personal ethics began to receive prominence.

> Sin was seen as an individual affair to be dealt with on an individual basis. Thus, attention was focused on personal vice—alcoholic beverages, smoking, theater attendance, prostitution, gambling, card playing—while social sin— slums, poverty, political corruption, fraudulent business practices, monopolies, hazardous working conditions, adulteration of foods—was deliberately ignored or overlooked. The result was that a mood of indifference settled over these churches as they withdrew from sociopolitical affairs and promoted the piety of the local congregations in almost total unconcern about social evils.[58]

Unaware of the ideology of the secularist religion of the megalopolis, evangelicals increasingly identified themselves and the gospel with status-quo capitalism. They could not offer the city a Christian alternative to the social and political structures it had created.

By the first half of the twentieth century, "the capture of the evangelical churches by business interests" had taken place. Dwight L. Moody was closely associated with the Philadelphia department store owner John Wanamaker. He received substantial financial support from men like Cyrus McCormick, Philip Armour, Jay Cooke, Cornelius Vanderbilt II, and J. P. Morgan. Billy Sunday's principal backer was John D. Rockefeller, Jr. These financiers could not complain when Moody preached, "I never saw the man who put Christ first in his life that wasn't successful," or when he advised his ministerial supporters in 1897, "Don't let Sunday be given up to talking on topics you don't understand such as capital and labor."[59] Alba

Johnson, president of the Baldwin Locomotive Works in Philadelphia, could say, "You know the widespread social unrest is largely due to the workingman's envy of those who make a little more money than he does. Now Billy Sunday makes people look to the salvation of their own souls, and when a man is looking after his own soul's good he forgets his selfish desire to become rich. Instead of agitating for a raise in wages he turns and helps some poorer brother who's down and out."[60]

In the wake of the theological controversies over liberalism in the early twentieth century, pietism's earlier mistakes had frozen into a static, evangelical, middle-class support of the religious value systems of the megalopolis. The "no politics" rule of the English Methodists of the nineteenth century had moved evangelicalism toward *laissez faire* conservatism without seeing the same religious ideology in it that they saw clearly in Marxism and socialism. "All the issues which were most important to working class people fell into the category where most Christians felt they must stay neutral."[61]

This was reinforced by the rise of extreme dispensational views, which strengthened a pessimistic outlook toward the future of the megalopolis and held out little hope for solutions apart from the return of Christ. The suffering of the city began to be interpreted not as a call for the gospel but as a sign of the end.[62] In 1914, R. A. Torrey wrote, "In the Return of our Lord is the perfect solution, and the only solution, of the political and commercial problems that now vex us."[63]

Revivalism as a feature of the evangelical methodology helped to reduce the complexities of the Christian faith to simple alternatives. Through their reduction of repentance from the public to the private sphere, the full implications of discipleship were not sufficiently stressed. "In time new elements crept into the evangelistic message such as the middle-class success myth, American chauvinism, opposition to actions of organized labor, and, of course, prohibition."[64] Privatization of religion as a cultural, Western given had moved within evangelicalism from a hidden presupposition to an explicit principle of what could better be called neo-fundamentalism.

### Christ-and-the-City-in-Paradox

Unhappy with both liberalism and evangelicalism, a new model for understanding the city, neo-orthodoxy, emerged in the first half of the twentieth century. A variation on an earlier theme, it sought to throw doubt on the nineteenth century's optimism by an analysis of humanity's despair, anxiety, and guilt.

From the Danish philosopher Søren Kierkegaard (1813–1855) it borrowed an existentialist orientation to the here-and-now, concrete humanity in its concrete situation. From Kierkegaard also came a revolt against the abstract religious goals of those content to know dogmas or ideas but not to live them. The real God of the megalopolis was to be found by the leap of faith from the dark abyss of doubt into the arms of Christ.

Karl Barth (1886–1968) gave neo-orthodoxy its systematic shape. But the American-born brothers Reinhold (1892–1971) and H. Richard (1894–1962) Niebuhr came closest to linking it to the social dimensions of the city.

Reinhold Niebuhr forged those links in a thirteen-year parish ministry among the working class in Detroit. Here, in an industrial community, he experienced the ruthless power of industry as it resisted unionization. Here also he re-examined his own liberal and highly idealistic creed, which he now found to be irrelevant. Marxism's cynical realism reinforced his concerns about social injustice and its roots in economics. But it had its own problems.

In the teaching years that followed in New York, Niebuhr's developing theology continued to focus on the urban world and its social problems. Kierkegaard's human predicament, the paradox of sinful pride and human freedom, became the center of his concerns.

Only in the dialectical relationship of love and justice could the paradox be faced. Justice makes its coercive demands, and love, the "impossible possibility" taught by Jesus, the suprahistorical norm, guides us in our struggle toward the goals of justice. Love overcomes evil by its vicarious identification with a suffering megalopolis. But the victory is always ambiguous, calling Christians to lift up their eyes to a still higher goal. "Christian realism" must recognize the ambiguity of the human solution. The tragedy of social life is that one must choose the lesser of two evils rather than an abstract absolute good. The mythical symbol of the resurrection of Christ affirms that such a choice is possible. Writes Niebuhr, "The hope of the resurrection embodies the very genius of the Christian idea of the historical. On the one hand, it implies that eternity will fulfill and not annul the richness and variety which the temporal process has elaborated. On the other it implies that the condition of finiteness and freedom, which lies at the basis of historical existence, is a problem for which there is no solution by any human power."[65] For all the good that Niebuhr left us (and there was much of it), he left us also an accommodating synthesis characteristic of the Christ-and-the-city-in-paradox model.

The Kierkegaardian dialectical opposition between time and eternity remains to frustrate.[66]

Richard Niebuhr's model operates in much the same way. The conclusion of his masterful work *Christ and Culture* points out that all the views he has set forth contain truth that ultimately must be synthesized by the individual's personal decision. His own view of Jesus Christ as the flowing of the eternal in the temporal, immanent divinity actualized in a human person, is not radical enough to set Jesus either over against culture or even as a transformer of the culture of the city. The *Zeitgeist* of existentialism, which is part of Niebuhr's working presuppositions, does not allow him to see Jesus as mourning the city.

Niebuhr's Jesus cannot function as the canon of the city. So Niebuhr sees the culture of the city as basically a relativizing instrument. No single conclusion can be the Christian answer. The claim of finality by any finite mind is said to usurp the lordship of Christ. It violates the liberty of Christians and the unconcluded history of the city. The problem for Niebuhr is not the conflict between the continuity of Christ and the discontinuity of the culture of the city, but "the conflict between the continuity of culture and the discontinuity of Christ, between man's present and God's future."[67]

Ultimately, Richard Niebuhr also sets Christ and the city in an unconcluded paradox. Operating from Kierkegaard's dualism of the finite and the infinite, he cannot ask, How does the eternal Christ look at pseudo-autonomous city culture? He can only ask, How can the believer, linked to infinity, live in finitude?

## The Church in the Global City

By 1950, almost 64 percent of North America's population was urban, and Europe's cities held over 55 percent of its people. As the pace of urban growth in these areas began to slow considerably, it exploded in the so-called Third World. The expansion of the megalopolis took on world dimensions.

The fourth great urban wave began to break on the shores of Africa, Asia, and Latin America. Africa's urban populace jumped from 14 percent in 1950 to 36 percent in 1990. Latin America's urban community has gone from 41 percent of the population in 1950 to 71 percent in 1990, Asia's from 16 to 32 percent.[68]

The mega-city phenomenon has come to the world, especially the southern hemisphere. At the beginning of this century only twenty cities in the world exceeded 1 million in population. As of 1980, that figure had reached 235, with some 118 located in economically less-developed areas. Since 1950, population in these cities has grown tenfold.

In 1950, only two cities in the world had a population of over 10 million—New York and London. By 1985, fifteen did, and only three of these were in Europe and North America. By A.D. 2000, say some, there will be twenty-four, all but three in the southern hemisphere.[69]

The "urban anguish" of the northern hemisphere in the nineteenth century has now become a global phenomenon. Old problems have become more visible: human dysfunction during rapid social change, the political domination of the powerful over the marginalized, the widening gap between rich and poor.

An estimated half the urban population in the southern hemisphere lives in slums or shantytowns. Everywhere the pattern is repeated. Slum dwellers form a third of the populations of Nairobi and Dakar; 415 squatter areas in Manila represent 38 percent of the population; 48,000—by official count—live on the streets of Calcutta (200,000 is the generally accepted figure); five hundred *ciudades perdidas* (lost cities) with 2.7 million people are in Mexico City. "In the year 2000, 2.116 billion or 33.6 percent of the world will be in cities in less developed regions and 40 percent (a conservative figure) will be squatters (846 million). This would indicate a world that is about 13.6 percent squatters by the year 2000."[70]

Compounding the problems of global urbanization for the church, we must remember, is population increase in areas traditionally hostile to Christianity. This, combined with growing nominalism in the northern-hemisphere centers of Christianity, has resulted in a significant drop in the percentage of urban Christians. In 1900, argues David Barrett, Christians numbered 68.8 percent of urban dwellers; by 1980, only 46.3 percent. By A.D. 2000, it will reach 44.5 percent.[71]

### The Church Responds

The 1950s and 1960s found the world church facing these challenges and demanding theological reflection on their significance. The superficial optimism of the social gospel movement had faded away under the impact of neo-orthodoxy. With it went the earlier fear of secularism as an enemy; a new emphasis on the vocation of the church in and for the world began to dominate.

Nourished by a particular interpretation of the prison saint Dietrich Bonhoeffer (1906–1945) and his posthumous call for the church to exist only "for others . . . in all the worldly tasks of human community,"[72] many in the world church embraced secularization as the key to the heart of the urban world.

Under the influence of optimistic theologians like Harvey Cox and Colin Williams, the church was displaced by the world as the object of God's first concern.[73] The theological slogan for this changed emphasis was *missio Dei*, the mission of God, and the person whose theology promoted it was J. C. Hoekendijk (1912–1975).

Fearful of what he called ecclesiastical introversion and its alleged threat to the essential character of mission, Hoekendijk warned against a church-centric interest. From this perspective, he argued, the world almost ceases to be the world and becomes a sort of ecclesiastical training ground.[74] His emphasis became the agenda for discussion in the world church as he called for a new sequence in missions that moved from church to world.

More quickly than the social gospel before it, the theology of secularization faded as a permanent solution. According to a later self-reflection by Harvey Cox, one of its advocates, it had misjudged the persistence of human religiosity and minimized the dark side of secularization as a process that could destroy as well as heal. It was also, Cox admits, a perspective on the city "of a relatively privileged urbanite. The city, secular or otherwise, feels quite different to those for whom its promise turns out to be a cruel deception."[75]

What the theology of secularization left behind, however, was a new agenda for the church that would not go away. Before the eyes of the church was not simply the city as the spiritual gathering place of the lost outside of Christ but also the city as the gathering place of the wretched and the oppressed, a center of racial, religious, and class struggle.

### Protestant and Catholic Conciliar Reactions

Within Protestant and Catholic circles, old perspectives on the city have reappeared, but this time with a darker hue. Despite the articulate protests of some within its ranks, the World Council of Churches, through the 1960s and 1970s, has revitalized something resembling the old Christ-of-the-city model. Increasingly the Council had seen mission as "world-affirming mission." The church's calling? "To affirm God's presence in all realms of life, to seek to discern his action there, and to seek obedience to his will through the action of Christians in the world."[76]

The Fourth Assembly of the Council at Uppsala in 1968 appears to be something of a climax in this emphasis. There, David Bosch argues, the model was expanded in three ways: a new definitional emphasis on mission as humanization and vigorous sociopolitical involvement; mission as the acknowledgment of God's activities in the world, the world said to be providing the agenda for the *missio Dei*; a positive interpretation of the world and of history.[77]

More than one evangelical commentator has seen the years following that Uppsala Assembly as one of modification and re-evaluation within the Council. Harold Lindsell could see the Fifth Assembly at Nairobi in 1975 as "a substantial improvement over Uppsala. The radical cast of the 1968 Assembly had yielded to a more centrist approach, a better balance, and the rediscovery of evangelism as an important part of the mission of the Church."[78]

Undoubtedly one factor in this modification toward a more evangelical cast has been the growing number of Third-World delegates to the meetings. Since Nairobi, the majority of the WCC delegates has not come from the West.

Another dimension to the shift, we suggest, may be the growing strength of the nonconciliar evangelical presence through the 1974 emergence of the ongoing Lausanne Committee for World Evangelization. Lausanne sponsored global gatherings in 1980 and 1989, both within months of similar gatherings of the Council's Commission on World Mission and Evangelism elsewhere.

The timing of the events has prompted comparisons.[79] Some have noted a growing exercise in self-criticism in both camps; Lausanne has become increasingly aware of the "horizontal" obligations of the gospel, and the WCC appears to be rediscovering the "vertical" dimension of evangelism. The perceived convergences, in fact, have been strong enough to prompt evangelicals attending the 1989 San Antonio gathering of the Commission on World Mission and Evangelism to issue an informal plea for fuller cooperation to the Lausanne II gathering at Manila.[80] Has the Council model shifted? Evaluation remains difficult, and final judgment will probably have to be postponed to future years, but there are encouraging developments that prompt hope.

In 1982 the Central Committee of the WCC approved and published a document, *Mission and Evangelism—An Ecumenical Affirmation*, that has received wide but cautious endorsement from evangelical circles. However, it was said to have received almost no attention at the Vancouver Assembly of the Council in 1983, and, according to Bosch, though Section I of the 1989 San Antonio Report made much use of it, there was no explicit reference to it in the remaining Sections of the Report.[81] Bosch, until his death in a car crash in 1992, remained cautiously optimistic that a new model was emerging within WCC circles. He hoped for a union between the Council's deepening commitment to the poor and a reappearing evangelical concern for the lost. The gospel's demand for believing all things, hoping all things (1 Cor. 13:7) requires no less.

At the same time, my own caution remains stronger than my optimism. I hope, but with great fearfulness. Modifications in the old model are surely apparent. But are they strong enough to bespeak a new model emerging? Continuing theological pluralism within Council circles, growing questions about the uniqueness and exclusivity of the work of Christ, and decades of commitment to a strongly socioeconomic and political agenda remain deterrents to a radical shift of models. Can the WCC break radically enough from its functional definitions of evangelism, structured in the past more around deed than word, to move in a new direction?

If it is fair to make generalizations on the basis of one agency's work, the Urban Rural Mission (URM), a Council ministry, offers little room for optimism. Mandated under a different name in 1961 at the New Delhi Assembly, URM has undergone a number of modifications in its mandate since then. But its nine priorities remain oriented to the support of people's struggles for justice and self-empowerment and to the development of solidarity with regional churches in social contexts of struggle, repression, and marginalization.[82] From an evangelical perspective, one notable absence from these crucial and needed concerns is any connection of the URM's agenda of social change with evangelization and the task of calling men and women to personal repentance and faith in Christ.

Protestants have not been alone in shifting back from church to world. Vatican II, the historic gathering of bishops of the Roman Catholic Church from 1962 to 1965, shows similar directions. Drawing some contrast to the preconciliar views of salvation theology as ecclesiocentric, the church in Vatican II criticized itself as detached from the world and self-serving, at least in the past.

Vatican II's perspective on the global megalopolis was touched, says George Lindbeck, by the insights of Teilhard de Chardin and his vision of a universe in movement toward the Omega Point of fulfillment in Christ.[83] In the shadow of that influence, it saw salvation as God leading the universe in all its aspects, including the so-called secular ones, toward the consummation. The church's mission is thus described in terms of the unification of all humanity and all genuine values of other religions and of secular developments in the fullness of its catholicity. "*The Church in the Modern World*, which is much the longest of its documents, is entirely devoted to this theme. It gives a highly positive evaluation of progress in all realms, not only ethical, social and political, but also economic, aesthetic, scientific, and technological. Its message is that Christians should throw their energies into the building of the earthly city. . . ."[84]

There are differences between the formulations of Vatican II and the World Council of Churches in this area.[85] But the similarities are equally striking. Houtepen, in fact, sees "sufficient building blocks for a common view of an attitude toward the saeculum" that there could emerge a new momentum for ecumenical progress between the two groups.[86]

### Liberation Theologies

This Vatican II call for dialogue with the world and its socioeconomic needs was heard loudly in Latin America. Encouraged by its vision of the church as a dialoguing servant, fed by the experience of destitution and repression in a region dominated by Christendom for centuries, came the diffuse movement we monolithically call liberation theology.

Making pastoral use of Marxism as an instrument of social analysis (as Thomism had used Aristotelianism before), liberation theologians like Gustavo Gutiérrez saw evangelism as the announcement of the presence of the love of God in the "historical becoming of mankind."[87] Mission to the city becomes denunciation, the confronting of the present state of social injustice. It becomes annunciation, the proclamation of the good news "that there is no human act which cannot in the last instance be defined in relation to Christ."[88] The church becomes a sacrament in the city of the convocation of all people by God, a theology of the church in the world refined into a theology of the world in the church.

Deeply oriented to the liberation of the oppressed, liberation theologians operated out of a new theological commitment to the poor. The poor become not the objects of gospel charity but the artisans of a new humanity—shapers, not shaped. Any ideological construction that finds the meaning and purpose of human history outside the concreteness of the historical "now" is spurned. True theology, in its search for hope in a world of poverty, asks, "Where is the God of righteousness in a world of injustice?"

Liberation theology fits well into the Christ-of-the-city model. It "cannot see the church as having any mission to build a separate history, but rather as leading the way in expressing and exemplifying the one meaning of the one history. The mission of the church is inescapably tied to historical struggles for liberation. Salvation does not occur elsewhere than in and through this struggle."[89]

Creating this theology, and created by it, was a new model for the urban church, the Base Christian Communities (CEBs). Described by Leonardo Boff as a form of "ecclesiogenesis," the CEB movement may number as many as 100,000 in Brazil and another 80,000 in the rest of Latin America.[90] Centered in the needs of the poor, the CEB typically appears in the shape of a small assembly of marginalized lay Christians. The elements of worship, Bible study, and community service revolve around the group's daily struggles as members corporately seek change in their personal and social situation. In an urban world characterized by massive poverty, they model the need for moving beyond almsgiving as social action to solidarity with the neediest.

Out of the United States and a similar setting of repression and social rejection has come another form of liberation theology, Black theology. One of the very few authentically indigenous American theological movements that were specifically urban in context, it began formally in the 1960s as a commentary on the civil rights movement and the struggle of Blacks for justice and self-identity.

Its most prolific writer, James Cone (b. 1938), defines Christianity as "essentially a religion of liberation" in a society where people "are oppressed because they are black." With his Latin American counterpart, he calls for a theology that will identify with the goals of the socially marginalized. He sees existential Blackness as a hermeneutical circle around which such things as Christology, ecclesiology, and eschatology must be reconstructed in terms of Christ as the liberator from social oppression and to political struggle.[91] Says Cone, "there is no place in Black Theology for a colorless God in a society when people suffer precisely because of their color."[92]

In the years since the 1960s, Black theology has continued to grow in maturity and global impact. Dialogue with Latin American liberation theologians and with feminist theologians has widened its agendas, and a healthy inframovement discussion has developed.[93] Cone himself sounds less strident and has come to see closer connections between racism, sexism, imperialism, and capitalism.[94]

Black theology has its own distinctives. Grounded in the African slave experience in the U.S., it is considerably more reluctant about close ties with Marxist social philosophy than is its counterpart in Latin America. Its stress, though modified by the years, remains on the socioethnic issues of the Black experience as the key to structuring theology. By comparison, Latin America's orientation is more politicoeconomic.

Liberation theologies, wherever they originate, carry all the deficiencies associated with a Christ-of-the-city model. The need for personal conversion stands in danger of being minimized. Liberation becomes the process of setting people free to help God build the future, God so historicized that he loses his otherness, and the poor so concretized by economics or ethnicity that they become a salvific category in themselves.

At the same time, liberation theologies offer powerful challenges for the development of a uniquely urban theology. How can we do theological reflection in a context of social, political, and ethnic oppression? What must the church say about the practice of justice and compassion toward the urban marginalized? Does the global city demand not only a church *for* the poor but also a church *of* the poor?

### Evangelicals Awakening?

The closing decades of the twentieth century have seen a new revival of interest in the city among evangelicals. A major role in this renewed concern has been played by the Lausanne Committee for World Evangelization. Its Theology Working Group has promoted worldwide study through the 1980s on such urban-related themes as the gospel and its relation to human culture, the simple lifestyle, and the relationship of evangelism to social responsibility. The Lausanne-sponsored 1980 Consultation on World Evangelization (COWE) in Pattaya initiated an extensive program of global consultations on urban ministry.

Ray Bakke, a Lausanne Associate, has led such gatherings in over one hundred cities to date. Spurred by his enthusiasm for a "responsible evangelism," regional networks of urban churches have been formed to search for new information and strategies.

Lausanne's achievements have been many. It has continued to underline the evangelical heritage of the past in evangelism as the primary focus of the world church. It has augmented this with a robust stress on unreached peoples as a strategy for carrying out that evangelistic task. It has been able to combine this theme with a growing concern for the social, economic, and political dimensions of mission to the city. And, in doing that, it has welded a stronger consensus in the world church on the need for putting together the horizontal and vertical elements of the gospel.

At the same time, the consensus has not been without dissensions. Particularly, some evangelical voices on the "right" have continued to question the propriety of its proposals for merging evangelism with social issues.[95] Some labeled "radical evangelicals" have in the past demanded better integration of the horizontal dimension,[96] although this criticism has lessened considerably, particularly in view of the achievements at Lausanne II in Manila, 1989, with its attention to urban mission in all its dimensions.[97]

How does one explain the continuing dissension within the evangelical camp? I suspect it reflects the continuing heritage of diverse models within the camp. The voluntarism and individualism that hindered some evangelicals in earlier centuries from dealing with secularism as more than an individual issue may still remain. The pessimism of an earlier dispensationalism toward pre-advent social change, though greatly modified through the years, may still thwart expectations of even partially realized reformation of the city's social structures. The note of repentance that permeates the Lausanne Covenant and the Manila Manifesto may still sound too triumphant for many evangelicals. Is the model of Christ as transformer of the city becoming dominant in Lausanne? Too dominant, in fact, for those who have made other choices?

Where will the future take us in cities of the world? Can and should God be served in all the culture and occupations of the city? Roger Greenway is right when he says,

> The biblical Gospel is far larger than either the liberal social activists or the traditional fundamentalists imagine. It is a Gospel which includes winning disciples to Christ, establishing churches, and building a Christian community with all its facets and areas of concern. The whole city, from top to bottom, must be called to repentance toward God and faith in the Lord Jesus Christ. This is the full Gospel which requires the total renewal of man and his society, and it is the only Gospel which offers any genuine hope for today's urban world.[98]

## Discussion Questions

1. Describe the integrating role of religion in the city as it was perceived in ancient times by both Christians and pagans. What happened to this perception in the course of history? What did Plato try to recapture? What does Conn mean by "Stoic cosmopolitanism"?

2. Compare Tertullian's Christ-against-the-city with the Gnostic Christ-of-the-city and Augustine's Christ-for-the-city. Argue the strengths

and weaknesses of each position and explain which one you consider closest to the truth.

3. Explain Thomas Aquinas's understanding of Christ's relation to the city. In Aquinas's thinking, what roles do reason, grace, and the church play in urban life? Explain what Conn means when he writes, "The seeds of the secularized city, the modern megalopolis, were sown by Aquinas and harvested in the more consistent efforts of the Renaissance and Enlightenment minds."

4. Describe the role of cities in the Protestant Reformation, which the author describes as "uniquely an urban event." What new vision for the life of cities did the Reformation encourage? Compare and contrast the models that emerged: Lutheran, Anabaptist, and Calvinist.

5. Explain Ritschl's idea of the kingdom of God and its eventual influence on theological liberalism and the approach to city ministry known as the social gospel.

6. Identify some of the nineteenth-century evangelical responses to the needs of city people and evaluate their strengths and weaknesses. In their rejection of the social gospel, what unfortunate mistake did American evangelicals make? Explain how it happened.

7. What place did Harvey Cox give to the church in the "secular city"? What has become of that viewpoint? What role do you believe the church ought to strive for in the city?

8. In Gustavo Gutiérrez's liberation theology, what constitutes urban mission? What place does the church play in this theology? How are the poor regarded? How do the Base Christian Communities fit into this scheme?

9. What was James Cone referring to when he defined Christianity as "essentially a religion of liberation" in a society where people "are oppressed because they are black"? How does Black theology differ from Latin American liberation theologies? What is the key weakness in all liberation theologies? What challenges do liberation theologies place before the church in the city?

10. How do you feel about the note of "Christ the transformer" of urban culture that can be detected in the Lausanne movement? How does that concept of the church's mission give shape and direction to the task of discipling the city?

# ENDNOTES

## Chapter 1: Genesis as Urban Prologue

1. E. M. Blaiklock and R. K. Harrison, eds., *The New International Dictionary of Biblical Archaeology* (Grand Rapids: Zondervan, 1983), 130.

2. For studies of such arguments, consult Don C. Benjamin, *Deuteronomy and City Life: A Form Criticism of Texts with the Word City ('îr) in Deuteronomy 4:41–26:19* (Lanham, Md.: University Press of America, 1983), 39–47; Frank S. Frick, *The City in Ancient Israel* (Missoula: Scholars, 1977), 1–23; John M. Halligan, "A Critique of the City in the Jahwist Corpus" (West Bend, Ind.: University of Notre Dame, unpublished Ph.D. dissertation, 1975); Isaac M. Kikawada and Arthur Quinn, *Before Abraham Was: The Unity of Genesis 1–11* (Nashville: Abingdon, 1985), 9–35.

3. Geerhardus Vos, *Biblical Theology: Old and New Testaments* (Grand Rapids: Eerdmans, 1948), 11–27.

4. Meredith G. Kline, *Kingdom Prologue* (Philadelphia: Westminster Theological Seminary, class syllabus privately printed by the author, 1983), 2:23.

5. Helpful discussions of these issues will be found in Mason Hammond, *The City in the Ancient World* (Cambridge: Harvard University Press, 1972), 6–53; Charles L. Redman, *The Rise of Civilization: From Early Farmers to Urban Society in the Ancient Near East* (San Francisco: W. H. Freeman and Company, 1978), 214–43.

6. Henri Frankfort, *Kingship and the Gods: A Study of Near Eastern Religion as the Integration of Society and Nature* (Chicago: University of Chicago Press, 1948, 1978), 252.

7. Paul Lampl, *Cities and Planning in the Ancient Near East* (New York: Braziller, 1968), 7.

8. At the same time, the Old Testament did not yield to the idolatrous religious connotations of the identification. The prophets made use of the tradition to condemn Israel's cities for committing adultery with foreign gods (Deut. 31:16; Ezek. 23:7).

9. Deryck C. T. Sheriffs, "'A Tale of Two Cities'—Nationalism in Zion and Babylon," *Tyndale Bulletin* 39 (1988): 21–29.

10. Geo Widengren, *The King and the Tree of Life in Ancient Near Eastern Religion* (Uppsala: Lundquist, 1951), 9–11.

11. Frick, *The City in Ancient Israel*, 30; Frank Zimmerman, "*'Ir, Kir* and Related Forms," *The Seventy-Fifth Anniversary Volume of the Jewish Quarterly Review* (Philadelphia: JQR, 1967), 382–92.

12. Jacques Ellul, *The Meaning of the City* (Grand Rapids: Eerdmans, 1970), 6.

13. John Goldingay, "The Bible in the City," *Theology* 92, no. 745 (January 1989): 5.

14. Roger S. Greenway and Timothy M. Monsma, *Cities: Missions' New Frontier* (Grand Rapids: Baker, 1989), 7.

15. Kline, *Kingdom Prologue*, 2:25. Kline also suggests that God's promise of the preservation of Cain (4:15) is "a virtual city charter."

16. For a similar but different accent, consult Bernhard Anderson, "Unity and Diversity in God's Creation," *Currents in Theology and Mission* 5, no. 2 (April 1978): 71.

17. Meir Lubetski, "*Šᵉm* as a Deity," *Religion* 17 (1987): 1–14, makes the interesting suggestion that the Hebrew term *sem* (most often translated "name") could very well be rendered here as "Let us make a god, an idol."

18. Goldingay, "The Bible in the City," 8–9.

19. Sibyl Moholy-Nagy, *Matrix of Man: An Illustrated History of Urban Environment* (New York: Praeger, 1968), 42.

20. Mircea Eliade, *The Sacred and the Profane: The Nature of Religion* (New York: Harcourt, Brace and World, 1959), 39–41.

21. Kline, *Kingdom Prologue*, 3:23.

22. John W. Olley, "God's Agenda for the City: Some Biblical Perspectives," *Urban Mission* 8, no. 1 (September 1990): 15–20.

23. The pairing of city and temple/house as the dwelling place of the Lord seems to be common in Scripture (cf. 1 Kings 8:44, 48; 2 Kings 23:27; 2 Chron. 6:34, 38; Ps. 127:1; Jer. 26:6, 9, 12). A more detailed study of this is found in Daniel E. Fleming, "'House'/'City': An Unrecognized Parallel Word Pair," *Journal of Biblical Literature* 105, no. 4 (1986): 689–97.

24. Many of these images are drawn together very helpfully by Richard J. Clifford, *The Cosmic Mountain in Canaan and the Old Testament* (Cambridge: Harvard University Press, 1972). In contrast to my argument, Clifford places great stress on the mythological continuity linking both the literary traditions of the ancient Near East and the Old Testament.

25. Some helpful comments on the significance of this naming (though unnecessarily linked to editing theories of the written record) are found in Allan K. Jenkins, "A Great Name: Genesis 12:2 and the Editing of the Pentateuch," *Journal for the Study of the Old Testament* 10 (1978): 41–57.

26. Claus Westermann, *Genesis 12–36: A Commentary* (Minneapolis: Augsburg, 1985), 74–77.

27. Cyrus H. Gordon, "Abraham and the Merchants of Ura," *Journal of Near Eastern Studies* 17 (1958): 28–31; John Van Seters, *Abraham in History and Tradition* (New Haven, Conn.: Yale University Press, 1975), 13–38. A full discussion of this question is found in Frick, *The City in Ancient Israel*, 188–93.

28. J. A. Thompson, *Archaeology and the Old Testament* (Grand Rapids: Eerdmans, 1957), 19–21.

29. Goldingay, "The Bible in the City," 12.

30. Delbert R. Hillers, *Covenant: The History of a Biblical Idea* (Baltimore: Johns Hopkins Press, 1969); Meredith G. Kline, *The Structure of Biblical Authority* (Grand Rapids: Eerdmans, 1972); Dennis J. McCarthy, *Old Testament Covenant: A Survey of Current Opinions* (Richmond: John Knox, 1972).

31. G. Ernest Wright, *The Old Testament and Theology* (New York: Harper and Row, 1969), 107.

32. Vos, *Biblical Theology*, 71–72.

33. Kline, *The Structure of Biblical Authority*, 155.

34. David J. A. Clines, *The Theme of the Pentateuch* (Sheffield: Journal for the Study of the Old Testament Supplement Series [10], 1978), 68.

35. G. Ch. Aalders, *Bible Student's Commentary: Genesis*, 2 vols. (Grand Rapids: Zondervan; St. Catharines, Ont.: Paideia, 1981), 2:163.

36. Clines, *The Theme of the Pentateuch*, 84–85.

37. Ibid., 84.

38. Several other suggestions of linking allusions, some more convincing than others, can be found in Kikawada and Quinn, *Before Abraham Was,* 121–22.

39. Walter Brueggemann, *The Land* (Philadelphia: Fortress, 1977), 26–27.

40. Stuart Murray, *City Vision: A Biblical View* (London: Daybreak/Darton, Longman and Todd, 1990), 42.

41. A more detailed study of the Lucan emphasis on Christ and the city can be found in Harvie Conn, "Lucan Perspectives and the City," *Missiology* 13, no. 4 (October 1985): 409–28.

42. Sverre Aalen, "'Reign' and 'House' in the Kingdom of God in the Gospels," *New Testament Studies* 8 (1961–1962): 215–40.

43. James C. DeYoung, *Jerusalem in the New Testament: The Significance of the City in the History of Redemption and in Eschatology* (Kampen: Kok, 1960), 63–74.

## Chapter 2: Confronting Urban Contexts with the Gospel

1. Harv Oostdyk, *Step One: The Gospel and the Ghetto* (Basking Ridge, N.J.: Son Life International, 1983), 223–36.

2. Waldron Scott, *Bring Forth Justice: A Contemporary Perspective on Mission* (Grand Rapids: Eerdmans, 1980), 209.

3. William J. Abraham, *The Logic of Evangelism* (Grand Rapids: Eerdmans, 1989), 103–4.

4. James Smart, *The Teaching Ministry of the Church* (Philadelphia: Westminster, 1954).

5. Ibid., 84.

6. Ibid., 86.

7. Ibid., 107.

## Chapter 3: The Role of Women in Discipling Cities:
## A Historical Perspective

1. Flora Larsson, *My Best Men Are Women* (London: Hodder and Stoughton, 1974), 17, 19–22.

2. Patricia Hill, *The World Their Household: The American Woman's Foreign Mission Movement and Cultural Transformation, 1870–1920* (Ann Arbor: University of Michigan, 1985), 2.

3. Catherine Booth, *Female Ministry: or, Woman's Right to Preach the Gospel* (New York: Salvation Army, 1975).

4. Margaret Troutt, *The General Was a Lady: The Story of Evangeline Booth* (Nashville: Holman, 1980), 22.

5. Catherine Booth, *Papers on Aggressive Christianity* (London: Partridge, 1980), 11.

6. Ibid., 14.

7. William T. Stead, *Life of Mrs. Booth* (New York: Revell, 1900), 195.

8. Larsson, *My Best Men Are Women,* 22.

9. Ian C. Bradley, *The Call to Seriousness: The Evangelical Impact on the Victorians* (New York: Macmillan, 1976), 48.

10. Edwin W. Rice, *The Sunday-School Movement, 1780–1917, and the American Sunday-School Union, 1817–1917* (Philadelphia: American Sunday-School Union, 1917), 37.

11. Leon McBeth, *Women in Baptist Life* (Nashville: Broadman, 1979), 78.

12. Albert L. Vail, *Mary Webb and the Mother Society* (Philadelphia: American Baptist Publication Society, 1914), 65–68, 107.

13. Timothy L. Smith, *Revivalism and Social Reform: American Protestantism on the Eve of the Civil War* (Gloucester, Mass.: Peter Smith, 1976), 169.

14. Ibid., 170.

15. Hill, *The World Their Household,* 45.

16. Mary E. A. Chamberlain, *Fifty Years in Foreign Fields, China, Japan, India, Arabia: A History of Five Decades of the Woman's Board of Foreign Missions, Reformed Church in America* (New York: Woman's Board of Foreign Missions, Reformed Church in America, 1925), 5–6.

17. Annie Ryder Gracey, *Eminent Missionary Women* (New York: Eaton and Mains, 1898), 18.

18. Carma Van Liere, "Sarah Doremus: Reformed Church Saint," *The Church Herald* (October 4, 1985), 17.

19. Carl F. H. Henry, *The Pacific Garden Mission: A Doorway to Heaven* (Grand Rapids: Zondervan, 1942), 25–28.

20. Ibid.

21. Norris A. Magnuson, *Salvation in the Slums: Evangelical Social Work, 1865–1920* (Grand Rapids: Baker, 1990), 115–16.

22. Christian Golder, "Mission and Aim of the Female Diaconate in the United States," in *The Nineteenth Century*, vol. 1 of *Women and Religion in America*, ed. Rosemary Radford Ruether and Rosemary Skinner Keller (San Francisco: Harper and Row, 1981), 271–73.

23. Mildred Cable and Francesca French, *Something Happened* (London: Hodder and Stoughton, 1934), 35.

24. Robert L. Niklaus, John S. Sawin, and Samuel J. Stoesz, *All for Jesus: God at Work in the Christian and Missionary Alliance Over One Hundred Years* (Camp Hill, Penn.: Christian Publications, 1986), 273.

25. Ibid., 266.

26. W. P. Livingstone, *Mary Slessor of Calabar: Pioneer Missionary* (London: Hodder and Stoughton, 1915), 9.

27. Cable and French, *Something Happened*, 28.

28. Louis L. King, "Mother Whittemore's Miracles," *The Alliance Witness* (January 21, 1987), 20.

29. Phyllis Thompson, *Each to Her Own Post, Six Women of the China Inland Mission: Amelia Hudson Broomhall, Jennie Hudson Taylor, Margaret King, Jessie Gregg, Jessie McDonald, Lilian Hamer* (London: Hodder and Stoughton, 1982), 78–79.

30. Elinor Rice Hays, *These Extraordinary Blackwells: The Story of a Journey to a Better World* (New York: Harcourt, Brace and World, 1967), 121–22.

31. Robert B. Mitchell, *Heritage and Horizons: The History of Open Bible Standard Churches* (Des Moines: Open Bible Publishers, 1982), 30.

32. Mary Lou Cummings, "Ordained into Ministry: Ann J. Allebach," in *Full Circle: Stories of Mennonite Women*, ed. Mary Lou Cummings (Newton, Kans.: Faith and Life, 1978), 9–10.

33. Charles Edwin Jones, *Perfectionist Persuasion: The Holiness Movement and American Methodism, 1867–1936* (Metuchen, N.J.: Scarecrow, 1974), 189–90.

34. Magnuson, *Salvation in the Slums*, 115.

## Chapter 4: Research: Matching Goals and Methods to Advance the Gospel

1. See chapter 11, "Research as a Tool for Evangelism," in *Cities: Missions' New Frontier*, Roger S. Greenway and Timothy M. Monsma (Grand Rapids: Baker, 1989).

2. James Engel, *How Can I Get Them to Listen?* (Grand Rapids: Zondervan, 1977).

3. Jack P. Gibbs, *Urban Research Methods* (Princeton, N.J.: Von Nostrand, 1961).

4. Leslie Kish, *Survey Sampling* (New York: Wiley, 1965).

## Chapter 5: Secularization and the City: Christian Witness in Secular Urban Cultures

1. Clark H. Pinnock, *Tracking the Maze: Finding Our Way Through Modern Theology from an Evangelical Perspective* (San Francisco: Harper and Row, 1990), 82–88.

2. John W. Bardo and John J. Hartman, *Urban Sociology* (Itasca, Ill.: Peacock, 1982), 326.

3. David Harvey, *The Condition of Postmodernity: An Enquiry into the Origins of Cultural Change* (Cambridge, Mass.: Blackwell, 1989), 110–13.

4. Sidney E. Ahlstrom, *A Religious History of the American People*, 2 vols. (Garden City, N.Y.: Doubleday, Image Books, 1975), 2:603.

5. Lesslie Newbigin, *Honest Religion for Secular Man* (Philadelphia: Westminster, 1966), 7–10.

6. Harvey Cox, *The Secular City—Urbanization and Secularization in Theological Perspective* (New York: Macmillan, 1965).

7. Gibson Winter, *The New Creation as Metropolis* (New York: Macmillan, 1963).

8. Jacques Ellul, *The Meaning of the City* (Grand Rapids: Eerdmans, 1970).

9. Martin E. Marty, *The Modern Schism: Three Paths to the Secular* (New York: Harper and Row, 1969).

10. Harvey Cox, *Religion in the Secular City—Toward a Postmodern Theology* (New York: Simon and Schuster, 1984).

11. Ralph D. Winter, *The Twenty-Five Unbelievable Years: 1945 to 1969* (South Pasadena, Calif.: William Carey Library, 1970), 11–14.

12. Robert Kuttner, *The End of Laissez-Faire: National Purpose and the Global Economy after the Cold War* (New York: Knopf, 1991), 36–53.

13. Beth B. Hess, Elizabeth W. Markson, and Peter J. Stein, *Sociology,* 2d ed. (New York: Macmillan, 1985), 363–64.

14. Kuttner, *The End of Laissez-Faire,* 36–53.

15. Lesslie Newbigin, *Foolishness to the Greeks: The Gospel and Western Culture* (Grand Rapids: Eerdmans, 1986), 76–81.

16. Walter Truett Anderson, *Reality Isn't What It Used to Be* (New York: Harper and Row, 1990), 3–4.

17. Harvey, *The Condition of Postmodernity,* 141–72.

18. Peter F. Drucker, *The New Realities: In Government and Politics, in Economics and Business, in Society and World View* (New York: Harper and Row, 1989), 3–9.

19. Alvin Toffler, *Power Shift* (New York: Bantam, 1990), 3–11.

20. Anderson, *Reality Isn't What It Used to Be,* 105–30.

21. Anthony Giddens, *The Consequences of Modernity* (Stanford, Calif.: Stanford University Press, 1990), 1–6.

22. Allan Bloom, *The Closing of the American Mind* (New York: Simon and Schuster, 1987), 25–26.

## Chapter 6: Being Disciples: Incarnational Christians in the City

1. Moises Silva, *The Wycliffe Exegetical Commentary: Philippians* (Chicago: Moody, 1988), 107, 112.

2. Vinay Samuel and Chris Sugden, "Agenda for Missions in the Eighties and Nineties: A Discussion Starter," in *New Frontiers in Mission,* ed. Patrick Sookhdeo (Grand Rapids: Baker, 1987), 62.

3. Nicholas Wolterstorff, *Until Justice & Peace Embrace* (Grand Rapids: Eerdmans, 1983), 77.

4. James F. Engel and Wilbert Norton, *What's Gone Wrong with the Harvest? A Communication Strategy for the Church and World Evangelization* (Grand Rapids: Zondervan, 1975).

5. Dick Taylor, "Discovering Your Neighborhood's Needs," *Sojourners* 8, no. 6 (June 1979): 22–24.

6. Ibid.

7. Paulette T. Beatty, from abstract of "The Concept of Need: Proposal for a Working Definition," *Journal of the Community Development Society* 12, no. 2 (1981): 39–46.

8. Manuel Ortiz, Interview with Amy Calkin, April 18, 1987.

## Chapter 7: Counseling and Discipleship for the City

1. See Luis Villareal, "Counseling Hispanics," and Edward Maynard, "Counseling Blacks," in *Healing for the City: Counseling for the Urban Setting,* ed. Craig W. Ellison and Edward S. Maynard (Grand Rapids: Zondervan, 1991).

2. David G. Myers, *The Human Puzzle: Psychological Research and Human Belief* (San Francisco: Harper and Row, 1978).

3. Ellison and Maynard, *Healing for the City*.

4. It is generally recommended that the pastor not spend more than eight hours per week in "formal" counseling and limit the amount of counseling to no more than ten sessions for each person or couple seen.

## Chapter 8: Authentic Strategies for Urban Ministry

1. The following books amply provide instruction on community organizing: Saul Alinsky, *Reveille for Radicals* (New York: Random House, 1969); Kimberley Bobo, *Lives Matter: A Handbook for Christian Organizing* (Kansas City, Mo.: Sheed and Ward, 1986); Robert C. Linthicum, *Empowering the City's "Rag, Tag and Bobtail": Community Organizing and the Church* (Monrovia, Calif.: World Vision International, 1990), and *City of God; City of Satan: A Biblical Theology for the Urban Church* (Grand Rapids: Zondervan, 1991); chapter 9 explores the biblical bases for community organizing; Felipe E. Maglaya, *Organizing People for Power: A Manual for Organizers* (Manila: Asia Committee for People's Organization, 1982), contained in Simpson and Stockwell's workbook; Gregory F. Pierce, *Activism That Makes Sense: Congregations and Community Organization* (New York: Paulist, 1984); Dick Simpson and Clinton Stockwell, *Congregations and Community Organizing* (Chicago: Institute for the Church in Urban Industrial Society, 1987); *The Organizer Mailing* (San Francisco: Organize Training Center [1095 Market Street, #419, 94103], periodic distribution of the best stories and articles on community organizing appearing in print since the previous distribution).

2. As quoted in "The Fund for the Self-Development of People," the General Assembly of the United Presbyterian Church of the USA, 1970.

## Chapter 9: Profiles of Effective Urban Pastors

1. See "What will the U.S. be like when whites are no longer the majority? America's changing colors," *Time* (April 9, 1990), 28–35.

2. Bernard J. Frieden and Lynne B. Sagalyn, *Downtown, Inc.: How America Rebuilds Cities* (Cambridge, Mass.: MIT Press, 1989), 66, 67. Apart from the brilliant overviews and masterful treatments in each chapter that are easily accessible to average readers, this book has a comprehensive annotated bibliography.

3. Ibid., 67.

4. Ibid., 70.

5. Not surprisingly then, Woodfield, the world's largest mall, would have its ecclesiastical counterpart in Willow Creek Church, which incarnates itself in that subculture as a church for "mall peoples," rather intentionally and appropriately so.

6. Frieden and Sagalyn, *Downtown, Inc.*, 86.

7. Ibid., 107ff.

8. In this section I am extrapolating or gleaning principles. Philosophers call this phenomenology. The purpose for this methodology is twofold: to identify some valuable data we can use and provide helpful examples for pastors, and to model a way some of us learn to grow and recycle on the job as pastors who seldom get furloughs and study leaves.

9. Ibid., 181.

10. Ibid.

11. Ibid., 187; italics added.

12. Ibid., 204, 220.

13. Bob Bufford, in an unpublished paper given at the Leadership Network Seminar in Denver, April 18, 1990.

14. Long-time Chicago pastor Dr. Bill Leslie makes this observation frequently.

15. Raymond J. Bakke and Samuel K. Roberts, *The Expanded Mission of "Old First" Churches* (Valley Forge, Penn.: Judson, 1986), 120.

16. Ibid., 99–100.

## Chapter 12: Church of the Poor

1. Based on research published in *Cry of the Urban Poor* (Monrovia, Calif.: MARC, 1991).

2. Mark 3:14; Christ's modeling in Matt. 4:23; 9:35; 11:1, 4–6; his calling of the Twelve in Mark 3:14; his training in Matt. 10:1, 7; his commission in Matt. 28:18–20.

3. Based on analysis of various anthropological theories on the nature of urban poverty. The most useful thesis remains that of Oscar Lewis in "Culture of Poverty," *Scientific American* (October 1966).

4. Based on observations in Brazil, where it is common to find three to seven Pentecostal churches in a *favela* but difficult to find a Baptist or a Presbyterian church.

5. For an expansion of this theme, see John Kenneth Galbraith's interesting monograph, *The Nature of Mass Poverty* (Cambridge: Harvard University Press, 1979).

6. See Milton Santos, *The Shared Space,* translated from Portuguese (London: Methuen, 1979), for one of the most comprehensive analyses of the economics of the squatter lifestyle.

## Chapter 13: Discipling White, Blue-Collar Workers and Their Families

1. Rich Thomas, "Is it Panic Time or Not?" *Newsweek* 116, no. 21 (November 19, 1990), 54.

2. U.S. Bureau of the Census, *Statistical Abstract of the United States: 1991,* 111th ed. (Washington: U.S. Government Printing Office, 1991), p. 401.

3. Ellen Israel Rosen, *Bitter Choices: Blue-Collar Women In and Out of Work* (Chicago: University of Chicago Press, 1987), 23.

4. Barbara Ehrenreich and Annette Fuentes, "Life on the Global Assembly Line," *Ms.* 9, no. 7 (January 1981), 52–59.

5. Rosen, *Bitter Choices,* 24.

6. Ibid., 40.

7. Bryant Robey, *The American People* (New York: Truman Talley Books, E. P. Dutton, 1985), 166.

8. David Halle, *America's Working Man: Work, Home and Politics among Blue-Collar Property Owners* (Chicago: University of Chicago Press, 1984), 58.

9. Ibid., 187, 205.

10. Kenneth Lasson, *The Workers: Portraits of Nine American Jobholders* (New York: Grossman, 1971).

11. Halle, *America's Working Man,* 34.

12. Ibid., 120–24.

13. Ibid., 165.

14. Ibid., 81.

15. Ibid., 43.

16. Lasson, *The Workers,* 6–8.

17. Halle, *America's Working Man,* 44.

18. Ibid., 43.

19. Ibid., xvii.

20. Ibid., 205.

21. E. E. LeMasters, *Blue-Collar Aristocrats: Life-styles at a Working-Class Tavern* (Madison: University of Wisconsin Press, 1975), 179.

22. Ibid., 24.

23. Halle, *America's Working Man,* 49.

24. Ibid.

25. Ibid., 208.

26. LeMasters, *Blue-Collar Aristocrats*, 34.

27. Halle, *America's Working Man*, 55.

28. Rosen, *Bitter Choices*, 108.

29. Halle, *America's Working Man*, 56–58, and LeMasters, *Blue-Collar Aristocrats*, 45.

30. LeMasters, *Blue-Collar Aristocrats*, 94–97.

31. Ibid., 81, 84–85.

32. Ibid., 111–14.

33. Heather L. Ross and Isabel V. Sawhill, *Time of Transition: The Growth of Families Headed by Women* (Washington: Urban Institute, 1975), 5.

34. Halle, *America's Working Man*, 60.

35. Otto Johnson, ed., *The 1900 Information Please Almanac* (New York: Houghton Mifflin, 1989), 61.

36. LeMasters, *Blue-Collar Aristocrats*, 116.

37. Halle, *America's Working Man*, 253.

38. Ibid., 254, 258–59.

39. Ibid., 254.

40. Ibid., 261.

41. Ibid., 262.

42. Ibid., 265–66.

43. Ibid., 267.

44. Ibid.

45. Ibid., 268.

46. Ibid.

47. LeMasters, *Blue-Collar Aristocrats*, 192.

48. C. Peter Wagner, *Spiritual Power and Church Growth* (Altamonte Springs, Fla.: Strange Communications, 1986), 37.

49. Ibid., 35, and C. Peter Wagner, "Spiritual Power in Urban Evangelism: Dynamic Lessons from Argentina," *Crosswinds* 1, no. 1 (Winter 1992): 38.

50. Steve Boint, "The Blue-Collar Worker and the Church," *Urban Mission* (March 1989): 17; Anthony Campolo, "The Sociological Nature of the Urban Church," in *Metro-Ministry*, ed. David Franchak and Sharrel Keyes (Elgin, Ill.: David C. Cook, 1979), 33; Tex Sample, *Blue-Collar Ministry: Facing Economic and Social Realities of Working People* (Valley Forge, Penn.: Judson, 1984), 107–8.

51. George G. Hunter III, *How to Reach Secular People* (Nashville: Abingdon, 1992), 82.

52. Paul Yonggi Cho, *Successful Home Cell Groups* (Plainfield, N.J.: Logos International, 1981).

53. Wagner, *Spiritual Power and Church Growth*.

54. Albert B. Lawson, *John Wesley and the Christian Ministry* (London: S.P.C.K., 1963), 168.

55. Hunter, *How to Reach Secular People*, 85.

56. Ibid., 84.

57. Ibid., 84.

58. Boint, "The Blue-Collar Worker and the Church," 17.

## Chapter 14: Getting to Know Your New City

1. Marvin K. Mayers, *Christianity Confronts Culture: A Strategy for Crosscultural Evangelism*, 2d ed. (Grand Rapids: Zondervan, 1987), 217–21.

2. James Spradley, *Participant Observation* (New York: Holt, Rinehart and Winston, 1980), 58–62.

3. Ibid., 82–83.

4. William F. Whyte, *Learning from the Field* (Beverly Hills, Calif.: Sage, 1984), 85–88.

5. Kevin Lynch, *The Image of the City* (Cambridge, Mass.: MIT Press, 1960), 46–48.

6. R. Lincoln Keiser, *The Vice Lords: Warriors of the Streets,* Fieldwork Edition (New York: Holt, Rinehart and Winston, 1979), 22–27.

7 James Spradley, *Ethnographic Interviewing* (New York: Holt, Rinehart and Winston, 1979).

## Chapter 15: Discipling City Kids

1. References in this chapter to the writer's church and neighborhood are to Burton Heights Christian Reformed Church, located in a racially mixed section of Grand Rapids, Michigan.

2. Two publishers that publish curriculum for urban children are David C. Cook Publishing Co., 850 North Grove Avenue, Elgin, IL 60120; and Urban Ministries, Inc., 1439 West 103rd Street, Chicago, IL 60643.

## Chapter 16: The Lifestyle of Urban Disciple-Makers

1. Ralph D. Winter and Steven C. Hawthorne, ed., *Perspectives on the World Christian Movement: A Reader* (Pasadena, Calif.: William Carey Library, 1981), 452–64.

2. Ibid., 461.

3. Jonathan J. Bonk, *Missions and Money: Affluence as a Western Missionary Problem* (Maryknoll, N.Y.: Orbis, 1991), 44.

4. Ibid., 58.

5. Ibid., 61.

6. Ibid., 125–29.

7. K. P. Yohannan, *The Coming Revolution in World Mission* (Altamonte Springs, Fla.: Creation House, 1986).

8. K. P. Yohannan, *Why the World Waits: Exposing the Reality of Modern Missions* (Altamonte Springs, Fla.: Creation House, 1991), 135–36.

9. Amy Carmichael, *Gold Cord: The Story of a Fellowship* (London: Society for Promoting Christian Knowledge, 1932), 64.

## Chapter 17: Theological Education for Urban Mission

1. Lewis Mumford, *La Cultura de las Ciudades* (Buenos Aires: Emecé Editores, 1945), 11.

2. Though in the United States *urban* is usually equated with inner city, in many Latin American countries the conglomeration of urban problems is found on the fringes of the cities.

3. Jacques Ellul seems to give the impression that the city is more evil than the country (see *The Meaning of the City* [Grand Rapids: Eerdmans, 1970], passim). There is also much romantic theology that makes God more accessible in the country:

> The kiss of the sun for Pardon,
> The songs of the birds for Mirth,
> You are nearer God's heart in a garden
> Than anywhere else on earth.

From "The Garden," by Dorothy Frances Garney, quoted in Herbert Hoyes, *Spiritual Suburbia: The Church in a New and Growing Community* (New York: Vantage, 1959), 14.

4. I have read in more than one book of a German proverb that says: "*Die Städluft macht frei*" ("The air of the city makes [men] free"). That was, of course, before pollution and refers to the exercise of human liberty without rural social restraint.

5. See Walter Kloetzli, *The Church and the Urban Challenge* (Philadelphia: Muhlenberg, 1961), viii.

6. Jose Comblin, *La Teologia de la Ciudad* (España: Editorial Verbo Divino, 1972), 41–42.

7. Ibid., 62. This excellent study by a Roman Catholic theologian merits serious consideration. I have found it helpful in the preparation of several paragraphs in this section.

8. Ellul, *The Meaning of the City,* 169–70.

9. Lewis Mumford, quoted in Constantino A. Doxiadis and Truman B. Douglass, *The New World of Urban Man* (Philadelphia: United Church Press, 1965), 56–57.

10. Carta, *Octogessima Adveniens*, quoted in Comblin, *Teologia de la Ciudad*, 248.

11. Gibson Winter, *The Suburban Captivity of the Churches: An Analysis of Protestant Responsibility in the Expanding Metropolis* (New York: Macmillan, 1962), 43, 81.

12. Ibid., 87.

13. Larry Krause, "Lessons from an Urban Church in Transition," in *The Urban Mission*, ed. Craig W. Ellison (Grand Rapids: Eerdmans, 1974), 138.

14. Ibid., 144.

15. Lewis Mumford, *The Culture of Cities* (New York: Harcourt, 1938) and *The City in History: Its Origins, Its Transformations, and Its Prospects* (New York: Harcourt, Brace and World, 1961).

16. Comblin, *Teologia de la Ciudad*, 122.

17. Cited in Juan Luis Segundo, *Acción Pastoral Latinoamericano: Sus Motivos Ocultos* (Buenos Aires: Ediciones Busqueda, 1972), 102. Segundo discusses the three aspects in the light of the Latin American situation, particularly for the Roman Catholic Church.

18. Ibid., 181.

19. See José Míguez-Bonino, *Doing Theology in a Revolutionary Situation*, ed. William H. Lazareth (Philadelphia: Fortress, 1975).

20. Gustavo Gutiérrez, *A Theology of Liberation: History, Politics, and Salvation*, trans. Sr. Caridad Inda and John Eagleson (Maryknoll, N.Y.: Orbis, 1973), 67.

21. Wilbert R. Shenk, "Theology and the Missionary Task," *Missiology* 1, no. 3 (July 1973): 297.

22. Segundo, *Acción Pastoral Latinoamericano*, 10.

23. G. Paul Musselman, *The Church on the Urban Frontier* (Greenwich, Conn.: Seabury, 1960), 1, 16.

24. J. C. Hoekendijk, *The Church Inside Out* (Philadelphia: Westminster, 1966), 113.

25. For a more detailed history of city missions, see Hoekendijk, *Church Inside Out*, especially chapter 6, "Mission in the City," 113–26. See also "Selected Bibliography on Urban-Industrial Mission," *International Review of Missions* 65, no. 259 (July 1976): 265–68.

26. These are described in Kloetzli, *The Church and the Urban Challenge*, 70–71.

27. R. Kenneth Strachan, *The Inescapable Calling: The Missionary Task of the Church of Christ in the Light of Contemporary Challenge and Opportunity* (Grand Rapids: Eerdmans, 1968), 108.

28. Ministers tend to foster this self-image. Gerald Kennedy speaks of his seven "worlds": preacher, administrator, pastor, prophet, theologian, evangelist, and teacher. Reference in David F. Wells, "The Pastoral Ministry 2: Preparation," *Christianity Today* (February 16, 1973), 8.

29. Kloetzli, *The Church and the Urban Challenge*, 69.

30. Quoted in Robert L. Ramsayer, "The Missionary's Response to Technological Society," *Missiology* 1, no. 3 (July 1973): 314–15.

31. Harold Brown, "New Religions for Old: A Study of Culture Exchange," *Practical Anthropology* 18, no. 6 (November–December), 248; quoted in Ramsayer, "The Missionary's Response," 317.

32. Harold O. J. Brown, "Can a Seminary Stand Fast?" *Christianity Today* (February 14, 1975), 453.

33. Quoted in Wells, "The Pastoral Ministry," 484.

# Chapter 18: The Kingdom of God and the City of Man: A History of the City/Church Dialogue

1. Quoted by J. Harold Ellens, "Church and Metropolis," *Missiology* 3, no. 2 (April 1975): 169.

2. Lewis Mumford, *The City in History: Its Origins, Its Transformations, and Its Prospects* (New York: Harcourt, Brace and World, 1961), 135ff.

3. Ibid., 138.

4. Gilbert Murray, *Five Stages of Greek Religion* (Garden City, N.Y.: Doubleday. Anchor Books, 1955), 72.

5. Wayne A. Meeks, *The First Urban Christians: The Social World of the Apostle Paul* (New Haven, Conn.: Yale University Press, 1983), 11.

6. R. J. Rushdoony, *The One and the Many: Studies in the Philosophy of Order and Ultimacy* (Nutley, N.J.: Craig, 1971), 71.

7. W. Warren Wagar, *City of Man: Prophecies of a World Civilization in Twentieth-Century Thought* (Baltimore: Penguin, 1963), 29.

8. Rushdoony, *The One and the Many*, 124ff. Harvey Cox, in *The Secular City—Urbanization and Secularization in Theological Perspective* (London: SCM, 1966), 21ff., speaks of this as "the disenchantment of nature" and "the desacralization of politics." Understood simply as another way of speaking of de-divinization, Cox's terminology has value. The problem comes with evaluating the correctness of the corollary he also sees attached to this, namely, that the early Christians were "relentless and consistent secularizers" (27), exhibiting a kind of holy worldliness.

9. Rowan Greer, "Alien Citizens: A Marvelous Paradox," in *Civitas: Religious Interpretations of the City*, ed. Peter S. Hawkins (Atlanta: Scholars, 1986), 39–56.

10. W. H. C. Frend, "Town and Countryside in Early Christianity," in *The Church in Town and Countryside*, ed. Derek Baker (Oxford: Blackwell, 1979), 34–39.

11. H. Richard Niebuhr, *Christ and Culture* (New York: Harper Torchbooks, 1951), 52–55.

12. Ibid., 87.

13. Charles N. Cochrane, *Christianity and Classical Culture: A Study of Thought and Action from Augustus to Augustine* (Oxford: Clarendon, 1940), 177.

14. Ibid., 185.

15. Greer, "Alien Citizens," 49–50.

16. James Dougherty, *The Fivesquare City: The City in the Religious Imagination* (Notre Dame, Ind.: University of Notre Dame Press, 1980), 26–27.

17. Niebuhr, *Christ and Culture*, 209.

18. Ibid., 212.

19. Ibid., 215.

20. Contra Niebuhr, *Christ and Culture*, 217. Niebuhr's own dialectical construction is critical at this point of Augustine's predestinarian dualism.

21. The reasons for this decline and for the emergence of the medieval city are complex. For a full discussion of the debate, consult Mason Hammond, *The City in the Ancient World* (Cambridge: Harvard University Press, 1972), 330–45.

22. Mumford, *The City in History*, 246–47.

23. Ibid., 265–66. For a full treatment of this period, see C. H. L. Brooke, "The Missionary at Home: The Church in the Towns, 1000–1250," *The Mission of Church and the Propagation of the Faith*, ed. G. J. Cuming (London: Cambridge University Press, 1970), 59–83.

24. Wagar, *City of Man*, 37, maintains, on the contrary, that in Aquinas "there is scarcely a word about the world state." This does serious injustice to the contributions of Aquinas then and now as an urban theologian.

25. Niebuhr, *Christ and Culture*, 129ff.

26. *Summa Theologica* I, question 1, answer 8. For a theological investigation of this dualism, consult Cornelius Van Til, *The Defense of the Faith* (Nutley, N.J.: Presbyterian and Reformed, 1955), 132ff.

27. Niebuhr, *Christ and Culture*, 135.

28. H. van Riessen, *The Society of the Future* (Nutley, N.J.: Presbyterian and Reformed, 1957), 47.

29. Steven E. Ozment, *The Reformation in the Cities: The Appeal of Protestantism to Sixteenth-Century Germany and Switzerland* (New Haven, Conn.: Yale University Press, 1975), 18.

30. Ibid., 34.

31. Bernd Moeller, "The Town in Church History: General Presuppositions of the Reformation in Germany," in *The Church in Town and Countryside*, ed. Derek Brown (Oxford: Blackwell, 1979), 263–64.

32. Ozment, *The Reformation in the Cities*, 39.

33. This thesis is unpopular among urban theologians like Gibson Winter, whose title, *The New Creation as Metropolis* (New York: Macmillan, 1963), 38–40, sees the Reformation as part of the trend toward modern secularization and not an interruption. Winter, like Harvey Cox, does not pay attention to the radical nature of the God-centered alternative the Reformers offered to both the shattered medieval synthesis and the emerging "secular city" of the Renaissance. Winter transforms the negative impact of the Reformation on the medieval model into a self-consciously directed synthesis with the megalopolis typology.

34. Ozment, *The Reformation in the Cities*, 44.

35. W. Stanford Reid, "Calvin and the Political Order," in *John Calvin, Contemporary Prophet*, ed. Jacob T. Hoogstra (Nutley, N.J.: Presbyterian and Reformed, 1959), 247; Ronald S. Wallace, *Calvin, Geneva and the Reformation: A Study of Calvin as Social Reformer, Churchman, Pastor, and Theologian* (Grand Rapids: Baker, 1988), 113–19.

36. Ozment, *The Reformation in the Cities*, 83.

37. Niebuhr, *Christ and Culture*, 174.

38. Ibid., 179.

39. John H. Yoder, "The Prophetic Dissent," in *The Recovery of the Anabaptist Vision*, ed. Guy F. Hershberger (Scottdale, Penn.: Herald, 1957), 101.

40. Harold S. Bender, *The Anabaptist Vision* (Scottdale, Penn.: Herald, 1944), 35.

41. Contra Niebuhr, *Christ and Culture*, 217–18. By making this assertion of Calvin, Niebuhr can list erroneously the views of F. D. Maurice as another example of the Christ-as-transformer model.

42. Full treatments of this area of Calvin's thought can be found in A. Bieler, *The Social Humanism of Calvin* (Richmond: John Knox, 1964); Fred Graham, *John Calvin, the Constructive Revolutionary* (Richmond: John Knox, 1971); Jeannine Olson, *Calvin and Social Welfare: Deacons and the Bourse Francaise* (Selinsgrove, Penn.: Susquehanna University Press, 1989).

43. Leonard Verduin, *The Reformers and Their Stepchildren* (Grand Rapids: Eerdmans, 1964), 82–83.

44. The place of the Reformation as a movement in this transitional stage is ignored in Lewis Mumford's history of the city. The omission does injustice to history and, we suggest, contributes to Mumford's despair over the future of the city in his pessimistic prediction of the downfall of the megalopolis. Cf. Lewis Mumford, *The Culture of Cities* (New York: Harcourt, Brace and Company, 1938), 267–92.

45. Paul Hazard, *European Thought in the Eighteenth Century* (Hammondsworth, Middlesex, England: Penguin, 1954), 34.

46. The adjective *religious* is used deliberately. The definition popularized by Harvey Cox—of secularization as a change from a religious consciousness to a nonreligious or areligious mind—is inadequate. Religion can never be discarded. What is changed is the form religion takes.

47. Harvie M. Conn, *Contemporary World Theology: A Layman's Guidebook* (Nutley, N.J.: Presbyterian and Reformed, 1973), 3–4.

48. James Spates and John Macionis, *The Sociology of Cities* (New York: St. Martin's, 1982), 144–49.

49. Friedrich Engels, *The Condition of the Working Class in England in 1844* (London: George Allen and Unwin, 1950 [1845]), 24.

50. Quoted in Niebuhr, *Christ and Culture*, 98.

51. Ibid., 99.

52. Joseph Schiffman, ed., *Edward Bellamy: Selected Writings on Religion and Society* (New York: Liberal Arts, 1955), xl–xli.

53. James Johnson, "Evangelical Christianity and Poverty," in *The Cross and the Flag*, ed. Robert G. Clouse, Robert Dean Linder, and Richard V. Pierard (Carol Stream, Ill.: Creation House, 1972), 162ff.

54. Earle E. Cairns, *Saints and Society* (Chicago: Moody, 1960), 36ff.; William N. Kerr, "Historical Evangelical Involvement in the City," in *The Urban Mission*, ed. Craig W. Ellison (Grand Rapids: Eerdmans, 1974), 32.

55. Norris A. Magnuson, *Salvation in the Slums: Evangelical Social Work, 1865–1920* (Grand Rapids: Baker, 1990).

56. David Ward, *Poverty, Ethnicity and the American City, 1840–1925: Changing Conceptions of the Slum and the Ghetto* (Cambridge: Cambridge University Press, 1989), 98.

57. Richard V. Pierard, *The Unequal Yoke* (Philadelphia: Lippincott, 1970), 29.

58. Ibid., 30.

59. Ibid., 30–31.

60. Quoted in John Reed, "Back of Billy Sunday," *Metropolitan Magazine* 41 (May 1915), 12.

61. David Sheppard, *Built as a City: God and the Urban World Today* (London: Hodder and Stoughton, 1974), 107.

62. George M. Marsden, *Fundamentalism and American Culture: The Shaping of Twentieth-Century Evangelicalism, 1870–1925* (Oxford: Oxford University Press, 1980), 66, 128.

63. Quoted in Pierard, *The Unequal Yoke*, 33.

64. Ibid., 32–33; Marsden, *Fundamentalism and American Culture*, 85–93.

65. Reinhold Niebuhr, *The Nature and Destiny of Man*, vol. 2 (London: Nisbet, 1943), 305.

66. G. Brillenburg Wurth, *Niebuhr* (Philadelphia: Presbyterian and Reformed, 1960), 40–41.

67. D. W. Soper, *Major Voices in American Theology: Six Contemporary Approaches* (Philadelphia: Westminster, 1953), 181.

68. J. John Palen, *The Urban World* (New York: McGraw-Hill, 1975), 4.

69. David B. Barrett, *World-Class Cities and World Evangelization* (Birmingham, Ala.: New Hope, 1986), 48–49.

70. Viv Grigg, "Squatters: The Most Responsive Unreached Bloc," *Urban Mission* 6, no. 5 (May 1989): 42.

71. David Barrett, "Annual Statistical Table on Global Missions: 1989," *International Bulletin of Missionary Research* 13, no. 1 (January 1989): 21.

72. Dietrich Bonhoeffer, *Widerstand und Ergebung* (Munich: Christian Kaiser Verlag, 1955), 261.

73. Colin Williams, *Where in the World?: Changing Forms of the World's Witness* (New York: National Council of the Churches of Christ in the U.S.A., 1963), 76.

74. Johannes Aagaard, "Some Main Trends in Modern Protestant Missiology," *Studia Theologica* 19 (1965): 248.

75. Harvey Cox, "*The Secular City* 25 Years Later," *The Christian Century* 107, no. 32 (November 7, 1990): 1028.

76. George Todd, "Mission and Justice; the Experience of Urban and Industrial Mission," *International Review of Mission* 55, no. 259 (July 1976): 256.

77. David Bosch, "Crosscurrents in Modern Mission," *Missionalia* 4, no. 2 (August 1976): 61–63.

78. Harold Lindsell, "Nairobi: Crisis in Credibility," *Christianity Today* (January 2, 1976), 10. See also Bruce Nicholls, "Theological Reflections on the WCC Assembly—By an Observer," *Theological News* 8, no. 1 (January 1976): 6; Paul G. Schrotenboer, "Fifth Assembly World Council of Churches, Nairobi 1975," mimeographed report (Grand Rapids: Reformed Ecumenical Secretariat, n.d.), 5–7.

79. For samples of such comparisons, consult David J. Bosch, "Evangelism," *Mission Focus* 9, no. 4 (December 1981): 65–74; Alan Neely and James A. Scherer, "San Antonio and Manila 1989: '. . . Like Ships in the Night'?" *Missiology* 18, no. 2 (April 1990): 139–48. See also the special

issue of *Missiology* 9, no. 1 (January 1981), devoted to an analysis of the 1980 meetings in Pattaya and Melbourne.

80. "Letter from Those with Evangelical Concerns at San Antonio to the Lausanne II Conference," *International Review of Mission* 78, nos. 311/312 (July/October 1989), 431–35.

81. David Bosch, "Your Will Be Done? Critical Reflections on San Antonio," *Missionalia* 17, no. 2 (August 1989): 132.

82. Hugh Lewin, ed., *A Community of Clowns: Testimonies of People in Urban Rural Mission* (Geneva: WCC Publications, 1987), 294.

83. George A. Lindbeck, *The Future of Roman Catholic Theology; Vatican II—Catalyst for Change* (Philadelphia: Fortress, 1970), 11–12.

84. Ibid., 39–40.

85. Anton Houtepen, *Theology of the 'Saeculum': A Study of the Concept of Saeculum in the Documents of Vatican II and of the World Council of Churches, 1961–1972* (Kampen: Kok, 1976), 147–52.

86. Ibid., 168.

87. Gustavo Gutiérrez, *A Theology of Liberation: History, Politics, and Salvation,* trans. Sr. Caridad Inda and John Eagleson (Maryknoll, N.Y.: Orbis, 1973), 205.

88. Ibid., 268.

89. Carl E. Braaten, *The Flaming Center: A Theology of the Christian Mission* (Philadelphia: Fortress, 1977), 144.

90. W. E. Hewitt, "Christian Base Communities (CEBs): Structure, Orientation and Sociopolitical Thrust," *Thought* 63, no. 249 (June 1988): 163.

91. Harvie M. Conn, "Theologies of Liberation: An Overview," in *Tensions in Contemporary Theology,* expanded edition, ed. Stanley N. Gundry and Alan F. Johnson (Chicago: Moody, 1979), 377.

92. James H. Cone, *A Black Theology of Liberation* (Philadelphia: Lippincott, 1970), 120.

93. J. Deotis Roberts, *Black Theology in Dialogue* (Philadelphia: Westminster, 1987).

94. James H. Cone, *For My People: Black Theology and the Black Church* (Maryknoll, N.Y.: Orbis, 1984), 78–98.

95. Samples of such criticism may be found in Arthur P. Johnston, *The Battle for World Evangelism* (Wheaton: Tyndale House, 1978); "Lausanne II and Missions Today and Tomorrow—A Forum," *Trinity World Forum* 15, no. 2 (Winter 1990): 1–4; David Hesselgrave, "Holes in 'Holistic Mission'," *Trinity World Forum* 15, no. 3 (Spring 1990): 1–4.

96. "Theology and Implications of Radical Discipleship," in *Let the Earth Hear His Voice,* ed. J. D. Douglas (Minneapolis: World Wide, 1975), 1294–96; Orlando E. Costas, "Report on Thailand 80 (Consultation on World Evangelization)," *TSF Bulletin* 4, no. 1 (November 1980): 4–5.

97. Samuel Escobar, "From Lausanne 1974 to Manila 1989: The Pilgrimage of Urban Mission," *Urban Mission* 7, no. 4 (March 1990): 21–29. See also "The Manila Manifesto: Calling the Whole Church to Take the Whole Gospel to the Whole World," in *Proclaim Christ Until He Comes: Calling the Whole Church to Take the Whole Gospel to the Whole World,* ed. J. D. Douglas (Minneapolis: World Wide, 1990), 25–38.

98. Roger S. Greenway, *Calling Our Cities to Christ* (Nutley, N.J.: Presbyterian and Reformed, 1973), 111–12.

# INDEX

293